Settle and

MW00785121

Settle and Conquer

Militarism on the American Frontier, 1607–1890

MATTHEW J. FLYNN

McFarland & Company, Inc., Publishers

Jefferson, North Carolina

LIBRARY OF CONGRESS CATALOGUING-IN-PUBLICATION DATA

Names: Flynn, Matthew J., author.
Title: Settle and conquer : militarism on the American frontier, 1607–1890 / Matthew J. Flynn.
Description: Jefferson, North Carolina : McFarland & Company, Inc., Publishers, 2016. | Includes bibliographical references and index.
Identifiers: LCCN 2016012697 | ISBN 9780786499205 (softcover : acid free paper) ∞
Subjects: LCSH: United States—Territorial expansion. | Indians of North America—West (U.S.)—Wars. | Land settlement—West (U.S.)—History.
Classification: LCC E179.5 .F59 2016 | DDC 978/.02—dc23
LC record available at http://lccn.loc.gov/2016012697

ISBN (print) 978-0-7864-9920-5
ISBN (ebook) 978-1-4766-2263-7

BRITISH LIBRARY CATALOGUING DATA ARE AVAILABLE

© 2016 Matthew J. Flynn. All rights reserved

No part of this book may be reproduced or transmitted in any form or by any means, electronic or mechanical, including photocopying or recording, or by any information storage and retrieval system, without permission in writing from the publisher.

Front cover: *Daniel Boone protects his family*, 1874 lithograph (Library of Congress)

Printed in the United States of America

McFarland & Company, Inc., Publishers
 Box 611, Jefferson, North Carolina 28640
  www.mcfarlandpub.com

For my wife and children.
A special thanks to Oscar Rothenberg
for his expertise.

Table of Contents

Preface: The War of Contact, 1607–1890

Working as a professor of war studies engaged in professional military education (PME) for the United States Marine Corps has allowed me to better gauge the effort within military circles to place in context the last ten-plus years of counterinsurgency (COIN) warfare in Iraq and Afghanistan. To its credit, the U.S. armed forces are is not content to allow only the American commitment in Vietnam during the Cold War to shape that understanding. Rather, many within its ranks look to extend that examination to encompass the nation's entire history and there find some good news, as it were. Invariably the desired moment lies in the war the U.S. Army waged against Native Americans on the Western plains roughly from 1860 to 1890. Here was success at COIN.

A number of books cover what experts frequently refer to as a guerrilla war in the West, and this is where attention falls within the PME community. These studies shape some of the story offered in the pages that follow. However, even should one accept the word "guerrilla" as the best meaning of the fighting that transpired on the plains, the question remains, was this clash an insurgency? Additionally, what of the history long before 1860, the struggle among New Arrivals and Natives that ensued after Europeans settled North America? Was this conflict different, or was it also an insurgency?

Few scholars have attempted to answer these questions, and when they have done so, the years after 1865 receive most of their attention. Andrew J. Birtle, in a book published in 1998 titled *U.S. Army Counterinsurgency and Contingency Operations Doctrine, 1860-1941*, lumps the post–Civil War plains conflict within his study of the U.S. Army's doctrinal response to COIN wars from that period up to the Second World War.[1] The time spent acting as a constabulary presence out West had a significant impact on the Army's counterinsurgency outlook going forward. Robert N. Watt in "Raiders of a Lost Art? Apache War and Society," published in *Small Wars and Insurgencies* in

2004, stresses the fact that the Apache captured their own people on behalf of the U.S. Army. Also in 2004, in *Defense Studies*, Wayne Lee broadens this view when he looks at what he labels "host nation" forces in "Using the Natives against the Natives: Indigenes as 'Counterinsurgents' in the British Atlantic, 1500–1800." In both cases, the point is that indigenous allies and scouts were a key to American counterinsurgency success then and now.[2] John M. Gates in "Indians and Insurrectos: The U.S. Army's Experience with Insurgency," casts success in surprising terms when he looks at soldiers engaged with Natives on the plains in the nineteenth century to find there a positive moral compass that contrasts with a more modern age, i.e., the twentieth century.[3] This brief list encompasses the extent of the parallels scholars have established, leaving the counterinsurgency of long ago that so greatly altered the Native world hidden in a compartmentalized history: from early colonization, to the expanding frontier, to the taming of the West. What follows offers an in-depth analysis of that Indian War, a synthesis of the entire *war of contact* that developed over some 300 years, from 1607 to 1890, from the founding of Jamestown to the tragedy of Wounded Knee. During this long stretch of time, Europeans and then Americans won their counterinsurgency.

The history of the Native American confrontation with settlers in North America places the writer in an interesting vortex. Gone is the triumphal march west that dominated this topic's historiography up to the 1970s. In its place came scholars condemning an act of conquest. Two books frame this dichotomy. Francis Parkman's *The Conspiracy of Pontiac and the Indian War After the Conquest of Canada*, first published in 1870 and re-released many times after that, typifies the view of the "noble savage," an individual bowing before the benevolent advance of European civilization.[4] In 1976, Francis Jennings openly countered what he calls Parkman's "consistently misleading" history by telling a tale of the harmful conquest the English visited upon Natives in the New England area in *The Invasion of America: Indians, Colonialism, and the Cant of Conquest*.[5] By extension, this fate befell all Native Americans. The vast literature in between these two extremes is referenced in the chapters that follow as the works pertain to waging a counterinsurgency. So too is literature over the last twenty-five years that reflects an effort by specialists to reach an understanding that departs from a too regimented view that has defined each side. Analysis featuring culture and race has led to an interpretive shift. A shared world existed along the frontier, an emphasis that backs away from a simplistic view of an "us versus them" confrontation that might characterize savage Indians and rapacious whites.

Following this lead of approaching early American history in a more complicated fashion adds counterinsurgency to a growing list of labels: discovery, exploration, contact, encounter, invasion, conquest, even genocide.[6] Clearly, how to understand these events is in flux, and the various terms suggest the need for a context offering a better understanding than what has been presented so far. The benevolence of discovery or exploration clashes with the negative connotation of invasion and conquest. The term encounter, even contact, suggests a compromise of sorts, and that may be so, but it also demands more explanation uncovering the nature of that encounter. That is attempted in the pages that follow, and the case is made that counterinsurgency best captures the realities of this conflict. In so arguing, a compromise is again reached, much like with encounter itself, but with the added benefit of resting on a key piece of analysis so prominent in the literature. For this COIN war was like any such conflict, requiring an exploration defining meaning between those tied together by the struggle, not retelling a tale where one party is expunged and the other triumphant. In short, experts have long since presented this clash as a counterinsurgency, but not recognized that reality.

Richard White's *The Middle Ground: Indians, Empires, and Republics in the Great Lakes Region, 1650–1815* is the most salient example of this approach. His "middle ground" thesis has dominated the historiography since that book's publication in 1991. It represents a significantly different view from that of an invasion and a conquest. Rather, settlers and Natives in the Great Lakes region engaged in cultural exchanges along equitable lines, so much so that Natives effectively managed their interaction with Europeans to remain in possession of a middle ground. That interaction was fragile and marred by violence but no matter the strife, and at times because of it, settlers had to contend with Native realities as much as imposing their own.[7]

The emphasis on a middle ground is invaluable in setting the stage for an examination of this entire period as a counterinsurgency. Clearly the conflict is not just one of expansion and conquest, but of something else as well. To advance in this direction requires further exploration of the middle ground, and in this book it comes from an unlikely approach—military history. While experts have discarded this focus as a narrative defining the "old" history of celebratory American expansionism, this line of inquiry can add a great deal more to the understanding of the conflict that raged between Natives and the new arrivals in North America. This richer picture is one where those settling the New World and then establishing the United States conducted a counterinsurgency. In this way, the Natives lost a war and a continent by failing to remain a part of this creation.

An examination of the *war* (not *wars*) that European nations, followed by the United States, waged against Native Americans from 1607 to 1890, makes it clear that Natives lost the struggle to define this shared world that witnessed their transformation from superiority, to parity, to dependence, and finally, to exclusion. Natives at times resisted that transformation or usually did not manage the transformation to first European and then American satisfaction, and so conflict ensued. Settlers justified that war in the name of coexistence with Natives, but that view was an empty promise repeated at each step of continental expansion. While the act of expansion was certainly conquest, its architects accomplished that task via a counterinsurgency enshrined in the labels of settlement, in the promises of an "Indian Country," and in the goal of Indian reservations. The hindsight of history may well have correctly identified a middle ground, one where the conquerors treated Natives as dependents in the new America, and the Natives actively sought out this end until such a time when settlers took that option from the tribes. This mindset left the Natives as insurgents.

What is striking in this outcome is the role of counterinsurgent played by so many accompanying settlement. The frontiersmen "opening the west" underscored the impact of settlers always moving west. Due to the remorseless expansion these intrepid few facilitated—indeed, made possible—too often soldiers found themselves facing confused realities and they responded with a litany of operations, including enforcing a Removal Policy as an attempt at winning over the targeted population, at winning the "hearts and minds" of the insurgents as COIN practitioners might say today. When the Army faltered, militia units sought out Native encampments in something like the search and destroy sweeps of more recent times. Army units followed the civilian lead and engaged in a self-proclaimed "total war" on the plains. This course of action meant soldiers eventually gave up on any effort at accommodation with or protection of Natives, blaspheming the Army's attempt at what might be called pacification. The benefit of the combination of military forces aiding civilian conquest surfaced over the course of this long war, eventually leaving the U.S. Army to enjoy a final success of ending the spasms of resistance in campaigns akin to security force or stability operations.

The counterinsurgency focus makes it clear that the U.S. Army and the variants that preceded its establishment at times showed great restraint when confronting the difficult issue of conflict with Native Americans. It is not an overstatement to say the punitive—at times criminal—acts inherent in expansion came at the behest of civilian operatives, not professional soldiers. The obvious exceptions to this view, the battles, the forced relocations, and the constant "wars," these blights stand opposed by more mitigating realities such as the reduction in size the U.S. government repeatedly imposed on the Army thereby limiting its reach, the massacres by either side that were few and far between given the long duration of the conflict, and that some of the vilest rhetoric directed at Native Americans by military personnel was later repudiated by those same individuals. Within military circles there was at least as much an effort to curb violence against Natives as there was among some portions of the civilian population. When military force became the desired option, civilians too often forced this to happen. Colonial and then American settlers offered a steady call for military action to deal harshly with Natives, all in the name of settlement, and when this support was not forthcoming, they often took matters into their own hands. The public's willful manipulation—then and now—often obscures this reality of the military's role in this war. Public perception holds the U.S. military responsible for the destruction of Native Americans when, in fact, the fault lies principally with the American people.

A military history of this event offers this insight, one that makes it clear that the American public's constant push for settlement was far more lethal to Native Americans than were the overt acts of militarism supposedly shaping this conflict. Consequently, forcing much of the legend and folklore so prevalent in this tale leaves the exploits of some famous figures advancing the means of a counterinsurgency. The frontiersmen Daniel Boone and David Crockett are notable primarily for their success in "opening the west." Mountain men carried on this tradition of expansion by pushing into and beyond the Rocky Mountains. Explorers charted the hinterlands of the continent and set the path of conquest. Militiamen, rangers, and volunteers sought to accelerate this process by engaging Natives in battle. Also, settlers and pioneers steadfastly overcame the elements to stand at the forefront of settlement and therefore complete the destruction of Native American peoples. Together, a civilian tide surfaced in North America that swept all before it, including the military arm of the burgeoning nation.

A focus on this struggle as a counterinsurgency makes this point and offers a historical parallel that reaches to the present. Several years into the Iraq war of 2003, Americans appeared willing to venture down this road again, that is, looking for victory that requires the obliteration of the enemy. The best example was the call among several experts in security studies to increase the use of violence to destroy those resisting the U.S.-led occupation. For instance, Michael Scheuer, an ex-CIA official, wrote an opinion piece in the *Los Angeles Times* in March 2008, suggesting that the United States use "lethal, overpowering force." Titled "Break Out the Shock and Awe," the author called for larger deployments of U.S. troops in order to kill more of "those that require killing."[8] Scheuer echoes the conclusions of scholars such as Gil Merom who asserts, in *How Democracies Lose Small Wars: State, Society, and the Failures of France in Algeria, Israel in Lebanon, and the United States in Vietnam,* that democracies struggle in "small wars" because they fail to "escalate the level of violence and brutality to that which can secure victory."[9] Merom released this book in 2003, the same year as the start of Operation Iraqi Freedom. I would argue that such a view met with great approbation among the U.S. body politic at that time and still does, a push for "victory" in the public mindset that entails the U.S. military establishment to completely eliminate "terrorists," yet somehow not harm the population endemic to the region. How this difficult balancing act is to be accomplished is hard to say, but it matters little. This harsh call meets firm resistance within the U.S. armed forces, as more reasoned minds check a vague public consciousness to bring the full military power of the United States to bear and "win" the war. This was the case in Iraq. Even in tough circumstances, the U.S. military refrained from such a perversion of "shock and awe," the mantra of restraint in terms of employing kinetic force that defined the start of the conflict. I make this clear in my study, published in 2010, *Contesting History: The Bush Counterinsurgency Legacy in Iraq,* and also show how this restraint runs contrary to the historical norms of great powers resorting to the use of kinetic military power to "win" a COIN war, something that eluded them no matter the recourse.[10]

That same dynamic of restraint arose in the long struggle to settle the nation, but at that time professional military forces were far less successful in staying the public's wrath. In *Settle and Conquer,* a civilian push for the decimation of their foe emerged in the war against Native Americans because of this failure. It is imperative to place this past experience before the American public, given its refusal to come to terms with the violence that civilians visited upon Native Americans in North America. The prospect that the founding of the United States rests largely on its citizens assaulting Natives leading to their destruction and to the rise of an entirely new people, this success in counterinsurgency hardly enters American consciousness. Yet, acknowledging this intent and recognizing the immorality inherent in this accomplishment may in fact curb some of the public sentiment to carry this practice into the future.

This insight offers a measure of the state of America today. Expeditionary operations are designed to foster stable and ideally like-minded states to better serve U.S. national interests, but to do so without a demographic change. There should be an intellectual even cultural transformation, not a physical one, a difficult outcome to achieve. These conflicts are usually prolonged and raise the public's ire given its preference of seeking a quick and complete "military" victory. It is a sentiment embedded in the nation's extended clash with Native Americans, a "success" enjoyed but not acknowledged. How could it be? That clash never witnessed a quick, military victory. Rather, it rested on civilians "settling" the nation, and during this long process, the home front held firm, producing a demographic destruction of Natives at times declared both friend and foe. This book ultimately makes this point clear and asks Americans to better understand what success is in terms of COIN wars. If one seeks a moral result, the enemy is not vanquished but neutralized, allowing accord and coexistence to follow. For Americans today, such a success would appear unique to their history and an uncomfortable outcome, if not unwelcomed. The sinews of history have indeed come to roost in today's "war on terror" but require exorcism, then emulation.

In writing this book, I also hope to better define what constitutes a successful counterinsurgency. I argue that a number of actions must be taken by the counterinsurgents and must be done in concert to achieve victory in such a conflict: sustaining military operations over a long period of time, isolating the enemy in the region in dispute, winning hearts and minds, taking advantage of the fragmentation of the enemy, demonstrating a will to continue this assault no matter the costs, and possessing the means to continue this assault. If this unity is achieved, the true aim of what leads to success in a counterinsurgency can move forward unimpeded, and that is when agents of demographic change are unleashed on a vulnerable opponent. These factors did indeed come to pass on the American landscape over the very long time period of 300 years. I characterize the overall impact of settlement on Natives as the ultimate counterinsurgency success, a phrase imbued with a tangible, clear understanding. The shift in population, the rise of settlers in terms of numbers and the creation of a dominant culture excluding Natives, this act of nation building formed the key principle of that success. Not only did one group prosper, but also the other group, Native Americans, faced utter vanquishment, meaning that nation building in this era had a divergent purpose from today—the invader did not protect or assist indigenous peoples to retain a homeland but in fact victimized them to ensure their loss of sovereignty.

This past success blasphemed the underlying premise of the new nation, the United States. Clearly given how settlers marginalized of Native culture, terms such as liberty, freedom, and entitlement only applied to that new society, and to select portions of that society. Therefore, the civilian-led effort that dragged with it the military elements accompanying the settlers and together obliterated the indigenous people of a region, this "success" story can never be duplicated. The temptation may be there in more recent times to seek such a victory, but the grave pitfall of this thinking is the moral cost.

Can a nation prideful of its role in world affairs as a moral guardian of justice inflict such a defeat on any enemy? The answer is no, and it helps explain why nation building in the hands of the United States now means something entirely different from the past: putting together the components of a successful counterinsurgency without the demographic consequence of this success.

Most studies trying to better understand the far reaching historical currents inherent in an analysis of the American counterinsurgency response to the 9/11 attacks reach for the familiar benchmark of the American failure in Vietnam, such as James H. Lebovic in *The Limits of U.S. Military Capability: Lessons from Vietnam and Iraq* and David Fitzgerald in *Learning to Forget: U.S. Army Doctrine and Practice from Vietnam to Iraq*.[11] Scholars lament that the United States did not learn the right lessons from that past war. As if conceding this point, there is also a renaissance of "classic" works on counterinsurgency, the French post–Second World War experience in Algeria leading this push with the re-release of books by David Galula, *Counterinsurgency Warfare: Theory and Practice*, and Roger Trinquier, *Modern Warfare: A French View of Counterinsurgency*.[12] Yet the French did not enjoy success either, and one should stress that the counterinsurgents habitually failed in a post–1945 era studded with numerous instances of insurgency. The English experience in Malaya is perhaps an exception, a "success" put in contrast to the American debacle in Vietnam by John A. Nagel in *Learning to Eat Soup with a Knife: Counterinsurgency Lessons from Malaya and Vietnam*.[13] The bottom line is success stories of counterinsurgencies are few and far between in this "modern" era, and the American track record is particularly suspect. Consequently, much of the literature reacting to the wars in Iraq and Afghanistan seeks a more hopeful outcome.[14]

This view lacks historic depth. As Max Boot stressed years ago, Vietnam possesses an undue hold on the American experience with COIN, and a negative one—the nation has struggled when confronted with this *kind* of warfare. This is not the case in wars it fought leading up to Vietnam, something Boot makes clear in his 2002 book, *The Savage Wars of Peace: Small Wars and the Rise of American Power*. The same is true of other authors who also stress Boot's point, such as Sam Sarkesian in *America's Forgotten Wars: The Counterrevolutionary Past and Lessons for the Future*, published in 1984, that is, well before Boot's own publication, and the 2011 book by Wayne Bert, *American Military Intervention in Unconventional War: From the Philippines to Iraq*.[15] These writers, like Boot, make it clear that the United States has a rich tradition of success from which to draw. Yet, in making this case, these books neglect study of the European and then American war against Natives in North America. Sarkesian offers a chapter on the Second Seminole War, Boot and Bert omit this continent-wide struggle entirely. This book, *Settle and Conquer*, puts what constitutes successful COIN operations into better perspective by focusing on that important period in American history. The synthesis I offer also speaks to present practitioners and theorists of COIN who seek answers to the question, what makes a successful counterinsurgency, but it leaves the modern period behind, i.e., post-1945. Thanks to the long period of settler-Native interaction examined here, an answer can begin to emerge that relates directly to the present and it is one that is more than an evaluation of the assumed guerrilla fighting engulfing the plains after 1865.

This comprehensive approach represents a timely study. Today Americans face unprecedented security challenges. Terrorist attacks and the American reaction to this continuing threat have led to questions about the American state: what it stands for and how it achieves security. To reach such an understanding and move forward confident in the future, a sound reading of the past is a necessary first step. Presenting a successful example of counterinsurgency germane to the American experience but also calling attention to its immorality (and therefore its inapplicability in current times) offers a liberating moment. The United States can recognize that it has shifted away from a barbarous practice and now seeks to use counterinsurgency as a means consistent with maintaining its moral standing in the world. By shedding haunting memories, not those arising from the Vietnam War, but the founding of the nation from coast to coast, current counterinsurgency operations are understood as having limits and therefore as successful. The ultimate counterinsurgency success is one where a people do not lose their soul to achieve victory. This calamity occurred once. Americans appear determined not to let that happen again, and the U.S. military is that guarantor.

*   *   *

Settle and Conquer requires a careful definition of several key terms. The characterization of this conflict centers on the use of insurgency and counterinsurgency. Chapter 1 explains why the Natives assume the role of insurgents. The remaining chapters detail key aspects of the counterinsurgency that defined the interaction of all those engaged in North America. It is important to stress that I consider guerrilla warfare a method of resistance frequently, but not always, adopted by the insurgents. Guerrillas do not exist as a separate category. Rather, the insurgents used guerrilla tactics. This understanding does not mean that all insurgents are guerrillas, but it does mean that, in this case, all guerrilla fighters were insurgents. I avoid using the term White altogether in the text, and use Indian only sparingly. Instead, I reference Europeans or Americans; Native is intended to group together all peoples in North America who inhabited the land before European arrival and who faced great changes after that event. Admittedly these are imperfect terms when looking to capture a complicated reality.[16] Where possible, I have used more specific labels. Similarly, the terms of engagement deserve mention. As will be clear in the pages that follow, the meanings of invasion and conquest are disputed among scholars. I clarify how I use them in the text. I do the same for settlement.

Sources

The analysis rests on secondary literature in that I am attempting to tell a very familiar story and do so across a sweeping compendium of time. The story is not uniform in the literature, of course, and I have been careful to report disagreements among scholars when they arise. At times, to try and resolve these disagreements, or when the story has been incomplete, the secondary writing not answering a key question or clarifying an event to my satisfaction, to overcome these problems, I have looked to primary research. Overall, the book offers a key synthesis for the reasons detailed above. It also serves as a demonstration where further research is needed to understand the the arrival, settlement, and expansion of new people across a continent in a more comprehensive fashion and to do so in the context of military history. In this way, the European and American interaction with the Native populations in North American can continue to add valued insight into American views of counterinsurgency.

Introduction:
Two Battles

Native Americans achieved their most famous military success near the end of their long ordeal with European and American expansion. At the Little Bighorn River in Montana in June 1876, over 2,000 Sioux warriors ambushed five companies of the U.S. 7th Cavalry under the command of Lieutenant Colonel George Armstrong Custer. The odds were overwhelming, with the Natives facing just a handful of troopers. Custer's errors had invited calamity. Always impetuous, he advanced rashly and upset his plan, which was designed to ensure that his three columns would arrive in the same place at the same time. Together, the columns amounted to 265 men. Momenturn did not guide this stratagem. Brigadier General Alfred H. Terry, leading a strike that included Custer's force and two others, wanted to ensure that the Sioux did not escape as he advanced. Custer shared this view, and he divided his already small command, a regiment, into thirds with the intention of first discovering the main camp and then encircling the enemy. His uneven advance allowed the Natives to confront him in segments, one portion of his command became tied down and unable to assist the men under Custer's direct control who faced an onslaught of hundreds of Natives who crossed the Little Bighorn River to meet him in battle. In about an hour, the Sioux annihilated Custer's soldiers, and he perished with them. His other two forces united and survived the engagement, although they too suffered heavy losses. A few days later, well after the Natives had fled the area, Terry's additional troopers arrived on the field to behold the carnage and take a reckoning of the defeat.

More than a few actions that day remain unclear. Why did Major Marcus A. Reno, leading the other two columns of the 7th Cavalry, not come to the support of the beleaguered Custer? Reno declared he was lucky to survive at all. While undoubtedly true, part of Reno's command under Captain Frederick W. Benteen managed to shift its position a mile forward but still remained within Reno's line, in the hopes that Custer could better locate it.

The Natives contained Reno's forces, but one wonders whether these soldiers could have reached Custer if Reno had advanced with his entire complement of troops.[1] Would this success have turned the tables, or would Reno simply have added his men to the slaughter? It is impossible to know.

The most important questions surround Custer himself. An ambitious, energetic commander, it is hard to assess his impetuosity as anything other than aggressive action in battle and, therefore, as a virtue. Custer did not know the size of the Sioux camp before him, and had he understood the numbers, he may well have waited for the other arms of his encirclement to unfold. However, even armed with this knowledge of his enemy, he also could have been just as concerned that the Natives would escape. Custer was too close to avoid detection, and should the Natives flee, as he expected, his reputation would have been soiled for not engaging the enemy. In fact, his superiors had given him command of the 7th Cavalry because they believed that he would act aggressively and forestall such an outcome. So Custer did what he had always done, advance into battle.

Aggressiveness hardly begins to explain Custer's behavior, however. Something more was afoot stemming from the fact that the futility of Native resistance was clear to all those involved in the struggle in the latter half of the nineteenth century. On the American side of this ledger, several developments had emerged to make the United States think in terms of a climax to this long struggle. The nation's internal ills had eased with the passing of the Civil War. Expansion west accelerated as the trails channeling that movement became clearer and safer. In fact, the Sioux that Custer faced in 1876 may well have remained unmolested but for a wave of prospecting in this

Gen. George A. Custer, circa 1865 (Library of Congress).

region as Americans searched for gold in the Black Hills. On the other hand, the Sioux had capitalized on American troubles during the Civil War by expelling U.S. military outposts from their territory. Now, settling an overdue score with these traditionally hostile Natives factored into Army thinking as well. Indeed, the U.S. Army considered the war that resulted in the destruction of Custer's command to be no more than a mopping up operation. In this regard, the clear vulnerability of the Natives to American expansion entitled Custer to an overconfidence that was not his alone. Reason dictated that the Sioux would capitulate and not fight at all. In his haste to ensure a clash, Custer upset the timetable of this scenario, producing the Battle of the Little Bighorn, which brought him glory and immortality along with defeat.

At this late date of 1876, the unprecedented degree of Sioux unity underscored the crisis atmosphere at large on the Native side of this ledger. In fact, coming to terms with their bleak future due to American settlement served as a reason for the rendezvous, and that it was so well attended speaks to a belated Native recognition of this reality. However, Custer's recklessness went a long way to ensure a last act of defiance on the part of the Sioux. The ease with which chiefs like Crazy Horse isolated Custer's command does not lessen the accomplishment of this military feat, but the context of the engagement does lessen the significance of the Native victory. In the wake of Custer's debacle, Americans accepted one more round of Native confrontation. A cry arose nationwide to avenge the heroic figure, and a punitive military effort soon vanquished the Sioux from the Northern Plains of the United States. Many Natives fled to Canada, although most eventually returned and surrendered to U.S. custody. Sioux resistance came to an inglorious conclusion in the years after Custer's death, and by 1881, the Sioux were a broken people. This end was discernible before the Battle of the Little Bighorn making it clear that in the summer of 1876, the Natives had won a battle while losing the war.

Similarly, in a confrontation with Americans in the early 1790s, the Natives emerged victorious on the battlefield but still lost the war. At stake were the upper reaches of the Ohio Valley, as well as a referendum on American strength in the post–Revolutionary War period. In this conflict, Shawnee warriors joined with Miamis, Ottawas, and Delawares to present a formidable alliance that scored a quick victory, turning back an American column under General Josiah Harmar in October 1790, one dispatched by President George Washington to bring peace to the area with hopefully a mere show of force. Rebuffed, the president determined that a second, reinforced army could accomplish the same end. When that second force under Major General Arthur St. Clair approached the Wabash River in the Old Northwest in early

November 1791, the Natives surrounded the American force, which totaled some 1,500 men. Three hours later, the Natives had killed, wounded, or captured almost 900 of that number, while losing maybe 60 warriors. It was the greatest defeat of American arms during the entire clash with Native Americans.

St. Clair deserves a great deal of blame for this disaster. For one thing, he was gout-ridden, and this condition limited his ability to command. On the eve of the battle, he retired early to rest after the long march of the day. Moreover, he had failed to adhere to President Washington's caution that he should always be ready for ambush. The night before the battle, his army made little preparation to enable it to repel a surprise attack. His soldiers camped in a box formation and did not fortify the position, leaving the army vulnerable to envelopment and assault from the start of the engagement. Two formidable chiefs intended to do just this. Little Turtle, a Miami, and Blue Jacket, a Shawnee, worked together in unprecedented fashion to ensure that their 1,000 warriors enjoyed a tactical advantage when the shooting started. Consequently, as the Americans rose on a cold November morning, shots to their front directed at militia were quickly followed by shots to their rear. Panic ensued as a careening militia slammed into the hastily formed ranks of Regulars now coming under accurate increasingly intense fire. St. Clair attempted to rally his force, a difficult thing to do given Native determination to fire upon the officers. A counterattack did go forward on St. Clair's right forcing the Natives to give ground there, but the American attack accomplished nothing except for further exposing the army to Native assault to St. Clair's left. This stand soon turned into a debacle. St. Clair and his army fled, leaving masses of equipment and heaps of corpses on the battlefield. It was a stunning defeat.

The Battle of the Wabash meant that the American effort to weaken, if not crush, Native resistance in the Ohio region had failed. In fact, many of the Natives now stood emboldened believing they had won the war. President Washington, enraged by what he considered St. Clair's incompetence, realized another army had to be sent to the area to restore American prestige, not to mention to lay claim to the area. Equally troublesome, the president worried that St. Clair's defeat would encourage overt British support of the Natives. Such an outcome could only prolong the conflict and threaten to escalate it, incurring great national expense. Only a new attack could prevent this end.

A third American army achieved victory at the Battle of Fallen Timbers in August 1794—almost three years after St. Clair's catastrophe. Following a plodding yet deliberate and steady advance, some 3,000 militia and a handful of Regulars under the command of General Anthony Wayne engaged that same confederation of Natives totaling close to 1,000 warriors in the woods near the British outpost of Fort Miamis, a strongpoint close to the Maumee River in the Ohio territory. Pressing ahead in such a thicket invited a sudden attack, and as Wayne marched his army forward, a concentration of braves surprised and overwhelmed a section of his soldiers. This assault had all the markings of the previous Native success against St. Clair. This time, however, panic did not ensue, primarily because of Wayne's precautions. For instance, just prior to the fighting, he ordered his men to defend in place if surprised. At the critical moment, they did just that. As the fighting intensified, the Natives could not capitalize on their first success since the Americans held firm and quickly counterattacked and regained the ground lost during the initial onslaught. This move shored up their defenses to such an extent that the Americans not only prevented an envelopment of their position, they soon forced the Natives from the field.

The thirty dead Natives and eight Americans hardly reflected either the severity of the fighting or the importance of the outcome. The fact was that an American column raised in haste and led by a one-dimensional commander, "Mad" Anthony Wayne knowing only one speed, advance and attack, had sought out this confrontation and traveled deep into Native territory to engage the enemy. True, Wayne had advanced cautiously, building forts for supply and defense at each incremental step into hostile territory, and he drilled his army relentlessly.[2] Still, other than a superiority of numbers, something a skilled enemy could easily neutralize given the heavily wooded ground, the Americans enjoyed few advantages—not terrain, not surprise, not the time of battle. Additionally, the Natives were skilled opponents. Yet Wayne prevailed, scattering the resistance to claim a decisive victory, which it was from the vantage point of morale. Feelings of elation and doom engulfed victor and loser respectively. Fallen Timbers represented latent American power, an aggression unleashed by militia formed in a perfunctory manner yet still able to increase American prestige and underscore the rising tide of that nation's expansionism.

As used here, "decisive" needs more explanation. The greater measure of defeat lay in the strategic outcome—the Natives soon abandoned a large portion of the Ohio area. They could in no way match American strength, no matter the victory Little Turtle and Blue Jacket had secured a few years before. The population growth of settlers sealed their fate. Little Turtle said as much prior to this third engagement. He feared the American ability to send new armies time after time and urged negotiation instead of continued fighting. This chief sensed that a demographic victory would produce an American hegemony in the years to come. Blue Jacket put his faith in English

Anthony Wayne's victory at the Battle of Fallen Timbers, near Toledo, Ohio, August 20, 1794 (Library of Congress).

support and overruled Little Turtle who dutifully took his place on the battle-line.[3] The result was disaster. Wayne marched to victory and English neutrality was underscored by their refusal to shelter those fleeing from the battle to Fort Miamis. With no allies and facing the inexorable advance of settlers, the Natives could only recoil and sign a peace treaty that forfeited huge portions of land. Defeat was disheartening in this respect but also in the inevitable consequence of this outcome: the loss of land meant a loss of a way of life and therefore extinction. As if to underscore this fate, Americans decreed the one recourse for survival that remained to Natives and that was farming the land left in their possession. Defeat forced the Natives to become more like their conquerors, accepting a mandatory assimilation that spoke to the decisive nature of the battle.

These two engagements call attention to the 100-year time span needed for the United States to completely end Native military resistance across the continent—1790–1890. But declaring winners and losers in these battles or any others offers an at best limited measure of the war unfolding in North America. The fact is, military confrontations of this large scale were few and far between and as is clear above, the Natives won two of them. However, they still faced obliteration in this long struggle. How was this possible? One reason is that Natives lost some battles. Even when noting failure in this respect, one must remember that ambush and raids were certainly part of this conflict as well and consisted of the majority of the fighting. But it is an exaggeration and an enormous simplification to say that guerrilla warfare characterized the Native response and in turn, that the American ability to defeat this kind of resistance explained the result. The main reason Natives faltered is the demographic reality that undergirded the battles detailed above, as well as the smaller ones. This reality was reinforced by a long war of attrition totaling some 300 years producing an outcome decided by much more than military confrontation. An increasing and aggressive colonial and then American population cunningly divided the Natives, isolated them from European support, adopted their mannerisms and imposed many of their own, and so embraced settlement as to strangle the Native ability to subsist on their own. As will be seen in the pages that follow, here was the key to the American victory, taking advantage of numbers and doing so faster than the Natives thought possible in what amounted to an unorchestrated counterinsurgency. While not recognized as such at the time, settler and Native interaction along the shifting frontier amounted to a counterinsurgency nonetheless. This remarkable occurrence is the focus of this book.

American dignitaries repeatedly invited chiefs and other Native representatives to visit eastern cities to thereby understand the magnitude of the

American advantage in numbers. For example, the war-like Sioux were treated to such an exhibition when Chief Red Cloud and other chiefs toured Washington, D.C., in 1870 and again in 1872. Each time Red Cloud spoke he struck a defiant tone describing himself as a wronged party to all who would listen and indeed he was. Treaties guaranteeing Natives land had proven false before; the then current offer of a protected reservation appeared as hollow. While his appeal for an end to U.S. military coercion met with great fanfare among the sympathetic crowds he addressed in the nation's capital and then in New York City, the Army's campaign to end Sioux resistance and force them onto reservations continued as well since U.S. policy declared that habitation for Natives best.

As President Ulysses S. Grant explained to Red Cloud when the two meet in 1872, this shelter was sorely needed since there was no alternative to the fate awaiting the Sioux due to the American tide of expansion. The sheer numbers meant that in the coming days the Sioux faced eradication at the hands of a civilian push, not just military action. Only sanctuary on a reservation could ensure their survival in the short-term and offer them the long-term benefit of slowly adapting to the new culture in order to re-enter the dominant society.[4] It was the perfect middle ground. Natives were to abscond to a locale out of the way until such a time as they re-emerged as model citizens, a gesture to a dubious future since that result entailed the complete loss of Native sovereignty that was the final price they must pay for their security. That shame, an abdication before American might, was also a *fait accompli,* the proceeds of an ongoing counterinsurgency. Red Cloud accepted his fate and after 1870, he did not wage war against the Americans again. More militant members of his tribe dismissed his dire warnings and shaped the path to the Little Bighorn. When Sioux resistance collapsed, and did so in tragic ways, the American promise of a middle ground obscured these costs by reinforcing the ideological bent of fair play that U.S. authorities insisted was implanted within the reservation system, but had never been the case no matter the rhetoric espousing this virtue.

At the behest of settlers, counterinsurgency evolved from an effort of accommodation to that of absorption in one-sided fashion—Natives accepting their conqueror's norms. Here was a perversion of the roots of the "encounter," where assimilation might have meant a shared new world after first contacts between Europeans and Natives. By the time the struggle on the plains unfolded, Natives were fighting for a right to simply exist. The reservation system was to force Native acculturation to American ways, not generate a shared culture. When reservations became a permanent fixture defining Native life, it was clear that Americans and Natives had managed to

Sioux and Arrapahoe Indian Delegations. Seated, left to right: Red Cloud, Big Road, Yellow Bear, Young Man Afraid of His Horses, Iron Crow. Standing, left to right: Little Bigman, Little Wound, Three Bears, He Dog (Library of Congress).

create something of a middle ground after all. It took a very long time to get to this point, to a permanent mix defining the interaction as the U.S. government forced Natives into a protected tributary status, but it happened. On the American landscape at the end of a very extended period of conflict, settlers finally accepted the insurgents as dependents of the whole, thereby offering them a reprieve from cultural effacement due to assimilation. When the fighting ended, Americans accepted that victory in a counterinsurgency is accommodation of the enemy, not their destruction.

President Grant labeled his effort to protect the Natives his Peace Policy. He believed that Native acquiescence to American terms was essential in order to end the violence on the plains between them and to do so before Natives no longer existed. With this purpose in mind, Grant presided over a number of meetings in the capital with delegations from various tribes. For example, Apache leaders visited eastern metropolises on several occasions, and roughly at the same time as Red Cloud. Cochise, perhaps the most famous Apache, refused to go "because of his fear of the military and the citizens [of the United States]."[5] A member of the delegation that went to Washington, D.C., on his behalf in July 1872, made it clear that the visit did make an impression; when he returned, he told Cochise that to continue fighting was pointless. This delegate advised acceptance of the American guarantees of security on a reservation, including living in houses, on farms, and benefiting from education.[6] However, many Apache kept fighting, the warnings of the men who had gone east were simply disbelieved or under-appreciated.

The inevitable defeat of those who continued to resist came in a generation, although Cochise stood apart from what became the end of the Apache way of life. He managed to secure a reservation for his Chiricahua Apache on a large swath of ground in their homeland in the southeastern region of the Arizona territory. This space in the midst of the spreading American settlements represented a singular achievement. Cochise had found peace, and at least for a time, he and his tribe remained intact and in possession of home soil, suggesting that he had paid close attention to the reports of the growing American population. However, Cochise gained this concession largely because of his reputation for fierce resistance; the American authorities thought it best to let him be. Consequently, he also served as a model for continuing to fight. Those Apache who did faced oblivion, deportation to Florida, or containment on reservations that forfeited the proud Apache culture and made a mockery of any middle ground supposedly inherent in adopting the settler's creed of self-sufficiency. These facilities were too often in locations where either the poor soil discouraged cultivation or disease flourished. Both factors greatly increased Native misery and hardships. This unpleasant reality did not prevent settlers from complaining that the Apache (and other Natives for that matter) had repaid government generosity with a slovenliness inherent in all Natives. In the opinion of most settlers, if the middle ground promise went unfulfilled, Natives had only themselves to blame.

The architects of the reservation system believed these refuges represented a humane response to the problem of Native assimilation. This conclusion was accurate, but still appalling. Life on these restricted areas remained a checkered one at best for too many Natives. American mitigation in terms of policy, such as it was, really indicated that the government realized the need to incorporate Natives into the new United States or inflict another exception on the American façade of widespread prosperity available to all. After a calamitous civil war ending with the elimination of slavery, the nation could not survive another besmirching of its name for racial intolerance, if Natives faced eradication. If that indictment of American freedom unfolded, a result that appeared more likely with each battle, the country's path forward as offering a haven to the weak and vulnerable, something defining its very soul, risked impairment should posterity mark the violence the great nation inflicted on Natives more than the promise of inclusion it bestowed upon these unfortunates. For the United States, providing a middle ground was essential because it justified the use of force so that Americans could extend their accommodation to Natives, a necessary outcome embedded in its counterinsurgency.

Of course, that effort emerged at the first attempts of colonization. When Native resistance surfaced at that time, the colonists resorted to violence in the face of that opposition, and their need for a larger paradigm that framed the conflict surfaced as well. What better way for colonists to assert their resolve than to understand their expansion as a movement to achieve freedom for masses of people imbued with a natural disposition in this respect? This belief had no basis in England, in Europe, or, as it turned out, in the colonies. No matter, that willful thinking did serve to drive settlement in a far-off land capable of being molded to that desired reality, to something believed lost in Europe. Europeans, and then Americans, would fulfill this cause by staking out a land for themselves and one where Natives could enjoy that dream as well so long as they did not get in the way. For settlers, the pursuit of American ambitions proved to be a difficult balancing act, one requiring them to mount a counterinsurgency in the name of securing a middle ground. That noble mission of inclusion could hopefully outweigh the expected violence and avoid the blight of having driven to near extinction Natives sharing the American experience.

A large American population created both the prospect of Native obliteration and the shame attending that sin, as well as the inertia to fulfill this ideological undertaking in practice and in principle. It was a phenomenal achievement. More and more bodies sustained the colonies, and the new arrivals validated the premise of the enterprise as one of molding a new world fit for all peoples. Consequently, settlers looking to make an impact on Natives with a show of numbers occurred from the beginning of contact. For instance, English colonists in the Chesapeake Bay region wished to impress upon the foremost chieftain in the area, Powhatan, the large population that supported the Jamestown venture in the New World. The initially small number of colonists made the opposite impact, so English authorities took comfort from the fact that Powhatan's representative in England could not keep a tally of the number of people he saw there.[7] Upon his return, that man relayed this unsettling news to his leader. The chief listened and tried to comprehend what he was dealing with when interacting with Europeans at Jamestown. The point was clear. Even as the English were first arriving and doing so in very limited numbers, the backing of the mother country called attention to the long-term threat these settlers posed to Native Americans. Powhatan failed to grasp that it would be a struggle of like-minded peoples as each sought to incorporate the other into a new power structure where the opposing sides sought accommodation with one another so long as the "enemy" became more like its overseer. The New World was to be one Powhatan believed tilted markedly to his advantage because of his large numbers unless a heretofore undreamed of population suddenly discharged itself upon the land and overran his empire. When this did happen, the middle ground became a prescription for Native eclipse, not continued dominance.

At times, Natives did not need an invitation to visit European or American population centers to draw the requisite conclusion. The large number of soldiers crossing the praire also made an impression. For instance, with the outbreak of the Mexican American War, General Stephen Watts Kearny marched an American army south and through Cheyenne territory and shocked Chief Yellow Wolf as he counted the thousands of tents marking the location of that force. After that spectacle, the chief accepted the futility of Native resistance. Yellow Wolf told an Army officer that extermination confronted Natives if they failed to heed American norms and become sedentary people by "forming permanent habitations, and living like the whites, by tilling the ground and raising cattle."[8] That dire prediction of extermination nearly came to pass despite Native attempts to do just that, look to European models of civilization. Native reluctance to do so was not nearly as much a factor in their demise as was the American intention to make them suffer this end as American soldiers herded scores upon scores of settlers across the plains. The predictable result was conflict and when it was over the violence netted a stark result: American ascendancy and Native misfortune.

Events took on more structure than Americans merely trusting the whims of a show of force to secure Native submission. Battle also drove home the conquerors' advantage in numbers, something Little Turtle faced up to in Ohio in 1794. Blue Jacket did the same a few years after his defeat at Fallen Timbers when, as part of a delegation of chiefs visiting Philadelphia, he submitted a letter to President Washington. He wrote to his "father," stating he had been deceived by the false offer of British assistance and now he encouraged his young men to seek peace. Blue Jacket's journey to the capital consummated the terms of the Treaty of Greenville that had ended the fighting and promised a Native refuge on their land. It was surrender, and Washington responded with a letter telling his "children" that their lands in "Indian Country" would be secure and they could live in peace with Americans if Natives raised cattle and planted corn—assimilate along settler norms.[9] Unfortunately, in the years to come, Americans did not enforce their guarantee of Native sovereignty in the Ohio region (or anywhere else for that matter) and more fighting erupted, ending with the same prescription for peace: Natives forced onto smaller holdings of land with the understanding that they adopt American culture in order to survive. This pattern repeated itself until U.S. territorial claims reached the Pacific Ocean, and Natives found themselves confined to reservations. By this time, the duplicity in U.S. guarantees reached the height of leaving Natives frozen in the ambiguity of the standard that had brought them to complete subjugation: an American promise to safeguard Native sovereignty so long as it expressed an adherence to American values and norms. In this way, repetition proved a key element of this success in counterinsurgency; the ascendant power's continual guarantee of a shared space for its conquered subjects that was realized only at the end of a very long period of conflict. This cathartic interaction ultimately won settlers a war and left Natives an identity as "Indians," one acceptable to the victors as a symbol of defeat.

The great disparity in numbers allowed Americans to recant on a mutually agreeable outcome of settlement. This demographic advantage was something on throughout the 300-year conflict colonials and then Americans had capitalized with Natives. And here lies the answer as to why Natives could win battles but still lose the war. Somehow the great military clashes between Americans and Natives did not measure up to the glory assumed to define the struggle. Rather, the Americans achieved a demographic victory. Their deliberate effort in this regard makes a statement more pronounced than the Columbian Exchange, where European diseases devastated the Native populations, a mere happenstance harming Native Americans. More than this, the European, then American, motivation and thinking pointed to a calculated reality leading to a decimation of Native populations. Here lies a case for counterinsurgency.

1

The Insurgents

First Contacts and the "Indian Way of War"

Chief Powhatan emerged from his shelter and faced the assembly. A handful of Englishmen from the Jamestown colony nervously awaited his decision. A considerably larger number of Natives, members of his Powhatan tribe, did the same. The chief approached his daughter, Pocahontas, led her to the fire, and gazed down at the captive prone before him. After a pause, he reached out and grabbed that man's shirt, pulled John Smith to his feet, and joined his hand with that of the princess. Relief and elation erupted in the crowd as the bystanders believed a lasting peace had come to the Chesapeake Bay region.

A number of years after the events impacting the fate of Jamestown in 1608, a different ritual netted a similar peace much further north. Metacom, newly declared sachem of the Wampanoags, entered an English town in the New England colony of Massachusetts Bay in 1671 with all eyes upon him. He and a small entourage filed into the meeting hall and faced the elders of the Puritan community who had summoned him. In a few hours they exonerated the chief of wrong-doing concerning his threatening display of violence against English settlements near his village. That verdict came with a price, the endorsement of treaty terms leaving the Natives beholden to colonial authority. Metacom, or King Philip as the settlers called him, accepted the judgment, passed through the chamber, and exited the town with the English looking on confident that justice had been served.

In either case, any parley was but the calm before the storm. Each chief would spurn the terms of agreement and act with force, violence directed at the settlers among them who were soon decreed enemies. However, "enemies" was too strong a term to define a war that sought both the destruction and preservation of the foe. This reality spoke less to confusion of purpose and more to design, a Native effort to enjoin with the English in a shared world along a common frontier. At least up to 1640, colonials often, but not always, responded in kind, fostering wars of accommodation where the winner set a peace that placated the loser. No matter the assumed equilibrium, by 1680, the Natives discovered that it mattered a great deal who won these wars. To better understand this result, the *kind* of war that defined European and Native interactions from first contacts to permanent English settlement on the eastern seaboard warrants close examination.

Invasion

To fulfill their destiny of settling America, Europeans had to contend with the Native populations already living there. Whether to include them or not in their vision plagued colonial and later American thinking, reflecting their belief in the duality of the good and bad, of defining what was civilized and what was savage. The new arrivals balanced these two sentiments in opposition to one another when deciding the fate of the Native civilizations in North America. Winning over the Natives to what became an American vision, was the key effort and the means justifying the goal of expansion. The attempt largely failed since expansion inevitably bred conflict. This tendency continued long after the initial contacts, until Natives had forfeited their chance of not just expelling Europeans from North America, but also of stopping them from gaining further territory at the expense of the tribes. Consequently, a long war pitting settlers against Natives ensued, a war that delivered American domination. This outcome hinges on a view of Natives as insurgents over the entire 300-year period of conflict.

The trouble with depicting these events as an insurgency is that the story also can be told as an invasion. Europeans first established coastal enclaves and from these "bases of survival," they extended their reach across a continent at the expense of Natives, as Ian Steele argues in *Warpaths: Invasions of North America*.[1] While there obviously is a measure of truth in seeing this meeting of worlds in this way, the small inroads made by the early settlers meant such an invasion was impotent in the extreme. The propensity of settlers to build forts underscores that the initial European penetration of North America witnessed new arrivals who could hardly do more than defend themselves, so their arrival was not much of an invasion at all. Within a month of landing and founding the first permanent English settlement in the New World at Jamestown near the mouth of the Chesapeake Bay in May 1607, the colonists had built a crude, triangular fort, and by 1622, they stood behind a defensive perimeter 2,700 feet long. To the north in the first colony of what would become New England, something similar occurred. The Pilgrims constructed a fort in Plymouth, completing a facile enclosure in March 1621, four months after landing, and by 1623, they had expanded it to 2,700 feet. This defensive posture both north and south served very deep-seated plans, hence Steele's reference to "bases of survival." With these structures, there arose a portent of the long-term threat to Natives that settlers posed by their arrival in the New World. That invasion was to be a slow process, marked by gradual advancement after colonials first staved off disaster and consolidated their positions.

Naturally the settlers' first responsibility was an act of defense, and these strongholds and many others like them proved impervious to Native assault, a fortunate occurrence given the conflict that arose and the vulnerability of European settlements to attack because of their small numbers. While the forts went mostly unchallenged by Natives because of the difficulty of reducing these strongholds or, as was more often the case, due to their lack of interest in eliminating the new arrivals, the danger the colonials posed to the tribes did not diminish. One way or another, these defensive positions meant the Europeans had arrived to stay. When they cast their eyes on the interior, the invasion began.

Still, forts hardly represented exclusion or conflict between the competing sides until one of them, the settlers, won. This view of an advancing frontier as a rationale for the expansion of colonial society offers too brittle a construct. Certainly the early settlers turned into expansionists, but not only were the outcomes of this offensive not as clear as merely assigning a winner and a loser, interaction was more the norm. This insight is present in the scholarship stressing the shared cultural meanings among Natives and the new arrivals. In this respect, James Axtell made a significant contribution with his books, *The Invasion Within: The Contest of Cultures in Colonial North America*, and *Natives and Newcomers: The Cultural Origins of North America*, arguing that the decisive battlefield was fought in terms of religion: who was converting whom became the foremost concern. Interactions shifted as time elapsed and events unfolded to the detriment of Natives. These shifts made it clear that the battlefield included more than the woods, mountains, and plains but also encompassed meanings that defined culture. The winner on this "battlefield" held the advantage. To put this another way, Axtell argues that the tensions persisted as long as they did between newcomers and Natives because of Native success on this cultural battlefield.[2]

Measuring this dynamic reveals more complexity and further questions.

The most important question is this: when did the power structure change, thereby allowing a beleaguered few to shift from mere survival to posing a looming threat to Native populations? Colonial motives in waging this struggle took time to crystallize. Carving civilization out of the wilderness represented the first step of this evolutionary process, an end redefining necessity as something else over time. The colonial mission of returning to England, a place soon to become uncorrupted after beholding the example of the virtuous civilization in the "New World," faded as permanent settlement became more desirable and probable.[3] The missionary zealousness of those in the New England colonies matched the economic motives of the inhabitants of Jamestown, at least in this respect: as the colonies clearly became long-term ventures, survival with the noble purpose of bettering the Old World through moral example or economic rejuvenation shrunk in favor of the settlers standing on their own for their own gains in the New World. Soon those colonists crafting this experiment directed their efforts inward, toward consolidation and expansion, not outward and toward a return to Europe. It was, as Vernon Parrington famously distinguishes in *The Colonial Mind*, the moment that Puritans living in the colonies but who associated themselves with the Old World deferred to "Yankees," or those making their way in America and doing so as a "product of native conditions."[4] When this shift in mindset occurred in New England and the Chesapeake Bay region, continued confrontations between colonials and Natives in North America loomed large despite the shared entity that was this emerging entity.

By 1680, the invasion had paid handsome dividends as the colonists secured a permanent lodgment on the continent, having overcome a valiant Native opposition conducted over an extended period of time. Nominally one would be quick to label the failed Native resistance a response to an invasion given the outcome: settlers no longer huddled along the coast and instead enjoying a large, prosperous expanse of territory. However, it was never just an invasion. In the New England colonies and in the area around Jamestown, as English settlements expanded, the relationship gradually reworked itself so that the Natives were the minority population in the various sections along the coast of North America now under the control of the new arrivals who looked to compel that Native world to submit to colonial authority. For this reason, the Natives mounted an insurgency, since most of them accepted the new presence and the mix that it entailed. Then Natives resisted the coercion that went with the establishment of an English hegemony. Indeed, for a time, all parties believed in a shared new world. The European arrival was less of an invasion and more of an overture to foster a mutually developing civilization, no matter how different the cultures may have been. This view explains why the Natives gave the colonials a chance to survive and become such powerful overlords, capable of dictating this relationship on increasingly inimical terms to Native interests. To better understand this shift in power requires a look at the Indian way of war.

The Indian Way of War

The Native military response to the newcomers mirrored how tribes had fought among themselves before any contact with Europeans. A complex pattern of warfare had been established to mask the demographic fragility that characterized the majority of Native settlements. By and large the fighting consisted of small raiding parties that attempted to outwit one another, inflicting a few casualties and fewer deaths. These results were considered a great success. This "Indian way of war," therefore, represented a virtual pageantry of conflict as tribes sparred with one another for hunting grounds and arable land that meant little to them if acquired with too much expenditure in blood.[5] A sudden drop in population could mean starvation from a paucity of land under cultivation or from a lack of successful hunting. The demands of survival required that the fighting not kill too many warriors. Some scholars contend that this pre-contact world at times deviated from the ritualized and personalized conflict and generated violence that can be likened to what awaited Natives when facing colonials and later Americans. A surprise attack could greatly increase casualties, and small clashes over time could produce crippling losses as well. In the right circumstances, Native warfare could achieve an "efficiency" that resulted in a large number of battle deaths. Even so, the Native approach to war, which preserved a demographic balance, contrasted with the European practice of waging war in the Americas which inflicted a great many casualties in an effort to vanquish a foe.[6]

The Native practice of the military art grew out of a desire of limiting conflict to protect and sustain pockets of settlement. This practice became the norm no matter the location on the continent, and some experts today are quick to equate the limited engagements to guerrilla warfare.[7] This label requires some further analysis. Clearly, Natives, most of the time, showed great restraint when making war. They often operated in small war parties, the low numbers of combatants designed to prevent large losses. Even when they confronted one another in big formations, the fighting seldom escalated to a point that produced many casualties. However, this effort to husband their manpower and resources hardly mimicked a modern guerrilla army, which avoids pitched battle and bides its time to facilitate a larger, more devastating attack. Instead, the purposely small scale fighting that characterized the engagement of Native military systems was designed to keep foes at bay and safely marginalized within an area of territorial claim. In this way, Natives sought coexistence with inferior enemies and this was the chief function of the Indian way of war. For this reason, there rarely was an attack designed to crush the enemy. This lack of a knockout blow was a key difference between Native warfare and guerrilla warfare as it is understood today, and it was a fatal flaw. The tendency to tolerate the enemy became a tremendous error when facing the intractable foe represented by permanent European settlement.

For eastern tribes, the forts they built underscored their restraint. Although crude in comparison to European fortifications, these structures effectively protected the limited concentrations of Native populations from attack by other Natives. While the powerful members of the Iroquois confederation developed sophisticated methods of assaulting these strong points, such Native attacks were infrequent and successes rare.[8] Rather, forts represented the general standoff characterized by conflict that did not produce large casualties. Yet, one could hardly claim that Native tribes were in possession of a clearly delineated territories. In contrast to their European counterparts, Natives held no aspirations of erecting borders defining separate domains. Land was in demand as tribes competed to control vast territory for hunting and farming, or a combination of these activities, crucial to sustain the Native communities. Rigid enforcement of these zones was impossible, undesirable, and unnecessary. Instead, large tribes staked out a claim and projected power across an expansive area, allowing lesser tribes a place among them. In the east, the Five Nations of the Iroquois including the Mohawk, and the powerful Algonquian tribes near the Great Lakes region such as the Huron, dominated the interior. This feat left tribes along the coast competing with one another to form malleable arrangements to achieve the goal of both sustenance and authority in a more limited locale. A charismatic leader or *sachem* could surface and bring some unity to a particular region, but the longevity of that power center was always in question given the mortality of the unifying figure. Moreover, the fabric of such an empire was elastic and its vitality in question. The need for a desired balance pointed to an Indian way of war: norms of warfare designed to foster coexistence among enemies. In this way, regional divides became pronounced.

The specifics mattered regarding the first contacts, for the tribes that greeted Europeans in Jamestown and Plymouth were those marginalized by the more powerful entities in the interior. This fact underscored the interchange, as well as factionalism, that beset all Natives in North America. Rivalry, often leading to warfare, arose in numerous places and at various times. An Indian way of war surfaced as well, but it fluctuated based on tribal needs. Protecting trade or land could be one such motive; another could be a determination to replenish the population by taking captives. Other attacks reminded some tribes of their inferiority to their neighbors and to mind their place in the existing complex political structure. On the coast, power blocks went to war with this aim in mind. The resulting clashes were capable of reshuffling alliances locally, but wars were hardly able or intended to reshape a coastal region existing on the periphery of larger and more vibrant Native entities. The compartmentalization of Natives in the east meant regional divides that favored the European arrivals. The feeble pockets of settlers could indeed survive should they find a niche among the rivalries that defined the coastal peoples but seldom involved their more powerful inland neighbors.

European contact fundamentally upset the balance in place along the coast and eventually in the interior as well, but not before Natives demonstrated an ability to react to the unfolding changes and maintain their norms of warfare. In this respect, the greatest Native success came west of the Mississippi River, where the European intrusion had the potential to radically change the status quo as early as the mid–sixteenth century when the horse arrived in North America after 1541. By the end of the 1700s, the horse had become a mainstay of life on the plains. More mobility when fighting might have radically escalated the military confrontations there due to swifter strike capabilities and the ability to range farther and attack previously unreachable villages. However, this did not happen. Instead, the plains tribes made sure to again establish an equilibrium that defined warfare as it always had been: a limited engagement with few casualties. The horse meant that warriors could attack with fewer numbers than required in a more risky ground attack and that the attacker could usually count on an easy escape. Individual glory was possible as well in the small raiding party as one challenger could signal a foe to a showdown.[9] As a result, personal acclaim became the ideal, not a struggle pitting one civilization against other.

The Comanche probably best exemplified this shift that quickly became self-regulating. Emerging from the northwest foothills in the early eighteenth century, their success as a mounted society allowed them to dominate an expansive tract of territory in the Southeastern Plains for a hundred years from roughly 1750 to 1850. To make room for themselves they expelled many tribes, the Apache the most victimized in this respect. The Comanche as a power was new, and the horse made this possible, the goal being coexistence with neighbors safely relegated to the periphery of their empire of *Comanchería*. Soon the Comanche turned the horse from an engine of war into a commodity of trade, and this exchange required partners, preferably Americans. This arrangement still demanded an enemy, and the Comanche found one in the south, raiding Mexican territory to secure the chief commodities of empire: horses and slaves. A test of strength decided on a battlefield that risked all, did not enjoin their thinking. Instead, to safeguard this loosely defined empire, Comanche warriors undertook an interminable struggle personifying the Indian way of war.[10]

In the southwest, the Apache remained dominant in a vast territory that from north to south extended a thousand miles. This huge expanse was the formidable land of *Apachería* and home to perhaps 6,000 Apache. However, allegiance to tribe determined loyalties, and conflict among Apaches was as frequent as their clashes with Spaniards and later Mexicans. Even the name Apache, or "enemy" (*apachu*) in the neighboring Zuni tribe's language, under-scored the lack of unity among these people beholden to a common cause only in the eyes of their foes.[11] Spread out, family centered, and quick to embrace a life of conflict and hardship in a barren land, the Apache inhabiting this empire underscored a decentralized existence unconsciously laying claim to an empire. The contrast with settlers could not be stronger. Among the Apache, a hierarchical impulse was lacking and, therefore, so too was a man-date expressing their suzerainty. Additionally, while conflict was a staple, conquest was never an objective. Only European arrival made clear the dimensions of Apacheria as something more than a sparring ground of rival tribes. That territory soon became land that had to be defended.

The Sioux rose to prominence by using the gun and the horse to such good effect that by 1850, as their contact with Americans intensified, the West-ern Sioux of some 15,000 people had laid claim to much of the vast Northern Plains. They had overwhelmed more sedentary peoples such as the Mandans and Hidatsas, and the Sioux had elbowed their way past the Blackfeet, Crow, and Pawnee.[12] These tribes and others suffered defeats that did in fact cripple their ability to challenge Sioux power. But weaker rivals were allowed to exist on the periphery; destroying them entirely was still alien to Native war prac-tices. This was not conquest but merely expansion for the sake of survival. The atomized living among like peoples such as the Sioux underscored this point. They did not concentrate so much as act as a conglomeration of peoples striving toward the same end, but not doing so in unison. It was a confused situation except in its more general and stark realities: an aggressive people able to project power across an expansive land because of a need to get out of the way of one another. That was the extent of tribal cooperation.

Once Sioux warriors forced an enemy to the perimeter, they kept that foe at bay with a sterling warning in the form of *counting coup*, the ability of a warrior to touch an opponent with a long stick, and escape untouched himself. Much like the Comanche, war was a contest of horsemanship demonstrating individual prowess. This competition persisted across the plains as Native empires like the Sioux became viable because these constructs were designed to withstand the permanent presence of rival powers safely marginalized on the outskirts of huge swaths of land. Raids and hunting expeditions performed vital economic service, but also kept tabs on enemies ensuring they did not recover or unite with other tribes to then challenge the dominant people. What the plains—and eastern—Natives desired was a means of controlling warfare on their terms. To ensure this result, tribes were comfortable with using raids and ambush to foster an almost endless state of war.

Those Natives roaming the plains kept a number of tribes more or less confined along the extensive western coastline. Just as in the east, these Natives on the west coast struggled among themselves and built alliances and fostered rivalries, but seldom looked beyond their homelands. In many ways, the horse crafted this separation; migrations occurred from north to south among the tribes embracing that animal, almost never from west to east or vice versa among more sedentary peoples. Geography, mostly deserts and mountains, and simply the vast plains, reinforced this compartmentalization, making some kind of unified Native resistance a fiction to the west as in the east. The result was a haphazard response across the continent when facing settler incursions.

Yet, something further contributed to this reality, and it stemmed from the Native war practices. A mentality of checks and counterweights dominated Native thinking during the pre-contact years and influenced each Native interaction with Europeans in North America. Once these newcomers arrived, more often than not, Natives decided to capitalize on their presence. Pitifully small in numbers, the early settlers hardly inspired fear. On the contrary, their firearms appeared potentially beneficial. An alliance with Europeans or, better, Europeans bound to them, could ensure Native ascendancy over neighboring enemies. A great shift seemed imminent: new technology allowing a weaker tribe to challenge its neighbor. Just as likely, European weapons offered the strongest tribe a chance to solidify the power structure in their favor in whatever region they resided. One way or the other, conflict would continue, but it would do so along norms of tempering violence, even when Natives encountered Europeans using harsher methods. The Native military response was designed to keep rivals as peripheral peoples, neutralized with a mixture of intimidation and punitive force. Should something be useful among those cast to the outskirts of a power center, those in the dominant position would co-opt it. For this reason, Native warfare sought coexistence with Europeans and frequently looked to benefit from this relationship. In so doing, Natives committed a grave mistake because their thinking allowed colonials a reprieve to survive and then to expand. The Indian way of war, understood as more than merely a guerrilla-like resistance and also as an effort to foster a deliberate state of permanent rivalry, cost the Native tribes not just a chance to defeat traditional enemies, but to defeat the newcomers as well. The carry-over from pre-contact to contact was an Indian way of war designed to project power via low-intensity conflict. This more sophisticated military practice, rather than merely limiting battle deaths, helps explain the results in Jamestown and New England.

Early Contacts

The confrontation at Jamestown starting in 1607 exemplifies how Natives missed a chance to eliminate the early English settlements because of an Indian way of war consisting of marginalizing enemies rather than destroying them. Chief Powhatan exercised the greatest power in the Chesapeake Bay area, and he stood at the head of an empire consisting of a confederation of thirty eastern Algonquian tribes totaling more than 14,000 people including 3,200 warriors. His subjects brought him tidings of the new arrivals early on, indicating his great influence. As the chief considered his options, he pondered how the colonials might augment his military power. From the outset, the obstreperous Virginians refused to augment Powhatan's military power, and so tensions arose, and an uneasy standoff soon characterized the situation in Virginia. The rudimentary forts and a handful of able-bodied men allowed the settlers to defy Powhatan's ultimatums, but only timely reinforcement in 1609 prevented the complete collapse of the colony. When Sir Thomas Gates sailed into the bay that summer, he found sixty survivors in such a desperate plight that he ordered the colony to be abandoned. This self-defined "starving time" was the closest the colony came to extermination. Just as Gates was leaving in June 1610, more ships arrived and landed a new complement of 300 men. The standoff continued.

The Native refusal to attack and completely destroy the enemy said less about the limitations of their strength and more about such thinking as simply alien to Powhatan, a position appearing acceptable because of the very small number of Europeans. For this reason, cooperation with these outsiders made sense to the Natives; their extermination did not. The logic flowed naturally enough to give rise to the Pocahontas folklore: Powhatan's daughter nobly sowing peace among rivals by saving John Smith from execution. An offer of alliance is surely the best explanation of her intercession on behalf of this

Pocahontas saving the life of Capt. John Smith (Library of Congress).

colonist. Powhatan's main concern was readying himself for a new clash with his enemies to the north and possibly in the interior. He could afford to hold off on a war intended to annihilate the new arrivals. In fact, because of their firearms, Powhattan believed that the Europeans might prove useful. Given what was to come, this hope proved a mistake; extermination may have been the best option. However, the point is that the Natives did not seriously consider this option. The Native world view in a military context was a fatal weakness; they were willing to continue to challenge the land controlled by neighboring tribes with raids and ambushes while tolerating, even fostering, the nascent threat in Jamestown because it might help serve this larger purpose. With settlers bottled up in mere enclaves on the coast, Powhatan correctly judged the situation, but failed anyway.

A change in leadership prompted a change in approach when Powhatan ceded control to his younger brother, Opechancanough. The new *sachem* planned a war of revenge given his ill treatment at the hands of John Smith years earlier. Smith had held a gun to his head and demanded corn; Smith got the corn and the colony got the young man's lasting animosity. Smith had not endeared himself to many Englishmen either. Many had chaffed under his firm rule, but looser strictures invited calamity, an inability to secure even basics such as storing food or preparing defenses. Long after Smith, the colony struggled in purpose and design, but it endured as other leaders imposed draconian measures. The shallow front was strong enough to prevent the colony's complete collapse, but in 1622, when Opechancanough planned his offensive, the English toehold in Jamestown was still feeble, with a small population that was beset by internal strife. Moreover, the colony continued to antagonize the Natives by requisitioning supplies and land and proving to be politically unreliable. If Opechancanough was not careful, he risked having the English upend his supremacy in the region.

Given its problems, the colony appeared ripe for a counterstroke to wipe it out. Instead, the new chief looked to some guile and surprise in order to hem in the colonials and keep them compliant to Native designs.[13] On March 22, 1622, the English awoke to a sudden ambush as Natives mixed among them as usual, but then suddenly turned and attacked all the colonists they could find in an eighty-mile radius. By nightfall, 347 settlers lay dead, a huge number given the entire population totaled only 1,240 and that few Natives had been killed in the exchange. However, there was no follow-up blow. Those colonists remaining retired to eight strongholds and girded themselves for the worst. More died from wounds or sickness. Reinforcements continued to arrive from England, and the surviving colonials held on.

What might be called guerrilla attacks seeking to limit colonial power had carried the Natives a long way and, on the face of things, back to parity. However, the balance was tenuous in the extreme. Once having weathered the immediate crisis, the colonists launched ten punitive strikes in a year and slowly re-established themselves in the Chesapeake Bay region. A tentative truce—ten years later—in 1632 spoke to renewed stalemate but found Natives on the wrong side of a demographic equation that favored the colonists. The Natives tried a final time to alter this trajectory when a very elderly Opechan-canough launched another attack on Jamestown in April 1644. This act of desperation again relied on surprise and guile and again netted results as the Natives killed 500 settlers. But this time, no crisis ensued, for the colonists were too numerous, perhaps 10,000 strong. Instead, a brisk English counter-stroke broke the will of the Powhatan Empire, and it disintegrated, having lost a long war. In just under forty years, Natives had vacillated between peace and war, between harassment and attack. Much as in pre-contact times, the Indian way of war had engendered a war of attrition that swung in favor of the most powerful tribe. In this case, the English were that tribe.

The Natives failed to control the newcomers, but they did succeed in creating a survival mentality that gripped the colony and fostered its own sense of justice among the colonists in the Virginia area. For this reason, the beleaguered citizens of Jamestown soon cast aside whatever morals they may have had when entreating with Natives. For example, when facing the onslaught in 1622, the Christians invited a number of Native dignitaries to dinner and poisoned the wine they served, killing over 100 of them. Those overseeing the colony from London questioned the treacherous methods in place to win this war but fell quiet when the inhabitants of Jamestown assured their overlords that the Natives merited no such consideration.[14] The perpetrators of this crime reasoned that the rules of war did not apply to the godless Natives. Whether this belief stemmed from a colonists' survival instinct or not, a European mindset when making war cast Natives in the ranks of heretics. The net gain was the acquisition of land, a paramount goal in Jamestown since it undergirded the entire enterprise. It was, after all, a colony granted a charter for the purpose of rewarding its investors via cash crops. The need to survive had indeed transplanted morality as colonials united economic purpose and religious conviction. This intellectual feat represented a great success, even if it was shrouded in hypocrisy.

That accomplishment also meant survival had transplanted reality. A dubious claim of the Natives as dependents accompanied colonial ventures in Virginia and had surfaced early on. In the first few years of the colony, despite pitifully small numbers that belied any claims of ascendancy, the settlers tried to force Powhatan to accept English sovereignty. The charter governing the colony declared that all efforts should be made to "kindly" treat the "savage and heathen Peoples in those Parts" and "use all proper Means" to "sooner bring them to the Knowledge of God, and the Obedience of the King, his Heirs, and Successors." This statement failed in the symbolism of the moment. At one point, Powhatan literally refused to kneel and be crowned by a colonist. Imposing English dominion also failed in the fallout of Native violence unleashed on the struggling colony. Scattered as they were in communities imbedded among Natives, in too many ways the English depended on Powhatan, who clearly saw himself in an equal, if not superior bargaining position. In response, the English looked to isolate Powhatan so that "all other weroances [*sic*] about him first to acknowledge no other lord but King James."[15] The colonials enjoyed only limited results, but their repulse of Opechancanough in 1622, and that chief's subsequent defeat in 1644, registered without fail the growing colonial might. While a mix of both settlers and Natives again became the norm, this grouping occurred along with a demographic factor decidedly in favor of the colonists. Because of this condition, the English in the Chesapeake Bay area at last could realistically demand Native subservience, as Virginians representing a new power established themselves after successful war in the "tribal zone."[16]

English willingness to engage in the Indian way of war came to a resounding end a generation after the bitter struggles of 1622 and 1644 when Virginia again fell into crisis as the Jamestown settlement faced a new conflict, this one stemming from an internal power struggle reaching unprecedented levels of violence. Continued Native raiding on the frontier victimized lands belonging to the settlers who were advancing further inland from the first Jamestown settlements. The clashes with Natives fostered tensions between the old and new parts of the colony. In April 1676, those living in the outlying areas responded to the failure of those representing the original lodgment to aid their neighbor's beleaguered state by sparking a civil war. Nathaniel Bacon, a property owner and a new arrival to Virginia, spurred on this revolt. Raising an army, Bacon lashed out at friendly Natives living peacefully within the confines of the colony. By turning on these people, Bacon inflicted brutality on a generalized foe, acts the colonists condoned only because the struggle had been long and traumatic. To many colonists, shared existence was no longer an option, and this outlook contributed to a willingness to resort to violence all too often. Jamestown's governor, William Berkeley, resisted Bacon's push for what historian Wilcomb Washburn in *The Governor and the Rebel* called a "crusade for extirpation" of Natives.[17] However, Berkeley's pleas were ignored by a significant part of the population which sided with the vigilantes. Assuming command of a punitive war against all Natives, the man leading "Bacon's Rebellion" threatened colonials and Natives alike. Only pestilence spared the Natives at the time; Bacon succumbed to an illness and died suddenly in October of that year. That illness spared the colonials as well. While the rebels managed to burn a part of Jamestown to the ground after a confrontation with Berkeley, Bacon's death shortly thereafter meant a temporary calm returned to Jamestown. The collapse of Bacon's Rebellion produced a cessation of hostilities in the vicinity of Jamestown, but in terms of Native and colonial coexistence, a mix of settlers and Natives was no longer the norm. It soon became clear that the English would not be satisfied with an Indian way of war of their own, one tolerating the existence of Natives within an assumed but as yet undefined frontier. The fiction of Native dependency had yielded to the reality of Native exclusion from the English communities.

Further north in the New England colonies of first Plymouth in 1620 and then Massachusetts Bay in 1628, the same desperation arose among the colonists and left scars. If more religious in intent than those inhabiting the Jamestown colony, Pilgrims and Puritans soon united survival with religious mission, and no act went unsanctioned in the name of god. For instance, the professional soldier Myles Standish helped defend Plymouth by meeting with a number of minor *sachems* in the area in 1622 and assassinating his Native guests, at one point lunging across a table and striking a warrior in the neck.[18] Massasoit, a leader of the Wampanoag tribe located adjacent to the new arrivals, had suggested the killing, proving his ability to use the newcomers to help weaken his rivals. Colonials condoned the savagery of the moment in the name of greater security, the English looking to ally with local *sachems* to better establish their position. While Plymouth's accords with Massasoit promised to curry the favor of his tribe, other powerful Native peoples in the area remained suspect in English eyes and for good reason. Many tribes plotted to crush the new arrivals. The mistrust was all the more intense because the Puritans believed their colonies were a function of god's salvation and required a defense to ward off the devil, a role they cast upon the Natives.

Those few Natives who remained near English settlements submitted to colonial authority as if to aid the great project underway. Squanto is a telling example of a Native who greatly helped the English by providing them with better methods of raising crops and spreading rumors among Natives that the English could summon sickness on demand. Given that disease had devastated Squanto's Patuxet tribe and greatly reduced other Native populations in the area, his warning to fear the new arrivals was a powerful advantage for the settlers; most Natives heeded his call and kept their distance. The colonies used that reprieve to consolidate their position as best they could. It was a wise "if obvious" step to take. Facing a struggle for survival and enjoying only a tenuous foothold in the New World, coexistence with Natives was the reality in the near term. Consequently, so as not to unnecessarily antagonize their neighbors, the colonials, for the most part, muted their ideological convictions that defined their colonization of the New World as a holy quest favored by god's providence. Any hope for suzerainty remained muted as well. Enmeshed in the local tribal power arrangements, the English accepted an uneasy stalemate, their dispersed colonies merely adding to the mosaic of power blocks now crowding the coastal area in the north.

Whatever equilibrium those in New England had established came to an end when another supplicant of the English, Uncas of the Mohegan, played upon English fears to seek an advantage. He followed the lead of Massasoit. If the colonists humbled a rival, Uncas' position would improve. Acting on this assumption, he told the English that his neighbors, the Pequots, threatened the new settlements south of the colonial power center of Boston and along the Connecticut River. When that tribe refused to submit to subsequent English demands that it extradite those accused of having murdered an English trader, the English looked to cow all tribes in the area with a sudden strike at the Pequot. New Englanders entered the Connecticut valley and struck the Pequot village at the Mystic River on May 26, 1637. Their Narragansett and Mohegan allies surrounded the camp as ninety men from Connecticut attacked the stronghold in the early morning and forced their way inside. The Natives resisted desperately, and soon the English grew confused and the assault stalled. Facing a multitude of Natives, the colonists set fire to the fort, killing at least 400 Pequots, including a large number of women and children. The attackers lost but two men and twenty were wounded. This spectacular act of military intimidation stunned the Native allies of the English, including those led by Uncas, by being far too excessive and outside the norms of Native warfare. They condemned the attack "because it is too furious, and slays too many men." The English rejoiced for having smote the heathens.[19]

The severity of the attack emphasized the larger aim of the assault, Puritan intimidation. In the wake of the violence, Uncas could not have missed the now obvious regional English supremacy. This rapidly accomplished victory trumped all morality since the Pequot War of 1637 allowed the landholdings of that devastated tribe to become immediate English possessions. The English also seized great quantities of *wampum* (beads woven into decorative belts) and forced a number of tribes to make payment in that prized Native commodity as tribute. The Mystic River attack had little to do with English justice and much to do with economic gain as the colonies, in this case Massachusetts Bay and an emerging Connecticut, vied with one another to benefit from territorial expansion.[20] With this result, Uncas, like the Wampanoags, found himself a minor player in local politics, dependent upon the English for good favor that included protection from neighboring tribes and shelter from overly punitive English retribution based on clearly flimsy, if not fabricated, affronts. As if to underscore this point, a few years after the Pequot War, the English reaffirmed their alliance with Massasoit but in a context that acknowledged his vassalage. Those Natives allied to the English could only blame themselves for their subordinate stature, having first aided English settlement and then encouraged the punitive English forays. An Indian way of war was now a means of expressing coexistence in the region largely on colonial terms. This shift underscored the English push to consolidate their hold in the New World, not as a means of survival, but as a stage for English demands of sovereignty further turning Natives into supplicants.

The English desire to play the role of overseer, exacting tribute from tribes, and to ally with Natives on a temporary basis (until further advances could be made), explained Native motives for war in New England in 1675. By this time, the Indian way of war spoke to a reversal of fortune, with Natives trying to hold on to mere pockets of territory and the colonists looking to further marginalize opponents and allies alike. The Native task was now one of remaining apart of the English colonies and this effort made Native dependence real. Yet the colonists would not adhere to this arrangement. When the next round of fighting erupted, the colonists closed in for the kill and largely eliminated the Native villages among them.

Metacom (also: Metacomet), the successor to Massasoit, inherited the Native struggle against European inroads in New England. Known to the English as King Philip, by the time this *sachem* surfaced as the titular leader of the Wampanoag, he led only 300 warriors; the colonies were able to field an army of 10,000. The great disparity in numbers made it unlikely that the new chief was plotting an all-out war as a Native convert to Christianity, John Sassamon, told the English. When that man was killed and the English executed three Wampanoags for that crime, tensions soon spilled over in June 1675 and pushed King Philip into a war he could not win. He did the next best thing by attempting to wage a protracted resistance from the swamps and hinterlands of New England. His sallies had some impact, and the New England frontier disintegrated into violence as the Natives continued to raid English settlements and the colonials responded with strikes against Native villages. Even when King Philip failed to engage the enemy in battle, as was his usual reaction to an English show of force, the Wampanoags often abandoned their homes and food stores, producing much hardship for themselves. However, the evasive measures ensured the war continued. This success, such as it was, posed great problems for the English as additional tribess joined with King Philip after witnessing the English inability to curb the fighting. The result was a destructive war, one of the bloodiest in American history, that claimed close to 9,000 lives, two thirds of them Natives, and left the New England tribes broken militarily. The English recovered; the Natives did not.

King Philip's strategic reality was hopeless, dooming him to defeat. He had one reason to continue fighting. The resistance he mounted was designed to conduct an attritional war so painful that the English would again accept him into the world shared between them. After all, some thirty years of peace between New Englanders and Natives had preceded the war. Fighting as a guerrilla force was the imperfect answer to redeem the Native existence as one of yielding political sovereignty with the understanding of an equitable cultural exchange with the nearby English communities.[21] King Philip wanted to force a stalemate, not pursue an impossible war of expelling the colonials from Native soil. Preserving their place on this changing landscape merited a war because King Philip possessed few options due to demographic collapse: only 18,000 Indians remained in the region facing over 60,000 colonials. No assembly of Native tribes could destroy the settlements. While the war challenged the colonials on an extensive basis and the damage of property and loss of life was extreme, they never faced annihilation.[22] Nor could Natives retreat from the coast; that would spark war with other tribes in the interior, particularly the Mohawk. King Philip was right. Better to face a war at home to secure a place on the periphery of English domains than to engage in a war with Natives outside of Wampanoag territory in a desperate attempt to start over.

King Philip, alias Metacomet of Pokanoket (Library of Congress).

The settlers did prosecute the war as one of extermination, however, advancing to eliminate those following or allied to King Philip. Even those claiming neutrality were not safe, most famously the Narragansett. One thousand Englishmen launched a surprise attack on one of their villages in December 1675, killing a comparable number of Indians and suffering ninety dead in the process. The English attack was prompted by the uncertainty in the area. Part of this insecurity was self-inflicted as Massachusetts Bay, Plymouth, and Connecticut remained rivals, each seeking advantage in the power struggle unfolding in southern New England. Conceivably, one or more of these colonies could become a victim of the Indian way of war and marginalized as a power center. In many ways, this twist of fate befell Plymouth, absorbed into Massachusetts Bay a decade after the war. But the common purpose of focusing the outcome of this practice on the Natives living among them ensured that the colonies maintained enough cohesion to defeat their rivals. This shared aim highlighted the other uncertainty: should the Narragansett join with King Philip, their many warriors would greatly complicate any favorable outcome of the war. The motive extended beyond a military calculation, however. The main reason for the attack lay in measuring English suzerainty in the region. The Narragansett had not conceded English supremacy. Yet, in the years leading up to King Philip's War, that tribe had suffered losses from disease and therefore a diminished status. This loss of power came at a time of increasing English demands for land. The obvious clash was pending, and the English decided that the ongoing war offered them a chance to end this rivalry on terms favorable to the colonists.[23]

The parallels of this attack to the Mystic River battle were clear, but less so in assessing the success of the action. Again, a colonial army, in this case, men from each colony as well as a small contingent of Mohegan and Pequot warriors, surrounded the stronghold, one protected by an earthen and masonry wall and located of an island in a swamp. They attacked immediately just as a blizzard descended on the battlefield. Forcing their way into the fort, confusion soon reigned, and as at Mystic, the attack stalled. The English then burned the village, a surprising act for two reasons. One, plunder was a key motive in launching the assault, and destroying the village forfeited that opportunity. Two, the attackers needed food to augment their meager supplies, and they needed shelter to protect them from the extreme weather. Soon after the attack, the English faced a perilous fate. Exhausted, hungry, and suffering from the cold, they withdrew in haste as more Natives rallied against them. This relief force came from a nearby fort housing the foremost Narragansett *sachem*, Canonchet. Their approach put the English in immediate danger and underscored that the colonial attack had missed its mark. A large village—perhaps the largest village—had been destroyed, but the main enemy camp remained intact, and its warriors were ready to attack. They did so, forcing the English into a harried retreat and inflicting a loss of life amounting to almost ten percent of the attacking force.

Unlike what happened at Mystic River, the Great Swamp attack did not end the war; rather it expanded it. As the new year unfolded, the English position was still one of superiority, but also one of waging a costly and ongoing war against King Philip and now the Narragansett and other previously neutral or peaceful tribes. Perhaps not surprisingly, King Philip's success as a guerrilla leader peaked in the aftermath of the swamp attack. Although he remained in command of only a few hundred warriors, the surviving Narragansett launched attacks of their own, easing King Philip's efforts in the vicinity of his village on the Mount Hope peninsula and to the west of his homeland. By the late winter and spring of 1676, the English appeared all but prostrate before the Native raiding tactics. But the colonies responded with similar raiding attacks, and these so disrupted Native food supplies that the colonials stumbled onto a strategic advantage to win the war. They could starve their foe into submission. In addition, the English enjoyed a tremendous boon from a Mohawk attack as this tribe descended on the coastal region at English invitation. That tribe's intervention robbed those Natives involved in King Philip's War of any chance of accommodation with their enemy. Instead, they faced extermination, caught between the unforgiving English and the longstanding animosity of a neighboring force.

The incremental consequences of English actions—that the Mohawk could find themselves the next target of the English—did not resonate with the Iroquois. Rather, the Mohawk could tell themselves they now enjoyed parity with the colonies, facing at the worst an extended war of attrition with their new neighbors and one waged with guerrilla warfare: in other words, a familiar war of coexistence. A shrewder assessment would have come from acknowledging the fate of the "praying Indians" in the New England area. This small group of some 1,100 to maybe 3,000 Natives scattered across ten communities in the Massachusetts Bay colony, were survivors of past wars or of disease that had otherwise wiped out their tribes. Unlike some other tribes allied to the colonies that had switched allegiance and joined King Philip, the majority of these converts to Christianity had done nothing to arouse suspicion and, in fact, had fought alongside the colonials. Regardless, the English met them with recrimination after the outbreak of King Philip's War and incarcerated over 500 of them on Deer Island in Boston Harbor where they endured a bleak existence. An imperative justified during the crisis of war, this draconian measure underscored the fate of any Natives found within the confines of the colonies. The English denied them sovereignty, instead demanding a crude assimilation requiring Natives to forfeit their political authority and territorial claims. Any semblance of an Indian way of war as a means by which Natives accepted dependency to stake out some form of existence within the colonies faded as settlers imposed an impossible uniformity. When the war ended and the English released the captives on Deer Island, it was clear that even absorption into the English polity offered no guarantee of survival and that destruction of these peoples was the English ideal of their interaction with Natives.

That harsh reality soon overtook King Philip. The English eventually caused enough calamity that Natives betrayed the sachem, and he faced death and mutilation at the hands of the triumphant New Englanders. Yet, his fall had not been due to betrayal more than it was an inability to prosecute the war successfully. How could he? The Native objective was never to eliminate the colonial presence. Rather, the goal was to wage a guerrilla war to maintain the Native's place in this shared world. Before the war, in 1662, King Philip had accepted the previous agreements with colonials that included giving up the right to ally with other Natives or to sell land without first consulting Plymouth. The terms cast the defeated as subjects of the king and so it appeared they were. If protection before this treaty had meant coexistence, after 1622, it now clearly meant dependency. In this light, King Philip's War represented the end of an interracial harmony in New England as Natives launched a vain insurgency, seeking validation of a supposedly mutually agreed upon world.[24] Instead, after this war, the emerging powers, the English colonies, enjoyed cultural as well as political and territorial gains that left no room for Natives to live among them as separate communities.

Benjamin Church's success in deploying small parties of colonials and Native allies in ambush and raids included leading the party that surprised and killed King Philip. Church, a self-proclaimed frontiersman and who was given expansive powers by the colonial authorities in the face of the emergency, recognized the effectiveness of this manner of fighting. While his peers frowned on what they referred to as dishonorable combat, Church took ownership of something he described as "skulking everywhere in the bushes."[25] His unconventional practices revealed that the English had grown very proficient at one aspect of the Indian way of war and also another aspect. Victory no longer meant a reliance on guerrilla tactics in a war of survival, one masking a weakness in numbers, and one requiring coexistence with Natives. Instead, the Indian way of war in the hands of Englishmen now meant a marginalization of the Native threat to the growing colonies. In New England, colonials had learned how to push their enemies onto the periphery of empire. Banished to this uncivilized wilderness, the settlers kept the "devil" at arm's length. The same result had occurred to the south in Jamestown, even if the settlers there had not cast that outcome in overtly biblical terms. In either case, the end was clear: the frontier would remain unsettled but the colonies would enjoy a base excluding Natives.

The population numbers bear this out. By 1675, hardly 3,500 Natives remained in the Jamestown area, while the colonial population exceeded 38,000. In New England, the numbers are as striking. Maybe 9,000 Natives remained of an original population of 75,000, and these survivors existed among almost 50,000 colonials. Europeans had indeed transplanted themselves near the turn of the seventeenth century, and while disease had been a key element of this outcome, so had a military practice duplicating an Indian way of war.

After 1680

After first contact with colonials, Natives never mounted a resistance that sought to expel the new arrivals, allowing settlers the opportunity to gain strength and eventually contemplate expansion far beyond their initial feeble inroads along the coast. It was an outcome made possible by the Indian way of war, less a *de facto* guerrilla resistance and more a tendency of allowing enemies to linger along an ill-defined frontier. Once given a reprieve, colonials made the most of the opportunity and their progression was significant, marked by a shift from mere survival to parity to dominance. Colonial inferiority early on did not prevent claims of superiority at Jamestown, even at first contact, and this outlook persisted until the English dominance there was pronounced by the time of Bacon's Rebellion. In New England, King Philip's War was one of Natives trying to remain within the colonial apparatus, not their attempt to destroy it. This kind of approach meant that shortly after the European arrival, the Natives found themselves waging an insurgency. They attempted to remain a part, if not in control, of the new world being assembled. North and south, the colonials denied the Natives this opportunity despite internal strife, looming tensions with Crown authorities, and opposition from other European powers. Consequently, what had been fiction, a land governed by European norms, became a reality for the most part, as a number of English colonies lay east of the Appalachian Mountains, competing Native populations west of this boundary. Things would get worse for the Natives since this pattern would repeat itself at every incremental advance of the colonials and then Americans. At each step, settlers would claim the Natives as dependents of the expanding tide of settlement. This mandate meant that the war for North America was a counterinsurgency from first to last.

2

Stopping Outside Intervention

European Foes and the "Permanent Indian Frontier"

Chief Pontiac eyed the row of soldiers at full attention in equal intervals along the rampart. He remained calm and collected in appearance, as he guided his entourage into the center of Fort Detroit, a British stronghold in the Northwest. However, a growing anxiety gripped him as he waited for his opportunity to strike. His plan entailed a sudden attack on the unsuspecting garrison, the onrush he would direct to coincide with a rush to the gate to allow more warriors into the fort. However, the garrison remained vigilant and the English commander defiant, bellowing instructions at him to state his business and get clear of the fort. After some tense moments, Pontiac indeed told his group to exit, aware his purpose had been betrayed to the enemy. Pontiac's scheme to win a quick victory had flittered away, and his brewing rebellion in 1763 faced an uncertain future as a result. Still, he carried on, confident that he could spark a movement wresting away from English control the allegiance of the Natives. The war that would bear his name would be both successful and unsuccessful in this ambition.

Many years later in 1813 and just over fifty miles east of Fort Detroit, Chief Tecumseh of the Shawnee emerged from his enclosure. He barked some orders to his attendants and studied the terrain that lay in front of him as it slowly gained definition as the dawn came to the battlefield. His warriors and a large contingent of English soldiers defended an extended defensive line, expecting an American attack at any moment. As Tecumseh moved about the defenses, approving of one position, shifting men at another, he, like Pontiac, hid his dismay. Outnumbered three to one, the hopes for victory were faint, the idea of a gain even from defeat was just as remote. Too much advance and retreat had brought about this sorry state, and the chief expected

47

his men to face dire circumstances in but a few hours. Tecumseh also expected to die, making this stand along the Thames River his last battle, and thereby spare himself the doom that he believed awaited his people. His own demise merely dismayed him; the prospect of the end of his struggle cemented his lament for an opportunity lost. A voice announced a movement in the American lines, and Tecumseh moved forward to find his place in the tumult and in history as a martyr to a lost cause.

These were the great figures leading Native resistance to first colonial and then American expansion in trans–Appalachia, the region west of the Appalachian Mountains and east of the Mississippi River. The cause of each man spoke to the optimism and futility that, after 1680, an accord between settlers and Natives could be reached somewhere on the North American continent. Their mutual fate revealed that this opportunity had passed, affirming the forlorn hopes of the beleaguered tribes. When these two chiefs departed from the scene, the insurgents had lost another round of the fighting. The fault lay less with a Native failure to unify. The idea of unity was, at best, a mirage, as these leaders discovered. Rather, much of the result rested on the American success of engaging, at the same time, both European and Native American power on the continent. Seeking divisions among the Natives and their allies said much of the American view of any middle ground, and they found the vulnerability that they sought among their factionalized foes.

Native Allies

Americans increasingly gained the advantage versus their Native opponents, and settlers strove to force Natives to live in seclusion from them by establishing a "permanent Indian frontier," a firm boundary between them.[1] It never came to pass because it was never permanent. Colonials and then Americans never enjoyed a complete physical break from Native Americans. Rather, interaction was the norm until Americans expelled Natives altogether beyond a supposedly firm border, a border invalidated in the next period of American expansion that again witnessed interaction and coexistence until expulsion. Any permanent Indian frontier spoke to an ideal more than a reality. Yet, in another way, Americans did create such a border. Survival in the international competition that was the founding of the United States helped that nation take a crucial step toward this goal when a series of wars produced a tremendous American military accomplishment. A permanent frontier did arise that expelled European nations from North America, rivals that could blunt or possibly end the forging of an American identity in the new world.

Indeed, the Americans vanquished a number of powerful states, from stymieing an advanced French program of colonization, to ending Britain's role as the overseer of the continent. To achieve this result, the citizens of what became the United States proved equal to the task of fighting Natives and warding off European interests. In consecutive order, the Americans defeated their European rivals, leaving the Natives as the final, overmatched opponent and any middle ground an endangered prospect. Here was a key counterinsurgency success of isolating the enemy from outside reinforcement or aid.

Colonial efforts to move further inland soon identified a European challenger to English expansion in North America, France. This competing interest meant both sides looked to establish zones of influence. The opposing power blocks resonated from Samuel de Champlain's rifle blast in 1609. This French explorer's salvo at the head of a Huron war party killed three Iroquois chiefs and left that confederacy seeking English support. The French helped rally those Natives in the Great Lakes region dispersed by the expansion of English allies. Of course, neat territorial divisions proved absurd despite the colonial effort to create borders markedly in their favor. The resultant wars, King William's War (1688–1697), Queen Anne's War (1702–1713), and the French and Indian War (1754–1763), among others, reflected what amounted to a long struggle of attrition, although its perpetuation came mainly from the English colonies hosting a growing population pressing for more land.

For a long period of time, the rival powers of England and France mirrored one another in purpose—accumulating Native allies to bolster their camp. The French and English competition in North America in many ways became a duel to see which nation could commit less of their forces but still advance their cause at the expense of the other. This made Native allies extremely important since a large contingent of warriors could tip the balance of power. As a result, the colonial task became that of defeating the French to then isolate the main enemy, the Native Americans. Denying Natives succor from the European enemy left the indigenous foes more vulnerable to subjugation. In this way, a new frontier could, in fact, come to pass—a push beyond the Appalachian Mountains to the Mississippi River.

The French held an advantage in this competition because they viewed North America in terms of commerce rather than settlement. The French focus on trapping and trade made them willing to tolerate and often adopt Native customs, which produced a less abrasive interaction with the tribes they contacted than might otherwise have been expected. Conversely, the English motive of settlement required land. This fact coupled with the all too frequent English cultural abhorrence of the Natives they encountered ensured a much more grating series of interactions.[2] The contrasting goals of the French and English gave many tribes an opponent superior bargaining position: an ability to choose one ally or the other. Of course, the down side to their efforts to gain favor with Europeans was that the competition exacerbated Native divisions. However, even while clashing among themselves over trade, Native power, when compared to the European, remained prominent. Yet, any European success at gaining allies meant a weakening of that collective strength which was a factor curbing colonial expansion. While, at times, equilibrium came to characterize this confrontation because of this dynamic, conflict erupted to arrest that very balance.

The series of wars wound up favoring the English colonies that soon hosted a large population that could present a formidable front and do so without Native allies. Population was a key advantage allowing both the mother country and its colonies, not to arm the Natives in too great of numbers; such an action could prove detrimental to the long-term English ambition—settlement. The contrast to France was profound in as much as an equitable trade blossomed between French trappers and Natives: beaver and deer pelts exchanged for pans, guns, rum, and even some religious instruction. This exchange meant the French relied greatly on the Natives and, therefore, the French armed them as much as possible. Soon, a string of French forts extended from Canada down to the Ohio country and then to New Orleans. In this way, the French tapped into a lucrative economic pursuit that bound many Natives to their presence and, in effect, augmented the French military presence. These forts were spread out and often hard to defend, and a shield attempted was never firmly established, but the intent was clear: a projection of French power surrounding the English settlements.

A series of French forts fended off the English threat to France's foothold in the New World for a long period of time. French success continued until 1760, when the English triumphed in the Seven Years' War and ended the French commercial enterprise. However, the French and Indian War, as that conflict was called in America, did not resolve anything; it led to more wars. Native resistance to colonial settlement continued, and the American Revolution had its roots in 1763, the official end of the war. This flow of events, conflict stemming from a vanquishing of French power in North America and the advancement of American supremacy, shocked all Natives. Those tribes supporting France realized they had lost a patron. Those backing the English now grasped the strategic importance of this last conflict: a great strengthening of Anglo-American power. These results came to the fore in clearest fashion in the measure of a growing isolation from external aid. There was, in the immediate term at least, no outside ally to turn to. The French were chastened, and the English recalcitrant.

When French defeat came in 1763, it meant the defeat of their Native allies as well, not just in military terms, but also in economic measures. The trapped areas were exhausted. Whatever bargaining power Natives had enjoyed given the active trading with France had been fading steadily for some time. Resource depletion was a key factor, but more unclear was the impact of assimilation on the Natives. France and England had used forts as a projection of power, but these outposts soon became a means of resupply leading to Native dependence and to a potential advantage for the European powers. If some tribes faced fundamental changes due to the disappearing fur trade, it was but a first step. Soon, the adoption of a European lifestyle became a dominant theme as well. Assimilation meant a Native dependency that equated to their vulnerability. So too did the intent—a sharing of items born of guile. Once Natives became dependent on European goods, their supposed benefactors could turn this relationship to great advantage simply by cutting off the flow of goods. Assimilation may have been the result, but it was a question as to what degree and whether that result was more harmful than not.[3]

Perhaps not surprising given this increasingly detrimental relationship, two great proponents of Natives separating themselves from settlers surfaced in trans–Appalachia and attempted to wean Natives away from what some of them saw as a harmful dependency. Two chiefs urged their followers to cling to a Native lifestyle and therefore end the assimilation process. The Ottawa leader Pontiac incited the first round of this effort as he found himself at the center of a Native uprising in the Great Lakes region in 1763. Tecumseh, a Shawnee chief, led another attempt in 1811, some 50 years later in the Ohio territory. The parallels are striking in what happened, less so in what each conflict meant. Pontiac's "rebellion" largely affirmed Native dependency and therefore the practice of trade as assimilation. Tecumseh's war started with his demand to chase settlers from the continent, but ended with his defeat, and this defeat meant the passing of the era of trade and the acceleration of the termination of the very fluid middle ground, at least that found in trans–Appalachia.

If Native interaction with European powers had been the norm there before this point, it was increasingly less so after 1815 as defeat left Natives reeling east of the Mississippi due to the establishment of a permanent frontier, allowing Americans a chance to deny Natives aid from France and then England. That success meant a chance for settlers to extend this border south and separate Spain from the Natives as well.

Pontiac

Pontiac found himself in a familiar situation when he launched his war in 1763. An Indian way of war designed to project power and foster co-existence with an enemy was supposed to bring him success in what he proclaimed to his followers a war of annihilation. Pontiac's method of fighting via raids and ambush left him at variance with his stated aim of expelling England, a crucial contradiction. At first, this goal of vanquishing the European presence in the north appeared feasible, and a great outcry of fear by settlers accompanied the onset of war, with good reason. An early flush of success meant Pontiac seized no less than eight English forts and outposts in the *pays d'en haut*, the upper Great Lakes region. This success came about mostly by guile. A game of lacrosse proved the ruse needed for Natives to take the largest of the forts, Fort Michilimackinac, located far to the north of the main British stronghold at Fort Detroit. English sentries allowed the few Natives enjoying this sport in front of the outpost to enter the gate while chasing the ball; these men then brandished weapons and in conjunction with others emerging from the woods overwhelmed the garrison. A number of small, disbursed outposts fell to Native assault as well, and British power in the region appeared to wane to an unprecedented degree.

Pontiac, chief of the Ottawas (Library of Congress).

The strategic bankruptcy of the situation doomed Pontiac, however. When he initiated his war in May 1763, he was without European allies. The French and English conflict in North America had ended officially several years before with the Capitulation of Montreal signed on September 8, 1760. England now controlled French territory in Canada as well as Florida and all land east of the Mississippi. Pontiac's key charge, in fact, was an attempt to get the French to reenter the conflict. Should the Natives succeed in reducing English power in the region, perhaps their former patron would be emboldened to do just that, or so Pontiac concluded.[4] His main objective was Fort Detroit, what had been the main French bastion in the heart of Ottawa territory that was now in the hands of the English. Natives believed that if that position fell, the French would join the successful offensive. Therefore, much depended on the fate of Detroit.

Pontiac's hope to take this position rested on a feigned parley with the fort's commander to gain entrance to the fort and then rush the unsuspecting garrison. He never got his chance. Although invited into the stronghold, Pontiac refused to signal the attack because English suspicions remained keen, their guns at the ready, so much so that Pontiac believed an assault would be suicidal. His plan foiled and his hostile intentions clear, over the next few days, the chief contented himself with harassing the outlying regions of the fort and interdicting its communications and resupply. One could not classify it a siege since the Natives failed to completely isolate the fort; the local inhabitants helped keep its communications open.[5] In short, Pontiac was reduced to using guerrilla tactics, something that could not force this key fort's capitulation nor, as it soon became clear, win the war.

With this failure, Pontiac's cause was stillborn. Worse, many in Pontiac's party believed Natives had tipped off the English as to Pontiac's intent when entering Fort Detroit, revealing divisions within his camp. This was not a universally accepted cause among the Natives, and the Ottawa chief hardly stood at the head of a unified people who answered to one man, Chief Pontiac.[6] Regardless, the reach of the war was impressive, ranging over an extended area and it spoke to the strength of the confederacy that he symbolized, if not led. Ottawas, Hurons, and Chippewas in the north and tribes to the south such as the Delaware and Shawnee, all found common purpose opposing England. The dissension and accord reveals that these Natives found themselves at a crossroads in 1763, and equivocated too long over what path to take. Pontiac preached separation from settlers in the tradition of Neolin, a mystic announcing this intention prior to the start of the revolt. Drinking alcohol was forbidden, and hunting should be done with bow and arrow, not guns. The aim was a complete break, something that would continue even into the afterlife. It was a radical assessment of the current state of affairs, essentially rejecting the British presence among them in an effort to divorce themselves from European influence by ending Native dependency on presents and trade. Still, many in Pontiac's loose confederation thought otherwise. Some Natives wanted continued ties with England to enjoy the exchange of goods, much as they had secured when the French directed trade in the region. The war was to force reconciliation, not separation. The two views advanced side-by-side, and the Ottawa chief found his name attached to a groundswell of Native resistance that broke into open conflict for these conflicting reasons. Even Neolin allowed the use of guns until the "expulsion" was complete. A closer look at the confusion suggested that the Natives sought a return to interaction as it had been with the French.[7] Whatever the case, Pontiac ended up straddling both visions for a time, and this position made him a powerful figure indeed.

For Britain, its recent success over the French could be undone by Native discontent sparking violence, and this danger is exactly what had come to pass. To this point, a French presence in the *pays d'en haut* had bolstered Native existence. Each needed the other as trading partners so economic avarice had remained muted for the most part on both sides. The English victory over the French had meant the loss of that equilibrium. Major General Jeffery Amherst, in charge of enforcement of English rule post-conflict and flush with success, showed little concern for his new subjects, French colonists and Native allies alike. He ignored the former and revoked the privileged trade status of the latter by ending gifts and restricting the trade of powder and rum. This brand of sovereignty discouraged Native supplication with Englishmen. With little attraction to the new overseer, and now that French power had left them, the growing calls demanding that Natives rediscover their own lifestyle gained momentum.

The Native appeal to a venerable nostalgia revealed a hollow purpose. The true aim was a rediscovery of equal status seen in concomitant trade. In the summer of 1763, Natives voiced outrage at the French desertion and the one-sided English claim of sovereignty over them. Pontiac found himself immersed in an amorphous rebellion that represented a spontaneous rejection of the British policy of halting presents and manipulating trade to ensure their domination over the Natives. Many Natives feared that this turn of events could end with their enslavement.[8] In seeking to capitalize on this discontent, Pontiac had proven himself more astute than the architect of English policy, Amherst. Disregarding the eruption of Native violence, Amherst stood firm, declaring harshly that the Natives should be exterminated.[9] Yet, neither he, nor any other Englishman, could stop this war in the name of assimilation, at least from the Native point of view or from the English viewpoint either. Pontiac's war soon recalibrated English policy in this direction. To end this outbreak of violence, London recalled Amherst and restored trading rights throughout the region in order to regain Native allegiance to the Crown, effectively hoping to return affairs to pre–1763 status. That, in effect, endorsed the French policy of trade so recently rejected in the just concluded war. This step meant England assumed the role of "father" to the Natives. Once the overlords extended respect and protection to their new subjects, the violence started to dissipate.

Pontiac struggled to prolong the war hoping for some change of personal fortune, an increase in stature resting on something more than an amicable peace. Unfortunately, Pontiac's efforts gained him no advantages. The chief continued skirmishing with English forces around Detroit, even defeating a detachment foolish enough to sally out of the stockade and test his strength. However, the Battle of Bloody Run in July 1763, changed little; deadlock remained in place at Detroit. It was the same elsewhere. The British avoided ambush at Bushy Run in August 1763, as a column came west under Colonel Henry Bouquet and reached Fort Pitt at the juncture of the Monongahela and Allegheny Rivers (modern Pittsburgh). Bouquet feigned retreat and then struck the advancing foe on the flank.

Here was a Native defeat. A month later, some warriors managed to destroy an English supply column near Fort Niagara situated on the southern bank of Lake Ontario at the mouth of the Niagara River. Yet stalemate descended about the entire theater of war. However, Native resolve was faltering. Pontiac's allies slowly faded away or threatened to, and the initiative passed to England by early 1764. Soon English and, ironically, their Native allies, boxed in the Ottawa chief. The English worked with the Six Nations of the Iroquois, and they advanced west and intimidated the Delaware and Shawnee. English columns ranged west as well heading to Detroit and beyond to the Illinois country. An army under Colonel John Bradstreet traversed the south shore of Lake Erie reaching Detroit on August 26. Bouquet advanced from Fort Pitt with a second column. These incursions underscored the limits of English power, however. Very little combat ensued, and even striking at villages failed to inflict much damage.[10] For the most part, Natives simply retreated, drawing the English forces into an interior where no tangible results could be achieved due to the elusive enemy and the threat of the approaching winter. The English refused the bait. They understood that they risked defeat by becoming overextended, any setback probably emboldening Native resistance. Instead, the English were content making clear they remained a force in the area, that peace was the wisest course of action for all parties, and that such accords included reestablishing presents, trade, and meeting Native needs and demands. In this uncertainty, the war petered out in 1765.

For the English, Pontiac's rebellion ended with a stalemate at best, an admission of weakness, if not defeat, at worst. In this sense, the Natives, but not Pontiac, won the war. He survived the struggle only to fall victim to lingering Native discontent when one of his companions clubbed him in the back and left him dying in a village in the Illinois country in 1769. His fate—perishing at the hands of Natives not the British—symbolized the war that bore his name. Pontiac's struggle remains an ambiguous conflict from start to finish, and the chief had managed to ride this dynamic during the war.

This feat in a real sense justifies naming the conflict after him. He was both the hope and failure of Native resistance: defiance in the immediate time frame and uncertainty in the long run. For even with a stymieing of English ambitions, what was the future of Native power in the Old Northwest? The English may have made concessions to cut the costs of managing their new empire, but the colonial population remained an obvious, looming threat to this peace. More settlement meant Native expulsion at the hands of the aggressive Americans, and for this reason, sovereignty under England, no matter how disrespectful, was a far better option than the futile rebellion that had ensued. Instead, Pontiac's efforts left the Natives and English exhausted, and ensured the Americans were in the ascendancy and could dictate peace terms in the near future, terms certainly unfavorable to Natives.

Assessing the fallout of the war underscores how Pontiac's rebellion stands out as a key example of the shared cultural dynamic among Europeans and Natives, one so at variance with the frontier paradigm of conquest and resistance.[11] Natives understood the primary reason to maintain contact was survival via trade. As Daniel Herman writes in his article, "Romance on the Middle Ground": "Only by trading with Europeans—and thereby establishing diplomatic relations with powerful outsiders—could tribes retain sovereignty in a world upset by epidemics, forced migrations, and an ever-changing balance of power. To refuse trade with Europeans was to render one's tribe powerless to control, or at least to retard, the forces of change." Herman continues by stressing that violence was the reality in the *pays d'en haut* since trade had made Natives dependent and they fought to maintain that dependency on something of their own terms.[12] A compelling if confused motive, it both empowered Pontiac and defeated him. Pontiac may well have helped the Natives regain an element of the middle ground, but given the ambiguity that plagued Native resistance at this time, this success was largely unintentional and increasingly insignificant. His overt effort to ensure Natives again enjoyed a position as a power between France and England, one where France was an ally and served as a counter to English advances, had failed.

Interlude

It would be quickly proven that this failure offset any success of a restoration of a cultural middle ground, save for the impact of the war on Anglo-American relations. In time, the Natives would see a new ally surface, the former enemy, England. This shift in allegiances came about because, fortunately for the Natives, the apparent harmony between Britain and its colonies leading to the defeat of France fell into disarray in a short period of time and resulted in open conflict in some twelve years. One main cause of the American Revolution was England's attempt to stem the tide of settlers moving west of the Appalachian Mountains. This Proclamation Line of 1763 was a border that London considered appropriate and manageable. With such a restriction in place, the chance of conflict between settlers and Natives was reduced and so too were the costs of defending the colonies. The colonial experience had come to fruition by 1763, at least from England's point of view. It was a rational view of the world that failed to account for the irrationality of the colonials: a willingness to go to war with the mother country, a preeminent world power.

England's inability to enforce this border and curb frontier violence became a main source of tension with its colonies. This failing underscored that in many ways, the French had served as a convenient enemy for colonial and Crown authorities. That conflict had distracted both from their diverging interests predicated on the exaggerated view colonials held of their tenuous security in the interior. Clearly, their survival was not at issue, nor had it ever been when measuring strength against France. A French victory in North America would have meant confinement, not vanquishment, of English subjects. With the French defeated, this fiction could not be sustained, and not too surprisingly after 1763, English authorities endorsed French war aims of keeping the colonials confined to the eastern seaboard. Crown rationale made more sense than did colonial aspirations. The land was vast enough to house the American and Native population. An accord could be reached, much as France had pursued in the Great Lakes region prior to its defeat in the Seven Years' War. After this date, once Pontiac's rebellion reminded England of the utility of the French position, the Crown needed only to curb colonial ambitions to secure a lasting peace. However, the Americans enjoyed too many advantages, which ensured that their rejection of the Proclamation Line would determine the future of Native-colonial relations. Their population superiority was pronounced, as was their mentality of entitlement. This reality and sentiment led Americans to brook no delay in their goal of establishing a new frontier beyond the Appalachian Mountains, beyond the Proclamation Line. In a short period of time, the settlers went to war against England to achieve this end.

As would become a familiar pattern, the American response was impressive in its ability to fight two wars at once, one against the declared antagonist, England, and the other against the longstanding opponent, the Natives. This was the greatest achievement of the Americans during the American Revolution, forcing England to acknowledge the independence of the colonies while dealing a blow to Native populations as well. Natives in the Ohio region declared their neutrality and stayed out of the fighting. Many tribes to the south did the same. But in the northeast, the Iroquois did enter the war. A few tribes of this alliance sided with the Americans, others with England. Consequently, that famed confederacy was engulfed by a civil war, and the alliance could not survive the harm stemming from this division or the ascendancy that greeted the American triumph after 1781. That fate testified to the lack of Native attention to the parameters of this struggle. Neutrality for some cost all Natives a key power-block. Still, a better option might not have been available. Was it the fiction of a great Native confederacy reaching west and south standing with England to finally stop colonial expansion? There was no reason to believe this scenario could come to pass given the unlikely unity of Native tribes. Nor was a replay of the wars prior to the American Revolution likely to work in favor of the Natives. The history of those campaigns had been their increasing marginalization, not empowerment. Only in retrospect was it clear that all Natives needed a chance to check colonial—now American—expansion and that the American Revolution may have been the best opportunity to do so. In any event, no such effort came to pass.

Consequently, by 1783, once an official peace ended the war between England and the colonies, a new strategic reality came starkly into focus, one revealing the extent of the danger facing Natives east of the Mississippi. To the European states that had done so much to give it birth, the United States may have appeared to be a fledgling nation, but to the Natives, the Americans were an established force no longer suffering from internal divisions that might impede their solidarity and growth. For this reason, acute Native trepidation greeted the new world shaped in the wake of the separation of the colonies from England. Another conflict was clearly imminent, with a sharp increase in the stakes since the Natives faced a war for their very survival as the Americans looked to push the permanent frontier to the Mississippi River and lay claim to the Old Northwest.

The American ambition to finish this process meant a new series of wars in Ohio and in the south. The hostility was rooted in the lost equilibrium between the European powers, the colonies, and the Natives since 1763. Up to this point, settlers had placated Natives when it was to their benefit. Once power swung in their favor, Americans excluded Natives more than they accepted them as equals. Settlement was now marked by exclusion, not assimilation.[13] This unfortunate development signaled the inevitable defeat of the Native cause, a reality Little Turtle recognized and bowed to even in the wake of his success of defeating St. Clair. Events soon made this inimical relationship not just clear, but decisive as a new crisis loomed and spilled over into violence in 1811.

Tecumseh

A rare visionary appealed to Natives across the trans–Appalachia area to join together and mount a military challenge to thwart American expansion. Tecumseh, a Shawnee, soon increased his fears to encompass—and represent—the perils threatening all Native Americans. Some fortitude of judgment could not compensate for the task at hand, however. It would take a great feat of arms to reverse the tide so readily in the favor of the Americans, a need at variance with any Native military ability. Tecumseh understood that even solidarity among Natives, north and south, could not deny the Americans a martial superiority. This advantage had to be countered with an alliance with England, and this Tecumseh set out to do. He met this challenge with some success. England, having retained control of many forts in the Old Northwest, could still mount a military threat capable of thwarting American ambitions along the frontier, and Tecumseh acted to capitalize on this possibility.

Ironically, Tecumseh had greater success tying his lot to England than to Natives as his efforts to rally southern tribes to make a common cause with northern peoples achieved marginal results. In truth, his rallying call was only a bit more effective in unifying Native resistance in 1810 and 1811 than at any time previously. An unwillingness among Natives to fight together continued to plague them. This was the case despite Tecumseh's efforts to help foment such an alliance by using his brother, Tenskwatawa. Nicknamed "the Prophet" due to his visions of Native purity that required them to live independent of Whites again (a view much like Neolin), Tenskwatawa's influence peaked after he vowed to block out the sun. When an eclipse of the sun occurred in June 1806, his prestige rose and so, too, did Tecumseh's appeal for Native unity.[14]

Despite some progress rallying Native support, Tecumseh wanted more allies, and he headed south to add Red Stick warriors of the Creeks to his coalition. Consequently, he was not present when war erupted in early November 1811 at Prophetstown on the Tippecanoe River. William Henry Harrison, governor of the Indiana territory, advanced with an army on this concentration of Native forces in the north. After a sharp fight, the Natives fled the area. When Tecumseh returned north in late December, he chastised his brother for sparking this war prematurely by being foolish enough to accept an American challenge of arms. Yet, Tecumseh's real frustration stemmed from his own failure to create a more formidable alliance among Natives. He again had had some success, buoyed up by an earthquake that shook the region on December 16, 1811. The Shawnee chief warned his audience that this omen made it clear that the decision-making hour had arrived. A number of braves agreed that a crisis was at hand and it was time to act, and they joined the forces of the Shawnee. However, Tecumseh understood that he commanded little beyond what his personal magnetism could assemble and keep in the field. He prepared to fight with a fading expectation of success.

Only the larger struggle could alter Tecumseh's doomed position. The United States and England allowed tensions to peak and by mid–1812, only a short period of time into the war that Tecumseh now waged, these two nations also went to war. The Native chief at last could look to a powerful ally, one that greatly impacted the situation and prophesied success, if not victory. There was a distinction between these two ends. The chief sought the formation of a seperate nation, and preached a race war against settlers. They were to be exterminated from the continent, Tecumseh told his followers.[15] Tecumseh's rhetoric when beseeching the aid of Natives contrasted sharply with the military reality he accepted: an alliance with England to achieve the limited success of stopping American expansion into the Old Northwest and possibly forcing their retrenchment to the Appalachian Mountains. Here was a more realistic end to Tecumseh's war. The conflating of a vague goal of Native liberation—really relief—with the means of having to ally with a European power (and a former enemy) spoke both to the desperate straits of Native peoples at the time, and to the apt vision of this one man, Tecumseh. The war was a referendum on his siren call of presenting a final line of defense to American expansion. By teaming with England, Natives could shift good fortune in their favor and against the Americans, a long overdue development from Tecumseh's point of view. In sum, he sought a recalibration of the historical norms that had too much harmed Native interests and allowed an American seed to sprout and grow into a plant threatening to choke off Native existence. The fighting would settle much.

The first task became correcting the strategic problems created by his brother. This Tecumseh rapidly and impressively accomplished. Harrison, now a general of militia, remained Tecumseh's main antagonist in this struggle. With that army still camped near Prophetstown, Tecumseh headed north, looking to lure the Americans into the recesses of the forest. The Americans gave chase but soon lost sight of their foe, a blunder that cost them the initiative since Tecumseh chose the location of the next major engagement, Fort

Detroit. Here the Natives captured an American garrison through ruse more than force of arms. Tecumseh marched his men around the fort twice to impress upon the American commander the hopelessness of weathering a siege. In August 1812, General William Hull surrendered to a combined English and Native army with hardly a shot fired.

This success did not portend of ultimate victory more than it underscored the limited role played by his British allies. Tecumseh had organized the attack, and the necessity of him using a ruse even with the backing of England strongly hinted at the tenuous support of his ally. This was the case despite the high qualities of the leader of the English army acting in support of Tecumseh, General Isaac Brock. This man, a formidable soldier in his own right, readily allied his forces with Tecumseh and supported the strike at Fort Detroit.[16] This development was all the more surprising since Brock was an unwilling participant in the war, objecting to London about his posting to the American frontier. However, this soldier took an immediate liking to Tecumseh, as did Tecumseh to Brock, and after Detroit, British-Native harmony was at an all-time high. Coordination of forces was exactly the point,

Tecumseh shields prisoners from another Native, on horseback, who is wielding a tomahawk. Another Native is about to scalp a dead soldier (Library of Congress).

and the personalities that had to make this happen could not overcome fate. Brock was killed in action a short time after the success at Detroit, a crucial loss and one inimical in the extreme to the Native cause given that Tecumseh had been away again trying to rally southern Natives with very little success. He needed English support more than ever. In any event, the favorable circumstances of receiving even limited backing from a powerful ally proved fleeting, and in just a matter of months, any gains were rendered negligible in the larger picture.

Once teamed with a less effective English commander, General Henry Procter, Tecumseh recognized the reality he faced. Procter did not share Brock's high opinion of Tecumseh, and the chief returned this feeling in kind, and for good reason.[17] To begin with, Tecumseh had to intervene and prevent the slaughter of defenseless prisoners at the hands of his forces after a clash outside of Fort Meigs, an American defensive position far to the north in the Ohio territory along the Maumee River near present-day Toledo. The Natives had intercepted a column of Americans looking to reinforce the fort and had taken many captives. Tecumseh berated Proctor for failing to control the situation. Proctor's refusal to better understand his Native allies explained his laxness in this respect. He also lacked the determination to attack the Americans. It was a point of high contrast to Brock, a man who had accepted battle at Detroit with little reason to believe he would be successful. He had risked much in support of Tecumseh. Under Procter, British activity soon waned, revealing that the British were content to leave Tecumseh to his fate.

That fate was not an envious one. Rebuffed at Fort Meigs, by 1813, it became clear that Native and British unity was too late and too feeble to stop American expansion. While circumstance made the heaviest inroads, the Americans also were quick to identify the potential danger of English support of Natives in the Old Northwest. The Americans looked to curb this strategic advantage by winning control of Lake Erie. Their naval victory of the Battle of Lake Erie in September 1813 ensured success in this vital aspect of the war. At that time, Native and English forces were again laying siege to Fort Meigs. Tecumseh had pushed for this attack, shunning the familiar guerrilla engagements, ones sure to drag out the war but also to allow superior American resources to efface Native resistance. Instead, Tecumseh looked to win a major battle. Taking this fort may have been that battle, one helping to retain Native unity and blunting American advances. However, with American naval power dominant in Lake Erie and his supply lines exposed because of this fact, Procter decided he had to retreat north above Lake Erie and position his forces near the river Thames. A stand here could stop the Americans. Yet such a move north also meant the English abandoned the attack on Fort Meigs and possibly the Natives as well as by essentially allowing too much land to come under the control of the Americans without a fight. Worse, even a successful defense would require an offensive later on to regain this lost territory. That action was dubious since Proctor appeared only interested in retreat. The old somber outlook of waging a futile struggle returned and gripped Tecumseh, and he feared having to face the Americans alone.

Once Proctor explained his need to retreat to protect his supply lines, Tecumseh supported the move, even leading the rear guard slowing the American pursuit. Procter's combined forces soon made it to the lower Thames, but a stand there turned to folly in a short period of time. English confusion was rife, compounded by Procter's indecision regarding where to make his defense. As a consequence, prepared positions and no artillery support existed, a bad state of affairs given that Harrison was at the head of a 3,500-man army, almost three times the men Tecumseh and Procter could muster. Still, a defense was made, with Tecumseh the central figure of that defense, the chief moving among the English soldiers to encourage them to stand fast, an unprecedented need and an unprecedented honor for any Native. However, Tecumseh also recognized their exhaustion, despair, and exposed deployment. The troops were bunched together and standing in the open, vulnerable to American fire and cavalry. Tecumseh warned Procter of these shortcomings, but little was done to correct these problems. For his part, the chief dispersed his 500 warriors skillfully, using good cover and soggy ground to thwart the expected American cavalry charge. Despite his efforts, Tecumseh realized his position was desperate and that he and his warriors would have to face the brunt of the American attack. The English were unreliable. A long trajectory had brought Native resistance to this point, and it was not a favorable situation.

When Harrison launched his attack, the predictable occurred. The English broke in minutes, leaving the Natives to mount a desperate resistance that did hold the Americans for a time. But the numbers were telling, and Tecumseh soon recognized his fate. As the fighting progressed, he sought death on the field of battle. Some say he fell while mounted on a horse, others say while running toward the American lines. Either way, he died at the Battle of the Thames on October 5, 1813. Now, decisive battle came to the Americans, the only combatant capable of earning this distinction given the circumstances.

This was Tecumseh's conflict. It was the last great resistance mounted by Natives east of the Mississippi, and when it was over, the plight of Native Americans had worsened. Even British success later in the war, including taking—and burning—the American capital of Washington, D.C., in August

1814, could not swing the strategic balance of power in favor of Britain and its Native allies. Instead, England settled with the Americans at the end of the year, accepting its inability to penetrate the permanent frontier separating England and the United States, spelling an end to British power in terms of impacting American affairs. This peace represented a sanguine result given that England did not face defeat so much as confinement to Canada. The Natives in the north confronted a much more negative result. The war's outcome affirmed their isolation. Divorced of a powerful ally, these Natives faced the American threat alone. Soon it became clear that in the aftermath of this conflict, Native peoples faced vanquishment throughout the trans–Appalachia region.

Jackson and the Southern Border

A disharmonious end to the War of 1812 reminded England of American resolve in defining the frontier as the United States saw fit. Foremost in this regard was the future president, Andrew Jackson, who earned fame by defeating the British at the Battle of New Orleans in early January 1815. The irony was that this engagement occurred after the war had ended because the declaration of peace in Paris, the Treaty of Ghent agreed to on December 24, 1814, had yet to reach American shores. Before this ultimately anticlimactic battle, Jackson did much to win the War of 1812 in the south. A ghastly scene greeted his effort at the Battle of Horseshoe Bend in March 1814, where Jackson's volunteer army collided with the Creeks. General Jackson sought to avenge the outrage of the massacre of Fort Mims the year before, when close to 500 Americans had perished after Creeks took the fort by a surprise attack. Jackson caught up to the Creeks at a natural bend of the Tallapoosa River and he recognized their stronghold as formidable in the extreme: "It is impossible to conceive of a situation more elgible [*sic*] for defence than the one they had chosen and the skill in which they manifested in their breast work, was really astonishing."[18] It was also a deathtrap, and Jackson surrounded and then assaulted the defenses. After a stout resistance, some 3,000 Creeks died in that construction, pinned between the river and the remorseless American advance. It was an unparalleled victory, even if the human carnage was horrifying to behold. However, that carnage was the point, Jackson having gone far in fulfilling his promise to "carry a campaign into the heart of the Creek nation and exterminate them."[19]

Settling a score with Natives was the dominant American mission in the Creek War of 1813 and 1814, as was advocating an end of English interference in American affairs, the larger parameter of the War of 1812. Therefore, Jackson's effort to capitalize on his success at Horseshoe Bend by taking the war into Florida coincided with the mandate of the War of 1812: striking at England.[20] Jackson earned an immediate dividend in both respects. Jackson's pursuit of Creek fugitives into that territory further scattered those Natives, and it blocked an English thrust inland at Pensacola and forced their subsequent strike at New Orleans. When the Americans repulsed this attack, Jackson formed a rapid defense force and leading this army as well; his active role in the war to the south appeared vindicated.

As a result, Jackson's reputation was greatly enhanced and for the most part justifiably so. However, blunting this lingering spasm of English military action launched Jackson's career in dubious circumstances. The remaining Creeks sought to continue the war in Spanish Florida, joining forces with the Seminoles, all of whom enjoyed resupply from England with Spain's complicity. The 3,000 or so Natives arrayed in the south and not sharing the fate of England's defeat still menaced that southern border. Soon it was clear that Jackson's efforts had merely forced a contraction of Native strength into a locale where they could receive material aid and even reinforcement from at least one outside power and possibly from two, England or Spain. Although the Natives were greatly weakened, the United States now faced an array of opponents who had a greater chance at gaining allies than prior to the American attack and in territory beyond any assumed frontier defining the United States.

The War of 1812 ended with Jackson becoming something of a national hero but not nearly the towering figure he set out to be. This search for a reputation soon had him in the field again, protecting the American southern frontier from a perceived growing threat. The importance southerners attached to this area hinged on land acquisition throughout the region and protecting the means of trade of commodities grown locally and shipped down river to New Orleans via the Mississippi. The route and outlet had been a long sought-after strategic goal inviting European interest from Spaniards to Frenchmen to Englishmen, and now from Americans. Thus, this part of the frontier came into focus as the next key area of the self-aggrandizement of American power, with this motive driving the struggle against ill-defined enemies.

Slavery also played a key role in what was to come since the region was a refuge for runaways. For Americans, this sanctuary was a problem for obvious reasons, but more than this, once having fled south, many Blacks took the opportunity to organize and arm themselves. Almost 400 former slaves defended an abandoned British fort on the Apalachicola River southwest of present day Tallahassee, having found guns and ammunition there. The Spaniards ignored this stronghold and the Americans feared it. The "Negro fort" testified to the threat such a group could pose to American ambitions in the south. British agents could stir up trouble by supplying weapons to both Natives and runaway slaves. These hostile groups could then launch forays back into the United States, using the Florida territory as a shelter for such illegal activities given the length of the border and the paucity of the Spanish presence. Because of this state of affairs, the United States had to act. Jackson, the ranking military commander in the south, sent an American flotilla to eliminate this threat in July 1816. As this small force moved up river, a lucky shot from one of its gunboats struck the powder room of the stronghold and destroyed it. The threat of armed Blacks dissipated in that moment, but not the potential of a reoccurrence made possible with British assistance, so brazenly on display in that fort.

Certainly opportunism drove English ambitions in the region, a chance to blunt American expansion by simply rendering that southern border too volatile to control. However, that effort underestimated the American determination to act and end this problem once and for all. Boasting to the Monroe administration that he could conquer Florida in sixty days if given the chance, Jackson settled for something much smaller. Compensating for a limited number of men and supplies, the general did the obvious: he assumed the offensive and entered Florida in March 1818 in search of English "agitators." He soon found two British traders as he advanced east of Pensacola to St. Marks. Jackson, always self-righteous when it came to his longstanding hatred of Englishmen, ensured a "border incident" by executing both men for plotting against the United States. The message, as far as Jackson was concerned, simply endorsed the imperative of refusing to allow Natives an ally. England was a continuing danger in so far as making this kind of support happen, and so the stern warning in the example set by executing the two "agents." Jackson then marched back to Pensacola, toppled the remaining Spanish centers of authority, and declared all of east and west Florida an American protectorate supervised by a U.S. military governor. The First Seminole War was over, and American citizens could now safely enjoy residence along this southern border.

Jackson's challenge made for good local politics. Many Americans hailed him each step of the way as he made his way back to Nashville. Less receptive were federal government representatives supposedly setting American policy. Monroe ordered his diplomats to answer Spanish and English protests in a desultory manner, hoping the entire affair could be forgotten. In a sense this tactic worked. Internationally, the gap between apparent lawlessness on the southern border and supposed Spanish authority was too great to merit war among the powers of Spain, England, and the United States. Only protests and denunciations came from Europe. Domestically, Jackson faced more of a firestorm, but this remained mere rhetoric since Congress excused the general by not acting as a body, although condemnation of Jackson came from partisan opponents of the administration in the Senate and House.[21] The final outcome of the entire affair was that Jackson was a general doing his duty on behalf of a grateful people—he defended the U.S. border with a strike into territory already threatening American interests given that that refuge harbored individuals seeking to harm U.S. citizens. The economic boon of a Florida and its neighboring environs as a part of the United States went unsaid; it need not have been any other way. Jackson, in attempting to serve his ambition, had done so in a way that tied his actions to the desire of the new nation—expansion. The economic bounty of such an endeavor was enough to excite Americans and mollify England.

Economic gain lifted all boats, except for those of Native Americans. Jackson's supposed defense of U.S. security in Florida set in relief the obvious target of such a policy. By mounting an attack to stop English agitation in the south and igniting this First Seminole War, Jackson further advanced the American war against Native Americans and did so in a two-fold manner that eased the American conscience. First, the Natives did not benefit from an ally as Tecumseh had enjoyed in the north. Second, the war continued to blur enemies and did so by conflating the presence of Natives, Spaniards, and Englishmen into one threat coming from a region of general volatility. American peaceful intentions were pursued in this war, at least to American satisfaction. The extent of this wishful thinking was revealed in a series of Seminole wars starting over a decade later. However, for now, in the wake of Jackson's triumph in 1817–1818, a peace could be determined that secured Florida as American territory in February 1821.

By adding Florida to its dominion, the United States curbed Spanish as well as English ambitions in the region. Again historical currents had worked against Native resistance, being that to the south, Spain, the weakest European power, had staked a claim. That ally proved feckless in the extreme. For Spain to stop American encroachment, its cooperation with Natives became a necessity, but that effort amounted to a limited response with dire ramifications.[22] Spaniards increased the flow of guns to the Natives in the south and American resentment of Spain. It was the French reality all over again, just in a different location and with a different European power: an ally backing trade that in reality meant arming the main enemy of American expansion. This situation drew American ire and action.[23] Fortunately for the United States, Spaniards were even less prepared than Frenchmen to defend their American possessions along what Spain believed constituted its northeastern frontier in the Americas. The tenuous Spanish union with the southern tribes was easily broken by the intermittent but aggressive American advances. This meant the southern border remained an Achilles Heel to Native resistance, and the people there were weakened, distracted, and then poorly served strategically by a European presence that offered few opportunities for the Native tribes to team with an outside power to stop the remorseless American expansionism. With victory in the south, the United States completed its conquest east of the Mississippi River.

Fall of Trans-Appalachia

Trans-Appalachia fell to the Americans by halves, first the northern portion and then the southern. Of course, this disaster for Native Americans occurred only after a ferocious counterinsurgency unleashed by the Americans had isolated the Natives. Up to 1815, the path had been steady and clear: colonials capitalizing on Native miscues of trying to balance Native allies, of assuming neutrality, and of allying with a former enemy. West of the Appalachian Mountains, the clashes initiated by the Americans engulfed and defeated a series of chieftains in the north. Greater American security had served the two ends of a push to expand and of a rejection of European interference when achieving that end. For Natives, the path forward was hard to see in any favorable light. Much as Tecumseh had predicted, a failure of the tribes to stand together and accept the American challenge realized a greater danger as the Americans prepared to even out their expansion west by claiming a rich reward in a southerly direction. After 1821, the isolation of the south was acute, and that region was now vulnerable to American consolidation. More fighting lay ahead, but the outcome could hardly be in doubt given the lack of outside assistance. No European powers of consequence were present to ally with in the south—or in the north for that matter. Continued resistance was a bleak option, as the Native prospect of enjoying a middle ground in trans–Appalachia faded due to the reality of a permanent frontier.

3

Paramilitary Forces

Frontiersmen, Explorers, Mountain
Men and "Opening the West"

Daniel Boone watched the warriors recede into the forest with much relief. The defense of the settlement he helped establish in the wilds of Kentucky, Boonesborough, had been a close thing. The bastion held out in 1778, and now Boone could think of returning to the woods and to hunting. That happy thought soon gained much urgency as many of his fellow settlers who had stood on the defense with him looked at him with recrimination. In their eyes, Boone was too much the Native in manner and appearance, a dangerous man in that he refused to abide by the strict divides between settlers and Natives. Boone knew that their estimation was correct, and he resolved to escape from civilization and take his chances in the wilderness, relieved to run the risk of clashing again with Natives because settlers had become a greater nemesis in too many ways. However, just as Boone needed this escape, so too did settlers need men like Boone, and they followed him into the backwoods expanding America yet farther.

Further south and a generation removed from Boone's exploits, the gun smoke cleared from a battleground to reveal David Crockett assessing his role in the fighting against Creeks in 1813. Certainly two of their number had fallen due to his bullets, and perhaps a third. The excitement and danger of the engagement having past, Crockett now realized that he stood among a number of bodies strewn about the field. He moved among them, recognizing women and children amid the dead. He saw few militia or Regulars, and this obbservation gave him solace as he contemplated the slaughter. The Americans had won the battle, a brisk shootout on the southern frontier. Here was payback for Native attacks on settlers, and Crockett accepted the necessary carnage. But he soon quit this campaign, ending his time in the militia, and went home. His sentiment about fighting Natives remained as conflicted as his understanding of going home, a shifting locale taking him farther west until his next great battle at the Alamo in Texas. On this frontier, Crockett ended his life as a defender of his own passions, but in the service of one emerging nation and another not yet fully created.

To many Americans, expansion became a seductive lure, and its pursuit generated its own rhythm and results. Boone, Crockett and others like them, including a host of explorers and a number of mountain men, found an innocence in the mission of opening the west, all the while denying this was their purpose. It found them nonetheless because these men represented a cross between the hunted Native and the empowered settler. The frontiersmen were both overt proponents of meting out violence and bashful advocates of pursuing the self-interest inherent in the homespun values of the American citizen. This willful intersection revealed a consequence, that impacted primarily Native Americans and resulted in an outcome that benefited all Americans, frontiersmen and settlers alike.

The First Way of War

Settlers took an active role in ensuring their own success, and part of this response came in copying aspects of Native resistance. Frontiersmen were the most fascinating in this regard, given their ties to the counterinsurgency fomenting in North America. As Americans looked to move beyond the Appalachian Mountains, some of these men ranged deep into the interior of the continent to strike at enemy encampments, responding in-kind to Native raids on the frontier. However, a handful of others also sallied forth into the wilderness and came to embody the promise of settlement, the key component of American expansion. All told, these backwoodsmen, followed by mountain men and then explorers, forged an American identity that seldom rose to this level of awareness—yet, this was the result. If their motives were innocuous their impact was certainly less so given their ability to serve as agents of a counterinsurgency. "Opening the west" to allow civilians to settle the land forced the Natives into a war of attrition across the continent, and it was a war they could not win. It was a crushing blow. The legacy of these paramilitary forces in the American consciousness spoke to this success. The result was that the Natives were on the defensive, and no amount of shared culture could change that disadvantage.

The too often savage nature of the struggle helped define this conflict from first to last and shaped a confrontation where the English became determined to take the war to the Natives in a process that historian John Grenier labeled the "first way of war."[1] While those inhabiting the colonies frequently took up arms as a militia force in the service of the Crown, Grenier referenced paramilitary forces ranging far inland and inflicting great harm on Native villages. Too often victimized by what the French called a "petite" war of raiding the frontier, killing civilians, and destroying homesteads, as a matter of survival, the colonials responded in like fashion.[2] These rangers did not directly target noncombatants, but women and children perished anyway because of the hardships these attacks created: a lack of food and shelter. For this reason, one way or another, the fighting too often focused on civilian rather than martial objectives. At times, colonial casualties were heavy, although a case could be made that the Native populations suffered more. Forced into longer campaigns than desired, strained in mounting these actions, and now subjected to punitive raids throughout their territory, the Natives found that the constant fighting was deleterious to their sustainability as a power bloc.

A war context helped validate the practice of a first way of war with a greater emphasis on this style of warfare accepted as commonplace by British and Americans during the French and Indian War. In August 1757, when the French struck the English at the southern end of Lake George and seized Fort William Henry, those Natives allied with the French attacked the surrendered British garrison, killing a great many defenseless men. In response to this outrage, the British looked to check the looming French threat to the Hudson Valley. The task fell to specifically recruited frontiersmen. An early "success" was Robert Rogers' punitive expeditions against French Native allies, something Grenier says made that man "North America's best known ranger."[3] By September 1759, with but a few hundred men, Rogers' command reached far to the north and burned an Abenakis village at St. François in the St. Lawrence Valley near Montreal. Rogers destroyed dwellings, crops, livestock, and food stores and otherwise terrorized those Natives into thinking twice before joining the French and launching raids along the American frontier. His impact was tempered by a devastation that was real but limited. Few Natives were killed, maybe thirty. Moreover, Rogers faced immediate retaliation and lost half his force retreating to safety. However, the destruction of that settlement ensured a long-term impact on those Natives. Hardship beset them when winter arrived. Additionally, Rogers' attack stressed that the French practice had become an English one as well, leaving the psychological aspect of war even keel.[4] Now, French raids into the interior would have an answer as colonials with England's blessing learned the first way of war.

Rogers' attack coincided with Britain's main effort to break this deadlock. Possessing sizable armies teamed with militia meant an ability to turn frontier warfare into military operations with strategic import. Seizing Quebec in mid–September 1759 represented this success, the famous clash next to that citadel on the Plains of Abraham—where both the respective commanders, British General James Wolfe and the Frenchman the Marquis de Montcalm, perished—a key moment in deciding that city's fate that fell to English assault a short time later. However, that triumph paled in the larger significance of the action. British control of Quebec spelled the bankruptcy of French policy, a reliance on Native allies in no way capable of delivering a counterattack that would net a comparable victory. While England had strained to mount this offensive, the French dared not consider such a sacrifice in response to the English success. French power in North America simply was insufficient to blunt English efforts. Decades of neglect before 1730 were not remedied in the years after this date, particularly in terms of demographics.[5] At the same time, seeing the war in global terms helped to propel the English to victory on behalf of its colonies in the New World. In 1759, the French accepted defeat in North America, even as European spasms continued this war until its final end in 1763.

The mentality of extending the war into the interior of enemy territory and engaging non-combatants carried on beyond this last conflict shaping French and English ambitions in the New World and helping to forge a new war. The fault lay mostly with the colonials. While they had assumed that Crown authorities would remain committed to defeating the Native population to speed American settlement, disputes over expansion helped ensure that the Anglo-American front that defeated France did not remain unified. By the mid–1770s, tensions between the mother country and its colonies boiled over into a clash of arms. England fought the Americans with the aim of retaining the 1763 Proclamation Line. The policy was designed to ease conflict between colonials and Natives, that is, arresting the very frontier warfare that had helped defeat France.

Such a goal left American ambitions incomplete. To pursue settlement at the expense of the Natives, colonials soon rejected Crown authority. As it was, the American Revolution unfolded as a war principally between the colonies and the armies England sent to the continent to quell the insurrection. Both combatants thrust Natives to the side. However, British expectations of a quick end to this "rebellion" soon faded; a combination of factors produced an extended conflict: early American success with the capture of Boston, English leaders unclear how to crush the resistance, and an American willingness to avoid battle in order to prolong the struggle. The dynamics of a long war brought the Natives directly into the fray.

To the Americans, the threat England posed to the colonies was genuine and would grow if the Iroquois, the most powerful block in the region, actively engaged in the war on a large scale and favored England. Therefore, the Americans looked to continue the neutrality of the Iroquois Confederation. The English, somewhat surprisingly, tempered Native ambitions early on, hoping that the latent threat of an uprising in the Old Northwest would deter American advances there. Only necessity provoked a shift in this view. In 1777, once British General John Burgoyne met resounding defeat at Saratoga while descending from Canada toward Albany via the Hudson River, England unleashed warriors against vulnerable settlements. In an effort to curb the now emboldened Americans, England turned the New York frontier into a battlefield. From the summer and into the late fall, the region entered a crisis mode as several Native war groups loyal to England moved south and inflicted great harm. Men, women and children perished in attacks known to Americans as massacres. The Wyoming Massacre resulted in 70 dead, and the Cherry Valley Massacre led to 30 dead.

The war in New York encouraged other tribes to abandon their neutrality. In territory along the Ohio River, Natives joined the ongoing war versus American expansion. For most tribes, the chance to maintain the favor of the English as allies was so great that they gave little thought to long-term consequences. Native reasoning was sound enough: they expected that any American force would have to respond to English threats and, therefore, be unavailable to protect colonists living in the backwoods. However, the faultiness of this logic soon came to the fore. The Americans did have soldiers available because frontiersman stepped forward to prosecute this war. Consequently, the Natives who willingly participated in this conflict were subsumed in a longer confrontation that they failed to realize was both inevitable and desirable from the point of view of the colonials who were attempting to forge a new nation out of the strife.

As the western theater erupted in violence, the Americans responded with a first way of war when General George Washington ordered punitive raids against the Iroquois tribes siding with England. In July 1779, Washington sent General John Sullivan on a large, three-pronged advance into the upper reaches of New York. Four months later, Sullivan's command had ranged far to the north and laid waste to a number of villages and large amounts of foodstuffs belonging to the Seneca tribe and several others. Sullivan killed only a few, but the damage was so great that his attack left thousands of the Seneca tribe homeless and desperate. Indeed, the physical hardships these Natives endured after Sullivan's raids were immense, but even more so was the psychological toll. As Starkey observes, "Spiritually the devastation of their homelands and burial sites was a disastrous blow to the Iroquois" and this blow was so harmful as to lead the Americans to conclude that Iroquois power could no longer shift the balance of the war in favor of the English.[6] It was not clear whether these tribes could have done so at any rate, for they were too small in numbers. Rather, these American actions suggest a look toward the future, a strike in the current war with England was really a measured blow in the larger war: that of expanding into the hinterlands of the continent.[7]

With this end in mind, the Americans extended their ranger attacks into Ohio. These units achieved some results and helped leave the Americans in a superior position to Natives when hostilities ceased with England. However, this result hardly constituted their full measure of their success. That these frontier units would go unneeded in subsequent conflicts spelled that achievement. When the rising power the United States again clashed with England in 1812 and battled Natives in frequent wars in the Ohio region and along the southern frontier, frontiersmen waging a first way of war largely had faded from view. Pitched battle became the norm. This shift occurred for reasons that had to do with something greater than military attacks no matter how vicious in intent. More significantly, American military efforts from the early 1700s to the 1830s had teamed with frontiersmen imbued with a different purpose altogether from those striking enemy territory to engage non-combatants by attacking villages. These other Argonauts traveled far into the interior paving the way for conquest via civilian settlement, albeit they did so for the most part unwittingly. Nevertheless, the frontiersmen's efforts dictated the flow of conflict in North America more than those rangers operating in any declared war. Thanks to these handfuls of men, a storied history arose featuring intrepid explorers assuming the mannerisms of Natives but remaining in the service of the emerging United States due to their role in "opening the west." This view polished the image of that crude individual who had been no more than a mirror image of his Native counterpart committing deprivations along the frontier during the wars against France and England. At least in retrospect, here was a uniquely American creation rendering any future battle with Natives a foregone conclusion.

Boone and Crockett

Legacy starts and ends this story because of the immense folklore surrounding men such as Daniel Boone and David Crockett. The fallout from legend deserves some perspective. First, many more individuals performed in a fashion similar to these famous men. This truth extends beyond the specific representations so endemic to the reality—frontiersman, explorers, and mountain men. From the perspective of settling the nation, however, it is hard to find two more famous names. So exploring something of an ideology growing out of the American experience as lived by these men assumes important dimensions. Second, if recent writing covering both individuals is accurate in portraying them as symbolic of what would be America, then it is fair to emphasize that they cannot hide from the consequences, which in this case is the American desire to settle the continent no matter the cost.

Daniel Boone's story exemplifies this mix of legend and consequence. Certainly his actions were benign enough, given his lack of ideological motives when functioning as a frontiersman. Much practicality determined his effort to move far into the wilderness, leaving him responsible for blazing a path from Virginia down the Wilderness Road through the Cumberland Gap. The frontier evaporated because of Boone's actions, his contribution being "opening the west" to the 300,000 settlers streaming into Kentucky.[8] However, this was not his intent, far from it. Enjoying a passion for outdoor living meant a reliance on hunting for both food and currency, this need defined Boone's ranging explorations from what is today Michigan all the way to Florida. The increasing population of the colonies did spur him to action, but only to avoid the reality of rapid settlement. His hunts took him away from settlements because of the paucity of game once settlers arrived in large numbers. Boone's ideology seldom extended beyond this practical recourse. Shunning this proceed of his exploits coincided with a lack of interest in farming, which was an American staple as assuredly as was exploring or opening the frontier. Instead, Boone embraced an itinerant lifestyle that facilitated the overall American dream. Doing what he wanted to do and what he was good at earned Boone a well-deserved reputation that was both rich and conflicted. His actions, regardless of his motives, left him a symbol of the American experience in opening up the west and dreading the consequences.

If something of a reluctant hero, Boone had other traits that made him a compelling figure. He was not a bloodthirsty killer of Natives. He slew very few and only when absolutely necessary. With this acknowledgement, his easy-going personality and generally likable disposition is easier to accept. In fact, if not ideology, a calling for the wilderness suited the man, and he preferred a solitary existence or one with but a handful of companions to that of large assemblies of people. Also, there was something more: a desire to be alone in the woods contemplating life as an insignificant factor in a larger world.[9] Should this sentiment shadow Puritan aspirations in creating civilization in the wilderness, it would have been a limited parallel; Boone was satisfied with the wilderness. So another contradiction surfaces in that the man leading this early portion of American settlement would rather have had nothing to do with those following him into that new space.

This "irregular living" meant a less flattering label from his contemporaries as an idler and, worse, as an "Indian," since settlers accused Natives of that same behavior. There was an ambiguity in Boone, an ability to identify with Natives more than Americans. This tendency reached a high point when he was captured by the Shawnee chief Blackfish who adopted him as a son. It is a period of great controversy in his story since he appeared content with the life, enjoying liberation from American society. Yet, Boone deserted his new family and did so to warn those occupying his creation, the crude Boonesborough settlement in Kentucky, that they had been targeted for destruction by the Shawnee. Blackfish followed him there, and Boone helped defend the settlement but not without raising suspicions that he was more Native than not. A series of parlays almost averted violence; in this instance,

Daniel Boone, circa 1835 (Library of Congress).

Blackfish was content to give up what promised to be a costly attack. The Shawnee's efforts to persuade the settlers to surrender and enjoy safe conduct out of the area failed when more than a few of the beleaguered defenders believed that only Boone would enjoy Native promises of safe passage. As it was, conversation turned to violence when shots erupted during negotiations, and the settlement had to endure a lengthy siege after all. Boone led the successful defense, but still stood trial for treason afterwards. He cleared himself of any wrongdoing, but the entire ordeal again cast this frontiersman in an awkward light: indispensable to wilderness survival but too prone to betraying an American future on the horizon.

No matter the accusations he endured at the hands of his countrymen, Boone maintained his jovial disposition. With his geniality came a genuine bravery. He very much led a discovery of a wilderness and this feat required him to take risks. The hunting Boone did for long periods of time often meant deprivation so a physical robustness accompanied his bravery. Attacks from Natives were a constant danger, as well as dangers from predators and simple bad luck. A sudden storm or mishap—a lost gun or injury—could leave one at the mercy of the elements. This fate overtook more than a few frontiersmen. In fact, Boone lost two sons in a more prosaic, expected fashion, in confrontations with Natives, one captured on a hunt and tortured to death, and the other shot dead right before Boone's eyes during a pitched battle on the Licking River in the wilds of Kentucky pitting American militia against a Canadian and Indian raiding party. This frontier clash ended the American Revolution. Boone survived all such close encounters, living to a very old age of 85. His longevity testified to his luck but also to his grit and determination, two key components of bravery.

After the high comes the low of accounting for those not as fortunate as Boone. He forced his wife Rebecca to move and follow him, and for the most part, she endured the resulting hardships of starting over in inhospitable, almost uninhabitable, land. Still, his family odyssey reflected a selfishness in Boone that revealed a character flaw of a never-ending adolescence. Maturity never caught up to him; only old age prevented him from continuing his long hunts that often kept him from his family for years at a time. His jovial disposition could not mask his increasing responsibilities and these he ignored to the detriment of his family. Boone's puerile disposition, however, mirrored the youth of the nation that he helped to forge and that benefited from his exploits. That emerging nation earned these benefits by depending on a number of individuals who mimicked Native culture in order to survive. This act did not negate the fact that Boone had bridged the duality of Americans as loners and builders, so earning an apt legend in this respect at least.

Even Boone's inability to cash in on the land bonanza unfolding largely due to his exploits (and this despite his best efforts to do just that) could not sour the progress of the emerging American nation. In fact, Boone's contribution earned him some charity and, with that, an accolade when Boone petitioned the U.S. Congress for land from the public domain. It was granted because he was "instrumental in opening the road to civilization." Also, it was a reward as a means of government sanction of a western aggression propagated by Boone and others. He soon sold the land to pay his debts and once again he was a "wanderer in the world," as his biographer John Mack Faragher describes him.[10] At this point in life, Boone was now more an observer than an active participant in ensuring that Americans consolidated their newly won gains. Another conflict with England came and so too did more spasms of Native resistance in trans–Appalachia, but Boone merely watched and faced his final years as a marked man, a symbol of an era gone by. He ended his days in 1820, as obsolete to the American vision as the Natives he had always emulated. He now shared their fate—oblivion.

The violence inherent in the frontiersman bookends the life of David

Crockett, another backwoodsman doing much to open the west to settlement. The enemy he vanquished in his youth to his death shifted from Natives to Mexicans. It was hard to surpass the legacy of Boone, but Crockett did so in his own lifetime and in many ways long after his death. An easy-going per-

David Crockett, frontiersman, circa 1839 (Library of Congress).

sonality and a comfort in the wilderness defined Crockett but so too did his violent service in advancing the frontier. Yet his participation in several wars with Natives left him ill at ease and seeking expansion for its own sake: for Americans certainly, but it was less clear whether he sought expansion for a future United States. The two ends caught up to him in the wilds of Texas and for largely self-defined reasons. First, Crockett managed to get more education for himself than Boone had and this knowledge empowered him to contemplate politics at the national level. Second, government service did little for his peace of mind, and a quest for more exploration led him to Texas in the name of wanderlust certainly but also to remake himself financially. Again Crockett's ambition exceeded Boone's, for Crocket enjoyed gains from land speculation, demonstrating an ability to remake himself on numerous occasions. However, his renewal never elevated him out of debt. The move to Texas, as it turned out, was his final effort in this regard. Still, no matter the motive, he sat at the forefront of opening the west.

Crockett enjoyed only a slightly better resume of killing natives than did Boone. Crockett was present when Jackson defeated the Creek nation in 1813 and 1814, these campaigns coming after Creeks struck Fort Mims on the Alabama River in August 1813. Shocked and alarmed by this attack, he volunteered for service in the militia. However, Crockett's role in that capacity is not clear. During one charge, he certainly killed a Native, perhaps a number of them, while helping his unit ambush a large war party in early November 1813. His own characterization of that fighting was, "we now shot them like dogs."[11] For Crockett, this slaughter of 186 Natives, including large numbers of women and children, was fair payback for Fort Mims. Still, Crockett quit the fight shortly after this clash, and so he missed Jackson's subsequent crushing victory over the Creeks at the Battle of Horseshoe Bend in March 1814. The success of this war belonged to Jackson, who used this battle to further identify himself with the nation. Crockett returned home looking for a breathing space to pursue his private interests.

Crockett's legacy says otherwise about his attitude toward killing Natives. More contemporary song and verse speaks of frontier success that emphasizes slaying his foe. Five of the first six verses of "The Ballad of Davy Crockett" reference his exploits against Native Americans, including in the sixth stanza, the exaggerated, "Fought single-handed through the Injun War/Till the Creeks was whipped an' peace was in store." As noted, Jackson led the way in defeating the Creek. Emerging in the 1950s, the ballad made it clear what memory Americans wished to impose on the Crockett legend—a heroic figure free of his many shortcomings.[12] This oversight continues as stanza seven of the ballad recounts Crockett's determination and success in allowing friendly to keep their land, a larger fiction than extolling his war record. Somehow, according to that mythical account, this frontiersman vanquished the enemy and dealt out a just peace. The reality is that men like Crockett spelled the doom of Native Americans, and for this reason, settlers owed Crockett a great deal. His constant roaming, like Boone's, meant an impact that lay in unconscious implications, aiding settlement in a profound way by "opening the west." This mantra first entailed identifying suitable country in which to live; settlers then followed the frontiersmen. In fact, new arrivals became so numerous that both men moved on. Too many people meant the area was simply too populated to suit these more nomadic souls. In this respect, these frontiersmen mirrored the Natives whom they helped displace. However, without the weight of settlement, their ability to become like the enemy may have hardly impacted the frontier. With settlement, their itinerant ways meant service with an expiration date, and rather than face this inherent contradiction in what they were and what they represented, they chose to look for new areas to inhabit.

Crockett's increasing fame and somewhat successful political career mitigated his predilection for playing the frontiersman. As was the reality, he both served this end and became victim to it. His ballad made good theater then, later on, and today, and rather than miss the accolades and the financial recompense that came from such performances, he sought to indulge his own legend. This he did to a point, even enjoying the theater presentation of "The Lion of the West; or, A Trip to Washington" in person, bowing in approval before the actor playing the wisecracking frontiersman, Colonel Nimrod Wildfire, that is, Crockett. He added an autobiography a few years later and told his tale as but a humble man making his way in difficult times. It was a high point made less exuberant by a fading political career. His affability and general common sense earned him recognition and enhanced his fame, a solid combination for winning office, and he eventually spun holding a number of local offices into two terms in the House of Representatives starting in 1827. This was a great accomplishment for the simple country boy from Tennessee. However, his inability to be more than an intriguing presence in Washington meant repeated failure on the legislative card. He was no political schemer, his aphorisms being genuine to a great extent. He was but a common man, and even if in the best sense—a kind, well-intentioned individual—this disposition left him unable to defend himself in the onrush of "modern" America.

Nothing made this situation clearer than Crockett's inability to muster a land reform bill through Congress. He hoped to allow the poor a chance to remake themselves via land acquisition, an objective he had in mind for himself. He recoiled at the requirement that states build a university on that land. Spying elitism in that condition, Crockett advocated revisions, but the bill languished

I have this rule, for others when I am so... Be always sure, you are right, then go ahead.

David Crockett

David Crockett, gentleman (Library of Congress).

in the House, bogged down in procedure. It was a failure that cost him his seat; he simply was unable to point to any success while serving in Washington. While he did win reelection in 1832, he never grasped the larger political battles swirling about his land reform bill. He did manage to alienate many in his own party, since the bill remained a hostage to Whig intrigues against the Democrat Jackson. Additionally, Crockett's, at times, open allegiance to Henry Clay, a prominent political voice oposing Jackson, further isolated him politically. Crockett did not seem to grasp that compromising Jackson by fostering political infighting among his own party to the delight of the opposition party was the true motive of such sympathetic supporters. Instead, he kindled a now permanent feud with Jackson, and he did not see the irony of opposing a president elected with the support of westerners like Crockett himself and those Crockett had helped bring west with his forays into the wilderness. In so doing, he played the role of frontiersman, a key figure—at least by reputation—who had wrestled the west away from the Natives but now was forced to face a new "enemy": the government supposedly perverting his purpose of opening the west to settlement.

When defeat in reelection again became clear, Crockett uttered another famous, oft cited line expressing frustration in career achievement: "You can go to Hell, I'm going to Texas."[13] The common man again was forced to move on and remake himself in the interior of an unchartered nation. At this point, he was frontiersman by circumstance more than by choice. Crockett's motives exemplified his part as victim at the end, choosing to defend Texan independence even though he was a recent arrival. Had he indicated his willingness to open the west by fighting there? Or was defending Texas another chimera of his loner mentality? Was Crockett in love with the land he only recently had come into contact with and now wished to defend? The existing evidence does not make the answer clear. However, Crockett sits astride the issue, a casualty due to his willingness to facilitate settlement even if not taking direct responsibility for the act.

Crockett died at the Alamo defending freedom as only Americans could define it. The outpost stood exposed far in Mexican territory, garrisoned by a small number of Texans and some *Tejanos*, native-born Mexican Texans. The purpose of this stand remained unclear, however. Defying Mexican authority was certainly one goal, but the meaning of what was to come from independence remained vague. Would Texas stand on its own or should the Texas frontier pass into the United States? Would Tejanos have rights and, if so, as a minority in their own land? This confusion was underscored by the lack of harmony among those championing Texan independence. Sam Houston, a key leader, ordered the Alamo abandoned and the troops to concentrate further north to be more responsive to his commands. Houston worried that his military rivals were looking to take his place, and he wanted them close by to control them. Instead, to defy Houston, his rivals, among them the leader of the garrison William B. Travis, and with at least the tacit support of Crockett, recklessly chose to stand and fight at the outpost. It was a politically based decision and a suicidal one since these men exposed themselves to an onrushing Mexican army 6,000 strong under the aggressive leadership of General Antonio López de Santa Anna, president of Mexico. The Texan factionalism was costly because the outcome was hardly in doubt. When the assault came, the post held for but an hour overwhelmed in early March 1830. Some 186 men perished, among them Crockett, Travis, and another famed frontiersman, James Bowie. Still, the stand validated Travis more than Houston. Santa Anna had to delay his march forward in order to reduce the stronghold, granting a two-week reprieve to the territory's new Texan government. Houston's strategy would have allowed Santa Anna a clear path to the heartbeat of the revolt at San Felipe in the northeast, possibly ending it.[14] Indeed, there was cause to remember the Alamo as *Texicans* now exclaimed, and they vowed to continue the war.

Also, there was another reason to remember the Alamo. Crockett's companions there reflected his now more unflattering persona. Together, they hardly represented a moral purity of the cause of freedom: Travis, a man crushed by debt who had deserted his wife and children but sought moral redemption in the defense of freedom; and Bowie, a man long having profited from trafficking slaves in violation of U.S. law and a slaveholder living as a Mexican citizen—thereby defying the laws of that state as well as leaving his participation in the defense of the Alamo mainly an endorsement of the controversial practice of slavery. Crockett entered their company when seeking new land in foreign territory and, should things go well, a renewed political career.[15] Supporting slavery was a given. He sanctified that option with formal resistance to Mexican authority. He welcomed that fight as a respite from his greater ailment, railing against the alignment of institutional forces now coming into their own and shaping economic realities at the expense of men such as Crockett. Like Boone, Crockett both helped to unleash and rebuke an onrushing modern America, his travels a prescription, as for permanent adolescence, as best seen in his journeys that often separated him from his wife and children. The transitory freedom enjoyed as a "paradigm of liminality" for living on the threshold of change, as one writer described Crockett's fortunes, could not remain the defining experience for him or the country, and it did not.[16] Maturity if not a sense of modernity, found Crockett at the Alamo, and it stalked the growing nation. A careless indifference to consequence of action soon evaporated in favor of a reckoning altogether unkind to the sensibilities Americans held dear.

The dubious moral purpose of Crockett's stand in Texas for any number of reasons meant that motives again clashed with intent, a shortcoming further emphasized by the fact that the racial barriers and cultural fissures that distinguished Tejanos from Texans remained intact. Only in the larger parameters of the fighting did the fate of this minority become clear. Texan independence foreshadowed the greater confrontation to come in a Mexican American War that served as a firm rallying point for the United States in the base motive of the prospect for more land. The last proceed Crockett secured by dying at the Alamo was opening the west to Americans and no one else.

Lewis and Clark

Figures not all that different from Boone and Crockett headed another band of frontiersmen who helped open the west. Meriwether Lewis and William Clark led a Corps of Discovery west in May 1804 at the behest of President Thomas Jefferson. So in this case, exploration received official government sanction. The prospect facing the forty or so members of the group was daunting in geographic scale, but even more so in terms of diplomatic recklessness. For Lewis and Clark were to explore the region of the Columbia River, that is, the northwest. In so doing, these men planned to reach the Pacific Ocean, well beyond the new territory claimed by the United States in the Louisiana Purchase, the enormous tract of land west of the Mississippi purchased from France in April 1803, land that more than doubled the size of the nation. By completing this journey, Lewis and Clark were to extend American territorial claims as far north and as far west as possible. This they did successfully, since the northern reaches of the Missouri River carried the party to the hinterlands of contested land. When they returned in September 1806, national acclaim greeted the expedition because the Corps of Discovery had accomplished a great feat of physical endurance and, in the process, produced a wealth of knowledge about the new U.S. land and its people there.

Bravery and scientific discovery could not hide the role of Lewis and Clark and their companions in opening the west to the benefit of the American populace. Of course, this was the expedition's real purpose. To conduct this effort, Jefferson turned to a member of his trusted inner circle, Lewis, who served as Jefferson's secretary, and Clark, a close confidant of Lewis. These two individuals meshed well for varied reasons. Lewis had served as a soldier for a number of years prior to being assigned to Jefferson. Clark had a military background as well and also concern about money. Wanderlust cemented the decision for both men. The journey reunited two friends in need of a grand adventure to ease their somewhat challenged station in life. The president chose well in that both men remained amendable toward Natives and quickly learned to complement one another. Each man could also act in the forthright manner of a soldier, punishing deviant members of the Corps if necessary and handing out similar treatment to foes encountered along the way.

Jefferson hoped to learn how difficult travel would be from the boundaries of existing U.S. soil to the Pacific Ocean. When completed, the mission offered bad news in terms of the lay of the land. No great river could carry Americans effortlessly to the coast. Instead, a great desert degraded much of the new territory secured from the French; the soil in this region was too poor to adopt as farming country. On top of these negative geographic indicators that diminished the prospects of settlement, there remained a mortal peril to this enterprise in that the two most powerful tribes in the region, the Sioux and the Blackfeet, openly opposed the mission entrusted to this small American expedition. In addition to traveling the unfavorable terrain to enjoy the minimal benefit of exploration, there existed the equally hard end of facilitating the nation's move west by overturning any claims to territory in the Pacific Northwest that England and perhaps Russia may have had claims that would curb, even disfigure the prospect of an America extending from one coast to another.[17] It appeared that no great payoff existed in the far west.

Jefferson had underestimated Americans. In pursuit of the "Empire of Liberty," the citizen emerging to inhabit the West endured these hardships and more. This mandate of securing liberty via settlement became most overt in Jefferson's thinking, less so in the consciousness of the frontiersmen executing the charge. Yet, that end was self-evident in the results. The settlers served as the tip of the spear of expansion, producing a "demographic imperialism" catastrophic to Native populations but excused by settlers imbued with a sense of American Exceptionalism. That ideology was formidable, shaping recurrent definitions of the "moving west" thinking that took this American tide to the Pacific Coast. For Jefferson, Native Americans caught in the wake of this advance could share the bounty of the American republic if they embraced a transformation requiring them, as one scholar put it, to "commit a kind of cultural suicide."[18] In this way, assimilation netted harmony between Jefferson, the architect of the Empire of Liberty, and the Native populations he so admired. It was an intellectual fiction designed to speak to posterity and it did so, save for the flimsy guarantee of a place for Natives in American society.

Americans championing their Exceptionalism in the West to the point of enduring great travail could not have been known to Lewis and Clark as they basked in the glory of their traveling feat. Once again, the frontiersmen had frequently exhibited bravery. The trait surfaced in the totality of their exploit—an expedition spanning 2,800 miles in twenty-eight months. The specifics were as impressive in terms of major rivers crossed, mountains tops overcome, and countless prairie acres traversed. The physical scope of the trip again meant facing threats from Natives and, with some luck and guile, the majority of their party survived the ordeal to report back to Jefferson. In this respect, audacity and bravery worked hand-in-hand, even if the celebrated science behind the mission came well after the fact, an effort by experts to shed a favorable light on an expedition that largely failed by this measure.[19] Lewis' suicide in 1809 underscored the assumed limited returns of the great adventure. Part of his despair stemmed from his fear of having wasted the government's money funding the expedition. Not so in its diplomatic charge. The horticultural compendium these two explorers produced masked the diplomatic mission of laying claim to more than the acreage composing the Louisiana Purchase. This mission succeeded very well indeed. With this expedition, President Jefferson put American "boots on the ground," the Corps serving as an "advance guard of a new American empire."[20]

The political importance of the expedition became clear in the attempted intimidation of the Sioux when the party found shelter that first winter with the Mandan along the Missouri River. Lewis and Clark believed they had caused the Sioux to cower by bolstering a tribe often victimized by these northern raiders. The Sioux apparently backed off and accepted the newly established American protection. However, those in the party failed to understand Native diplomacy. These hostiles were simply waiting for the small party to move on before the Sioux reestablished local supremacy. The explorers' mistaken assumption in this respect demonstrated the party's poor ethnography as James Ronda emphasizes in his study of the expedition, *Lewis and Clark Among the Indians*.[21] This observation may be true, but this error in judgment mattered little since the diplomatic end of the mission was served by the U.S. representatives reaching the Pacific Ocean.

Accommodation helped the cause. As the party continued west after wintering with the Mandans, the Nez Perce provided essential aid to the Corps of Discovery in the form of horses and food and even information about traveling along rivers and path ways. This parley was the high point of the expedition since afterward the tone of the interaction became tense between the Corps and Natives along the Pacific Coast. These tribes proved circumspect and essentially hostile to the small party and not for reasons of shock of contact. Indeed, these Natives had established trade with Europeans along the coast. In fact, the threat Lewis and Clark posed was replacing established and trusted traders, or worse, displacing the Natives' role in that trade. The possibility of these negative outcomes was clearly understood by the tribes, and only the caution shown by the party kept hostilities in check. This deference was needed since the party also openly confirmed its trading ambitions, and therefore the very fears of the Natives—the arrival of a new, uncertain trading partner and one advertising the tenuous, flimsy mandate of the party, a reconnaissance on behalf of a faraway government. Lewis and Clark formalized the claim with a published "list," setting their names on a marker that read: "sent out by the government of the U'States in May 1804. to explore the interior of the Continent of North America."[22] Here was stated the intent of opening the west as a government mandate.

With much relief, the party debarked for the return home after a long, hard winter on the coast. The cold and damp made all present fondly remember the winter spent with the Mandans, although that winter had been as inhospitable in climate. That memory consisted primarily of the better accord with those Natives who had helped pass the time in study and amusement the year before. No such recreations surfaced along the Pacific Coast, and so in early March 1806, the party eagerly headed back. It did so assiduously avoiding adventure and as many dangers as could be identified, that is, until deciding that the mission was underachieving. Rebuffing the virtually absent entities of first Spain, the state originally claiming the area being explored in the northwest, and then France in the interior, paled in comparison to having to humble Native power. The outcome was uncertain, and so the two captains made the momentous decision to split their command and take divergent paths until reuniting at the Missouri River. Separating their troops allowed a final effort to engage, if not intimidate, the Blackfeet and Sioux tribes. It also invited disaster if the Natives decided to strike the now dispersed explorers who probably could not repel even a small war party. The gamble made clear the feeble authority exerted by the party on behalf of the United States, since inferiority was the norm the group experienced among the Native peoples it contacted. This desperate act of diplomacy also acknowledged the expedition's understanding that Native tribes still opposed the newly minted claim of American authority. The explorers were a mere visiting novelty, and not emphasizing this truth became the party's diplomatic mandate and succeeding in this end its triumph. When the party did in fact reunite, the homage Americans paid to discovery continued the obfuscation of limited diplomatic returns. The Corps reached St. Louis at the end of September amid thunderous praise for scientific discovery born from physical endurance, not for having won passage west.

The celebrated exploits of Lewis and Clark advanced along some familiar ground: a few brave individuals changing the course of American history for the better. If not true in the immediate act of discovery, the long-term import was inescapable. The Americans had explored the interior ostensibly for the sake of knowledge, all the while advancing their project of settlement. The scientific mandate had not completely blighted the military backgrounds of Lewis and Clark, since these frontiersmen hardly embodied a mix of Native and European worlds, as if their advance across the continent suggested an equitable division of power. Exploration was to be a continent-wide effort by all those inhabiting the western hinterlands as symbolized by the mixed composition of those present in the party. Accounts extolling the contributions of other members of the group, such as Sacagawea, a woman from the Shoshone tribe who traveled with them in the company of a French trader, suggest this view.[23] Rather, Lewis and Clark claimed the opposite: uniformity would define ordinary citizens, not diversity. They saw themselves as explorers in the pay of the government and therefore very much charged with ending Native ascendancy by starting a process of opening the west on behalf of an expanding nation. Ronda strikes this cord by writing, "Lewis and Clark had done their work well" since the exploration brought a flood of Americans to the northwest. In this case, Ronda inadvertently echoed Bernard DeVoto's *The Course of Empire,* a book casting Lewis and Clark as executors of "imperial policy."[24] Native acquiescence mattered little given the chief tool of conquest, settlement. Opening the west had taken a giant step forward with Lewis and Clark, and it would not be thwarted by the Natives.

Mountain Men

The last great contribution of the frontiersmen in opening the west is found in following a number of men who headed off into the Rocky Mountains in the mid–1820s and initiated a lifestyle that played a key role in assisting settlement. These thousand or so mountain men hardly possessed this goal or even the aim of exploration for that matter. They went to trap beaver and sell this prised commodity to European markets. So an economic purpose and a loner mentality were the guiding qualities of the mountain men, just as they had been for Boone and Crockett. Never large in numbers, these men had a remarkable impact on settlement while applying their craft. However, this result came only after some harrowing episodes of survival and endurance. Both the famed Jedediah Smith, who probably did more to discover the Rockies than any other trapper, and the lesser known Hugh Glass, suffered head wounds from bear attacks and only emergency field dressings and some luck accounted for their survival. Glass had to traverse hundreds of miles to make it to safety after his companions left him for dead. Others faced recrimination at the hands of the mercurial Natives. One experienced trio, Edward Robinson, John Hoback, and Jacob Reznor, set out on a hunt but never returned, presumably meeting their doom in an ambush. Two other men almost met the same fate except that one man lived to tell the tale of his miraculous escape. After Crow warriors shot his companion, John Colter surrendered but then faced a "race for life": released but chased by his captors. He evaded his pursuers and after an epic journey covering 200 miles he found refuge and a chance to heal. Due to this feat of endurance, Colter deservedly took his place as a legend among mountain men.

Natives aided these mountain men as often as they molested them. The benefit of trading with these newcomers was certainly one reason for accord. Warriors often demanded guns in exchange for guaranteeing safe passage or for helping the trappers find a river flush with beaver. Yet the effort of these Americans to become more Native than European was a factor as well. In some respects, turning on a mountain man meant that Natives lashed out at their own kind. In these men existing on the fringes of American society, Natives could claim a triumph of sorts, a referendum in favor of their way of life. While mountain men scorned the Natives they contacted, they integrated with them due to circumstance, largely that of seeking cohabitation with women. This duality left them "agents of expansion" but "not fully trusted by those Americans who followed." Their mostly unacknowledged impact on "opening the west" mitigated any harmony they shared with Natives to a great extent.[25] Even if denied or unconscious, Native suspicion of these men hit its mark in this respect. Fanning out at the forefront of American settlement, mountain men offered a perversion of the Native way of life in its very embodiment.

The tales of valor were one thing, sustaining a way of life another. With each success, these men destroyed their own enterprise. Trading for furs had self-imposed limits. In some fifteen years, the beaver were gone, and trapping in the Rockies collapsed as an economic endeavor. Consequently, these men were looking for other ways to make a living. This transition was not easy to do. Too often illiterate and now obsolete in craft, mountain men faced a bleak future. Ironically, some found solace in a poetic stoking of the frontier dream. Skilled at tracking and knowing the mountains and the dangers of Native attack, these men became a coveted resource in terms of reestablishing the American frontiersmen as a tool for opening the west. For if that dream had died with Crockett at the Alamo, the mountain men now added one more refrain, and in so doing, they completed the groundwork for the settlement of the United States. After 1840, mountain man turned trailblazer did in fact embrace settlement as a purpose and their role in aiding this process was overt: intrepid souls opening the west at the behest of an aggressively expanding population.

Jim Bridger perhaps best filled this purpose as he led Americans beyond the Rocky Mountains. Indeed, his ability to find a better way than the "south pass" over that formidable mountain range gave impetus to American expansion. Finding the Bridger pass in what is today southwest Wyoming was one thing; leading Americans across it was another. Bridger did this as well. For example, he accompanied a Momon mission and encouraged that party to settle in the Salt Lake region, which it did. He also aided the reputed first wagon train west, the Bidwell-Bartleson group of thirteen wagons heading to Oregon in 1841. His trading post, Fort Bridger, sat astride the trail leading to Oregon and California benefiting these first travelers and others that soon followed. Bridger had revealed a fine eye of an entrepreneur because his post was all but unavoidable. Indeed, that man helped open a floodgate of sorts. The only shortcoming was that the building was often in a state of ruin, since he was frequently absent as he wandered the area or led travelers west. The beaver trade had died, but not Bridger's willingness to maintain as much of the lifestyle of the mountain man as he could. His reputation remained intact as did his trading fort which helped expansion west to continue apace.

A lack of violence complicates Bridger's story, however, much like the frontiersmen in the tradition of Boone and Crockett and Lewis and Clark. Bridger hardly clashed with Natives, though the danger was constant. Much later, in 1866, he stood in Fort Phil Kearny and watched Sioux warriors annihilate troops near that fort. His circumspection then at what became known as the Fetterman massacre underscored that, like Boone, he had endured wilderness hardships that required some luck to escape. Bridger's courage and physical strength served him well, too. Finally, the fallout from his exploits—opening the west—remained a constant, but for the shifting circumstances that greeted Bridger's accomplishments. The Natives were in dire straits as he led travelers west, a doom stemming from the hopelessness of resistance. Bridger, in contrast to Boone initiating this process, or Crockett accelerating the impact, helped administer the *coup de grâce* to Natives west of the Mississippi. So the absence of violence meant a swan song of epic proportions, a bell tolling for dying peoples and a way of life, one that included the frontiersmen. Dressed in buckskin, nomadic in tendency if not in the consequence of their actions that spurred settlement by opening the west, the last contradiction of their personas was that they helped a nation make war against their apparent ideal, Native Americans. Mountain men always had embraced a mission of serving American interests, given the implications of their actions—settlement—even as their legacy, which cast them as nomadic souls embracing a divergent lifestyle, belied that truth.

To the West

A unique mix of adventure and exploration subsumed the overt act of expansion whether at the hands of the frontiersman, explorers, or mountain men who ventured far beyond the initial colonial gains along the coast. Much acclaim had been present early on, as frontiersmen practicing a first way of war targeted Natives and helped produce a counterinsurgency that was rich in its origins and effective in its overall results. Striking enemy villages is only part of this legacy, however. By 1840, and thanks to another brand of frontiersmen mirroring aspects of Native culture, Americans could embrace clear avenues of advance past the Appalachian Mountains and beyond the Mississippi River and even the Rocky Mountains. This handful of men, so often praised in song, verse, and rhyme, formed an unlikely vanguard of the American counterinsurgency effort, but they did function as part of that vanguard nonetheless. This was all the more the case when men like Bridger transitioned from mountain men to trail blazers, underscoring their importance to opening the west. Settlement required a helping hand. The impact of this mandate coupled with the ugly ramifications of the budding giant of expansion went far to subdue the Natives. There is no disputing the impact of the paramilitary forces leading this effort because the frontiersmen helped to produce a demographic shift favoring only Americans.

4

Winning Hearts and Minds

Removal and the Promise of "Indian Country"

The saga of Removal injured all parties, the victors and the victims. Andrew Jackson, chief proponent of the policy, saw this in some ways lifetime goal become a further affliction as he sat in the White House. The expurgation of Natives from trans–Appalachia to the west of the Mississippi River left him intellectually challenged, resolute, and supposedly vindicated. Yet, the Removal decree tested a hardened Jackson at a time in his life when he believed himself past such torment. The machinery of government went into motion, and hundreds of miles away, U.S. soldiers enforced that policy. Many Natives went peacefully. Others ran away, and some fought. With each outcome, the sagacity of the U.S. government buckled, and Jackson felt the reverberations.

John Ross, a key leader of the Cherokee, finally accepted Removal. He exited his home to make his personal journey to the "Indian Country," an undetermined tract of land set aside in the west by the U.S. government for Natives removed from the east. Ross turned his back on one life hoping for a better one, but close to despair over how such upheaval could be made good. Sauk chief Black Hawk endured his own rite of passage as he led a band of 1,000 Natives *east* across the upper Mississippi River to reclaim their homes in defiance of Removal. His desperation mounted, calmed only by his refusal to consider life beyond the west bank of that river. Amidst the swamps of Florida, Osceola stepped away from the chief he had just killed, a man consenting to Removal. Osceola looked forward to more violence, embracing the coming struggle as his lone comfort in a conflict making enemies of settlers and Natives.

In the abstract, the Removal Policy eased the conscience of all those involved. Ending the coexistence of Americans and Natives east of the Mississippi merely recognized the tide of history to this point. In terms of specifics, the policy eviscerated any middle ground, and did so in a legal manner that insulted those seeking more from human interaction. Given this trauma, those who could afford to believed that Natives traded the solace of living unmolested in the United States for a promise of sanctuary west of the Mississippi in the Indian Country. The exchange proved a poor one due to the harmful ambiguity always plaguing Native relations with settlers. With separation or assimilation left unclear as the guiding purpose of this act of American benevolence, Removal meant exactly that, removal, a policy beyond redemption in the vastness of the West and therefore a harsh decree rationalizing the ongoing creation of the United States.

End of the Civilizing Policy

As Americans multiplied and expanded their territory, the frontier they advanced consistently and purposely looked to exclude Natives. Resettlement west of the Mississippi River again raised a geographic obstacle as a separation point, allowing Americans a notion of conflating the frontier conception that the English had articulated with the Proclamation Line in 1763, with something of their own creation, the Empire of Liberty. Beyond the frontier in Indian Country existed Natives of no consequence. Inside the new boundary defining the United States lay those meriting eradication for interfering with the Removal mandate. How genuine such a break would be remained in question because the Empire of Liberty also applied to Americans outside the confines of the United States, but not to Natives, leaving those tribes removed to the West in an uncertain status. Removal inherited this confused purpose and, for that reason, dictated a hearts and minds verdict shattering any idea of a reprieve extended to the victims of American expansion.

After the American defeat of England, Natives in the trans–Appalachia region were clearly subordinated to the new power, the United States. Rather than incorporation or protection, however, expulsion was the near universal solution as far as settlers were concerned. This goal created a singular problem, given that so many Natives saw their doom and the futility of resisting, but held out hope of assimilating into American society. The frequency and numbers were impressive, the pointlessness of the act equally so, for settlers simply ignored these efforts and targeted Natives for elimination. The U.S. government could not protect Natives where they were due to the encroachment and continued Native resistance appeared futile. The physical relocation of all tribes east of the Mississippi River to the west of that boundary seemed the only option and a humane option. For Natives, to accept Removal appeared the best choice, albeit a dangerous one. What would happen to them if that assumed compassion disappeared?

Military success legitimized Removal for reasons that were not hard to understand. After the Battle of Fallen Timbers in 1795, with the Treaty of Greenville in that year, the Americans claimed the land to the north beyond the Ohio River. This treaty repudiated the Treaty of Fort Stanwix entered into in New York in October 1768, where the English had claimed all rights to territory south of the Ohio River, but assured Native control of the land north of the river. The Delaware and Shawnee certainly had opposed these concessions, but war rendered both treaties valid. These documents proffered a judgment of dependency since in each the U.S. government solemnly swore to safeguard existing Native lands. However, the guarantees evaporated and would under the weight of American population growth, meaning dependency equated to Native vulnerability. The Natives did not overcome the right of conquest inherent in the right of preemption that had surfaced as the deciding factor of settler-Native interactions in 1795. This meant that land vacated by Natives would first be amendable to Americans, a claim that would thwart European inroads into what had evolved into an American domain. In effect, this principle acknowledged Native ownership. What they lost in a future conflict, U.S. practitioners of this longstanding American policy concern were ominously not clear.[1]

To the south, the tribes there endured a painful process of having land stripped from them in the aftermath of conflict and for similar reasons as in the north: losing the war. It was a truth on the ground and one the Americans drove home with the treaty process. These accords stated that the Natives had made war against the United States. At the same time, the call was for an offer of peaceful coexistence. The treaties at Hopewell in 1785–1786 imposed these terms upon the Cherokee, Chickasaws, and Choctaws. The Creeks accepted similar conditions in a treaty they agreed to in New York in August 1790. In exchange for land concessions, these tribes received a federal guarantee of their current territorial holdings. The agreement appeared a good one. For instance, it recognized the Creeks as an independent nation. In this respect, the treaty was binding. However, also in the treaty were provisions leaving the Creeks "under the protection of the United States," an acknowledgement of their loss of sovereignty.[2] Such an arrangement undergirded all of these treaties, simultaneously advancing dependency and sovereign status. However, Americans preferred the dependency inherent in the right of preemption more than sanctioning any Native claims that might accompany independent nation status. As Americans multiplied and therefore expanded their land ownership, dependency would be the only result, since a growing nation could dictate to increasingly feeble peoples what their place was.

Repeated war in North America also meant a willingness on the part of Americans to redefine the frontier, one so ill-defined that the leaders of the new nation could understand the need for some order. Jefferson's Northwest Ordinance reflected this impulse—a desire to expand into a vague fulfillment of America but in an orderly fashion. The clinical plan that Jefferson advanced in 1787 to settle the newly won Ohio territory also exemplified his lament for the plight of Native Americans, and his understanding of the root cause of that sorry plight—economic advancement. This motive rang true particularly in Jefferson, whose desire for an Empire of Liberty relied on the yeoman farmer. This great American citizen settled the continent in republican fashion, given the individualism garnished from land ownership. Self-representation would overcome the aggression clearly evident in expansion, so that empire paled in the face of liberty, in Jefferson's view, the true motive of settlement.[3] His rarefied and lofty vision, worthy of his scholar mentality, completely broke down in a dual movement of ecstasy and agony at once celebrating the bounty of the earth and decimating its current landholders, Native Americans. Few faced this ugly dichotomy as Jefferson did. He, unlike the nation, contented himself with Native preservation by learning about that culture.[4] The more accepted narrative safeguarded American interests only—celebrating what was gained, ignoring what was lost.

In response, Jefferson looked to removal. To Jefferson, such a call was best because the Native race was then beyond the reach of settlers. This belief explained his support of George Rogers Clark and that frontiersman's efforts at a "first way of war" when raiding in the Northwest during the American Revolution. Removal spared Natives there from "extermination." This belief also explained his support of William Henry Harrison's aggressive military posture when facing Tecumseh's rebellion. Such a challenge to American sovereignty could not be tolerated, but removal soothed the concomitant fate of Native destruction. They would endure away from the reach of American expansion.[5]

Jefferson's vision for the rest of the landmass clouded this happy ending. He clearly looked to a future when settlers would cover the entire expanse of North America, an American tide cementing what he started with the Lewis and Clark expedition. What sprang from this result did not have to be one nation, but any creation must host Americans joined by a common interest in republican values.[6] This view of expansion meant Removal was a calamity in waiting for Natives as Americans spread throughout North America. An American reality extending from one coast to another eviscerated this policy as a long-term solution that allowed two great cultures to coexist by moving those in danger to the west where they would enjoy a sheltered existence. Sooner or later, that shelter in the far off "west" would become an American domain as well. This potential betrayed the promise of Indian Country for what it was, a hollow gesture to posterity. Removal, in the end, would be what its name intended, the exclusion of Natives from the American creation. It would not be what its architects promised: either coexistence as a state within a state, as had been the struggle initiating the policy, or as assimilated peoples, as Jefferson hoped could be the case.[7] It was an awful spectacle to behold: noble rhetoric seeking to justify a looming human disaster with the pledge of a better future, a future compromised by the very source of the problem, Americans imbued with an entitlement of founding an Empire of Liberty.

Few wanted to face this looming contradiction. Jefferson certainly did not. Only when Andrew Jackson was president would the leadership at the top of the American political establishment act in the name of Removal, and then only in immediate terms: the incompatibility of expansion and the preservation of Native population centers east of the Mississippi. Removal now became the operative American understanding of the clash in trans–Appalachia. War, past and present, gave the policy legitimacy. By the 1820s, Shawnee, Creek, and Cherokee power was broken after a series of wars, some of them with Jackson playing a direct role. He had been instrumental in the defeat of the Creeks, so that by 1815, in the wake of Tecumseh's defeat, Americans could look to consolidating the south as well as the Ohio region. Jackson had chastised Seminoles in Florida so that by the early 1820s, the United States could talk of adding this territory to its nation-state. Trauma and duplicity greeted Jackson's every act, either driving hard terms with Creeks and even the Cherokee allied with him, swallowing almost two thirds of their land, or spurring international crisis after his heavy-handed treatment of English citizens in Florida.

With each American victory, the tone of the conflict had shifted as well. In the name of progress, of advancing civilization, the settler had to prevail. Settlers looked to Removal to ease their conscience and, therefore, do the bidding of the nation, but also to allow the new, growing country to escape its hypocrisy. Inexorably, Jackson found himself at the center of the Removal issue. It was his policy as president. Still, Jackson spoke sympathetically of Natives, claiming to sympathize with their plight even after having made his reputation as one of their foremost antagonists. In this respect, he revealed his great understanding of American mentality, that of economic gain no matter the ideological contradictions that might entail, and he personified that thought as an agent of democracy.[8] The Age of Jackson spoke to this reality and defined Removal as Jefferson did: an act of kindness to avert the greater blot of Native destruction at the hands of settlers.[9] The civilizing policy of the United States, one advocating that Natives attempting to live as Americans could remain in place, and one active since 1790, fell as a result.

Removal

Jackson only partly succeeded. His conviction that Removal was best because it was humane, may indeed have been merely good politics. Settlers got what they wanted—land—and Jackson got votes. However, many Natives, especially in the south, had declared in favor of American culture, an admission of vulnerability if not racial inferiority. John Ross was the most famous Native seeking to emulate Americans and, therefore, win a respite from their efforts to seize Native land. Under his stewardship, the Cherokee conspicuously spoke the English language, taught English in their schools, adopted American dress, created farms and lived in houses, and even used slaves to operate their farms. Here was a Native protégé of American southern society. A final step, that of crafting a constitution, decreed self-government and defined specific boundaries. The Cherokee exalted in being a nation apart from the United States; there were two distinct peoples, but one seeking accord and therefore desiring co-existence. In other words, the Cherokee sought protection in the middle ground established between treaties and the realities on the ground. Their safety, they believed, lay in forcing Americans to live up to the ideals of the Enlightenment era of favoring equality among men and fair government.[10]

Ross soon discovered the flexibility of American ideology as the Cherokee stand invited attack from a new mantra of human ideals altogether different from those sanctifying human decency. The racial ideologies blossoming in the early 1800s topped Enlightenment sentiment by decrying that inferior people could not remain within an American state for fear of debasing that state. Cherokee accomplishments in civilizing themselves confirmed the futility of assimilation by exposing the ugliness of nationalism. To Americans, Cherokee efforts at civilization meant they were no longer aspiring to be American, but acting as an unwanted, dangerous rival to the new American success story. When gold was discovered on Cherokee land, American agitation reverberated all the more loudly as did the assault on Native lands. The Cherokee soon learned that even a subjugated people accepting their lot could not remain among Americans who still coveted the land. Removal declared that the tribes had to move to survive. This was certain, even if Removal did not specify the motive that served as the groundspring of what would become U.S. policy. This decree was aggression in the name of acquiring property; race allowed the justification for Removal but played a subordinate role to that economic purpose.

The state of Georgia did the most to advance the threat of Removal. A series of state laws questioned and revoked Cherokee sovereignty. Georgia owned the land, some five million acres, and could do what was in its best interests. In so arguing, race became paramount, both the facile argument that Natives could not become civilized, and the more categorical assertion that with a permanent difference between the two races, any Cherokee nation represented a threat to state control. Georgia's stand was effective only in that it capitalized on federal inaction. A state claimed authority to preside over Native affairs, and in the process it rejected previous treaties sanctified by the federal authority. Jackson ignored these broader issues, and he focused on the danger of a rival Native state. This could not endure. To disarm the Cherokee meant compliance with state law, and Jackson endorsed Georgia, and with it Removal. Jackson signed the Removal Bill into law on May 28, 1830. Under its terms, Natives were to surrender all of their territory in the state and move west of the Mississippi River. Interestingly enough, Georgia was not a state in step with its neighbors. It was on the fringe. For example, North Carolina, in contrast, protected its Cherokee population. Other states did not claim the Natives' now confiscated land; it fell to the jurisdiction of the federal government. However, Georgia dragged these states with it, with a helping hand from Jackson. By siding with Georgia, the Jackson Administration was advocating Removal of all natives east of the Mississippi River.

Jackson embroiled himself in legal complications because of his support for this legislation. John Marshall, Chief Justice of the Supreme Court, pushed the judicial branch of the U.S. government in the opposite direction of the administration. Marshall made clear American responsibility for Natives, first regarding the Natives themselves with *The Cherokee Nation v. The State of Georgia* ruling, then in his effort to rebuke Georgia's punitive implementation of Removal with *Worcester v. The State of Georgia* decision. In these famous cases, the Supreme Court defined Natives as "domestic dependent nations," a people living in dependent states, enjoying their own autonomy but still within the borders of the United States and, in a recurring theme, deserving protection due to that status. The rulings were more clever than effective. Legalisms hardly stopped settlers from seizing Native lands. Additionally, Jackson defied Marshall by having the U.S. government accept responsibility for Natives only on the condition that those Natives submit to

Removal as expressed by the state of Georgia. In other words, if Georgia did not act in compliance with Marshall's ruling, neither would the federal government. This lack of action was a far more subtle step to take than was his apocryphal denouncement of Marshall: "Marshall has made his ruling, now let him enforce it."[11] The subtly was uncharacteristic of this dynamic statesman but eminently effective. Native territory was not protected by the federal government in Georgia, where the ruling directly impacted, nor elsewhere for that matter. What Jackson's inaction meant was Removal would proceed given the *de facto* and increasingly violent reality of settlement. Natives would have to move to survive.

Legalism now sustained the collusion of those determined to garnish land for profit via settlement, not a precedent establishing equitable guarantees among nations.[12] Jackson's program of Removal went ahead and targeted Native civilizations east of the Mississippi regardless of the Supreme Court's opposition. Marshall's ruling captured the dilemma facing all Native tribes in existence at the time and ominously extending into the future. They had to submit to American power, even if the main benefit of living under that power—protection—was not forthcoming. In other words, Natives were now legally subject to the United States even if they did not enjoy the distinction of being citizens and therefore enjoying protection under the law. Marshall had recognized this pitfall. Yet, no matter the distinction of extra constitutional standing as awarded to Natives with Marshall's decisions, one has to agree with Frank Pommersheim in *Broken Landscape: Indians, Indian Tribes, and the Constitution*, that Marshall's classification of "domestic dependent nations" did little in practice, and in theory. Pommersheim writes, "The nature of a tribe's sovereignty or its domestic dependent nationhood status remains as unclear in the year 2009 as it was in 1831." One can bring the date current to 2016, and continue to follow Pommersheim's analysis: "It [the unique relationship between the tribe and the federal government] continues to exist, but its particulars, its contours, and its borders remain elusive."[13] More harmful to Natives would seem the norm of defining these "peculiar and cardinal distinctions," as Marshall labels them, in any way Americans saw fit. Removal added one more distinction and it was certainly a blow to Native hopes because treaties, not the Constitution, set the norms of the relationship, such as it was.[14] The historical basis of treaties was that the colonists and Americans cast aside or simply amend treaties when it suited their purposes. Consequently, tribal rights existed outside the Constitution but within an arbitrary sovereignty. This guarantee proved tenuous if not ingenuous given that it allowed Natives only an assumed dependency subject to enforcement by Americans and, as was the case of Removal, a savage enforcement if desired.

The legal discourse only delayed the inevitable, and Removal soon spelled the end for the Five Civilized Tribes east of the Mississippi: the Cherokee, Choctaw, Chickasaw, Creek, and Seminole. Even as this great moment of crisis impacted entire civilizations in the south, Natives could not unify. Part of the divisions arose from the military hopelessness of the situation; resistance could only lead to their destruction, an almost assured result if hostilities broke out. Recurring patterns advanced this outcome of ruin nonetheless: some scattered resistance, a few leaders signing agreements binding entire tribes to Removal, including the Treaty of New Echota (the Cherokee capital) that meant Cherokee compliance with the Indian Removal Act. The Natives had no good choices and the source of their dilemma was far beyond their control. There was, however, the promise of relocation to the Indian Country where Natives would shape their own destiny free of American interference. In this sanctuary lay the salvation of beleaguered peoples.

The Cherokee again symbolized much of this calamity in all aspects. They resisted the most, attempting to do so via legal posturing that cost them dearly. The U.S. government forced the remaining tribes out of the southeast, but it was the Cherokee who endured the infamous "Trail of Tears" where some 4,000 of their number perished when 16,000 of them made the long trek of 800 miles to a reservation west of the Mississippi. Starting in the fall of 1838, thirteen different columns emerged from Army camps established to organize this movement, and the various start times for the numerous groups meant that some Cherokee experienced the worst of weather: limited rainfall negated river travel for those starting later in the year, meaning traveling longer distances on foot, more time spent traveling, and more exposure to both the heat of summer and the chill of winter. The elderly suffered tremendously, as did the very young. Soldiers oversaw the forcible expulsion and the misery they enforced weighed on their consciences. They told themselves that their presence spared these Natives from deprivations at the hands of settlers. Had settlers conducted the move, perhaps greater atrocities would have occurred.[15] As it was, General Winfield Scott employed only one company of volunteers. Instead, soldiers answered a legal decree as a tool of a federal mission, as was their chief function. For this reason, they could understand the cost of the execution of the Removal Policy if not condone it. Moreover, once soldiers forced Natives from their camps and started them west, the Cherokee directed the movement. Because of this combination, soldiers were not the immediate cause of the suffering that ensued, or its catalyst. Settlers had forced the issue. However, it was a shallow separation between act and consequence, leaving Native redemption in Indian Country far from the thoughts of the soldiers orchestrating Removal.

Tragedy in 1838 did not capture the totality of this experience. That came from realizing that two previous waves of Cherokee, approximately 3,000 in total, had emigrated before the forcible move of the entire Cherokee in that year. These earlier groups had avoided the suffering that cost the remaining 16,000 a quarter of their number. John Ross, the foremost advocate of legal defense, appeared to have clung to a denial of the future and that exacerbated the Native plight. This end came with a note of truth, since Ross did seek a moral victory in the future: that treatment flouting the sovereignty of a people seeking to remain in the United States undermined the premise of that state. A Cherokee failure was in fact one shared by the United States. No doubt true in posterity, a reality framed by historical recollection, Ross traded a future moral victory for a disastrous present. The immorality of planning for the future at the expense of the present was not merely an intellectual conceit; it was a victory only Ross could appreciate in the present. This thinking also exacted immediate, physical loss. Ross buried his wife on the Trail of Tears, a personal cost that many of his people faced as well.

Cherokee actions, ineffective as they might have been, did produce an enduring victory of commemorating a tragedy endorsed by the American people. Americans cared little of the consequences, as land acquisition remained the key economic lure and spurred on the deluge. This more bottom up viewpoint exonerates Jackson to at least some extent. Removal, its approbation from below, was the worst face of democracy, a process working "for the people" as it vanquished a minority. As might be expected, some political dissent arose, but much of it could be accounted for in seeking merely to rebuke Jackson and his party. That Jackson's chosen successor to office, Martin Van Buren, presided over the Cherokee expulsion, spoke to the failure of the political opposition. A few voices rose above

John Ross, a Cherokee chief (Library of Congress).

the politicking, such as Senator Theodore Frelinghuysen of New Jersey. While Frelinghuysen drew from a Christian tradition and was morally appalled by Removal, he advanced a view that championed the sovereignty argument: that treaties were federal guarantees and states could not overturn them. Frelinghuysen declared, "When, or where, did any assembly or convention meet which proclaimed, or even suggested to these tribes, that the right of discovery contained a superior efficacy over all prior titles?"[16] The answer came in the right of preemption that said just that, by allowing the stronger group to redress a shared sovereignty among Natives and settlers due to expansion. The eventual failure of the senator's argument made it clear that no legal recourse existed to stop Removal. Also, no moral outrage arose among Americans to stop it either. Instead, removal endorsed an unfolding human misery shrouded in a racial ugliness that served as a referendum on the triumph of democracy. Jackson was adamant, the Supreme Court ineffective, and the military personnel followed orders. By 1838 removal became a reality, as Jackson's second term ended.

The Black Hawk War

As the push for the relocation of Natives in trans–Appalachia became a reality in the 1830s, in the north one Sauk chief, Black Hawk, railed against his fate. However, Black Hawk's rebellion in the upper reaches of the Mississippi River fizzled out almost as quickly as it had surfaced. In fact, Black Hawk had struggled to raise a following; the futility of the resistance was clear to the majority of the Sauk and their Fox allies who had acquiesced to living in Indian Country. Some 1,000 discontented souls did not. Dissension within Native ranks was always present, of course, but the reasons some chose to fight in this case centered on Black Hawk's personality. He was a leader past his prime but still seeking influence by increasing internal unrest. A prophet also emerged appealing to a past apart from settlers, a hope for a resurgent Native community. This now familiar dream was supported by an expectation of British intervention, creating a hopefulness very similar to the hope Tecumseh had responded to years before. Black Hawk and others in his group were veterans of that fighting. They should have known that thinking was more fantasy than not. But, concrete disturbances perpetrated by settlers occurred as well. At the mouth of the Rock River, Black Hawk's village suddenly possessed an American population, and his very dwelling became a habitat for settlers who had occupied it in his absence as he hunted in the north. For Black Hawk and many others, returning home meant fighting.

Black Hawk gathered in his following almost 500 warriors and in April 1832, he crossed to the east side of the Mississippi into Illinois to return home to Rock River. This bold act was enough to spark fears among Americans of an era gone by when Natives could terrorize the land. Terror did not greet this incursion, however, since a great many "volunteers" could be found who were anxious to engage the Natives. The assembled force included a small component of Army Regulars. Both of these approached Black Hawk's stronghold on the Rock River, only to find it abandoned. The soldiers took out their frustrations on the corpses found in a nearby Native burial ground. Symbolically, the act made it clear that there was no place for Natives east of the Mississippi. Tangibly, Black Hawk had continued to move east and now advanced north seeking refuge at the prophet's village.

Ma-Ka-Tai-Me-She-Kia-Kiah, or Chief Black Hawk, a Saukie brave (Library of Congress).

There he hoped to remain undisturbed. Black Hawk reversed himself only when he realized he stood alone, facing recrimination from other Sauk and Native tribes, expecting a confrontation with an American army, and accepting the realization that his appeal to England was delusionary.[17]

Before Black Hawk could retrace his steps and retreat across the Mississippi, he received reports of a group of militia closing in on his position. These militia were led by officers responding to the exhortations of Governor John Reynolds of Illinois, who desired a clash or at least a confrontation with Black Hawk to both end the tensions caused by his foray and to gain what political limelight could be had in the process. To wait on some Regulars advancing under General Atkins would only delay this favorable outcome. The result was a showdown of sorts as some 280 militia under Isaiah Stillman and David Bailey surprised Black Hawk's camp in mid–May. When the Sauk leader learned of the militia's presence, he ordered a trio of men to parley with them. Violence ensued. Black Hawk insisted that his subsequent attack was meant to avenge the wrongful treatment of those he had sent forward to ease tensions. Stillman declared that the Natives attacked his prepared position and overwhelmed it. The collapse of the Americans was the only certain outcome, as the militia scattered and Black Hawk won a "battle" that accelerated a confrontation into a war.

After the defeat of the militia, a crisis atmosphere descended upon the entire area, and Black Hawk's party killed many of the settlers it encountered. However, in a short time, an energetic leader emerged, Henry Dodge. This man led only 29 volunteers. Still, he went after Black Hawk. Dodge's group scattered a detachment of Sauk, a victory that revitalized the frontier. More militia were soon on the trail of the now retreating Natives who continued north. Then, Black Hawk, in desperation, fled west toward the Mississippi River hoping to cross to safety. This retreat enjoyed an auspicious beginning when his warriors held off a rush by militia who had caught up to his retreating column, occupying some high ground overlooking the Wisconsin River. As the militia drew near, Sauk warriors attacked them in an apparently unplanned effort to scatter their pursuers. The militia held firm and a number of the attackers fell. The total is in dispute, but something close to 40 braves may have perished; American estimates of Native dead are twice that number. Black Hawk, presiding over the battlefield from atop his horse, considered this engagement a great success because the women and children with his group safely crossed the Wisconsin and evaded capture or slaughter.

Black Hawk was not so lucky once he reached the Mississippi, which he did at the end of July. There, two miles below the junction of that river with the Bad Axe River, Black Hawk planned his last moves. With the militia closing in behind him, he was shocked to find a steamboat in the water. Black Hawk appears to have desired surrender, at least of his women and children, but this did not occur. Instead, having evaded destruction for a number of weeks, the end came. Black Hawk watched as his remaining warriors, approximately 200 of them, were decimated by fire on land from militia closing in for the kill. The steamboat added to the destruction as it targeted warriors, women, and children all clinging to the shoreline. Survivors struggled to cross the river and many did so only to be killed by Sioux warriors waiting for those who struggled out of the water and thus violated Sioux territory. Annihilation was the result, and Sauk enemies purposely sought this out. More than a few settlers relished this endgame, the call for extermination of the Sauk, but articulated in terms of all Natives. In fact, this zeal for total extinction had imbued Black Hawk's pursuers from first to last. While the militia rejoiced in this outcome, the professional soldiers remained mute. True, they had missed the slaughter on the banks of the Mississippi, and a desire to minimize the militia victory may have explained much of their revulsion. However, it was also clear the militia represented the growing gap between soldiers and civilians, between those performing a job of achieving security and those cleansing a land for settlement.[18]

Possessing a strategic advantage and wielding a tactical ruthlessness, American actions doomed Black Hawk's attack. His discovery, made too late, that a war party had no place east of the Mississippi, was tragic and significant in lessons learned. Forced from their homes but refusing to move beyond the Mississippi, renegade Natives faced only destruction, and this is what came to pass. This reality explains the body count as a large number of Black Hawk's warriors died and only a few Americans perished in that climatic battle along the Mississippi River. Black Hawk was not among this tally. As the end became clear, he fled north to surrender at a later date. A failing of leadership accounted for this act of cowardice, as did his recognition of his fate. Black Hawk had been conflicted from the start of his war, so to again center the events of the summer of 1832 upon his person was fitting in many ways. His now personal humiliation served as a testimonial to the doom that awaited those who rejected the Indian Country. Ironically, given this ignominious end to the war that bore his name, Black Hawk went on to enjoy some fame among Americans for having played such a large role in these events. The Jackson Administration sent him on a tour of the east, a symbol of the end of the threat of Native savagery and therefore to Native resistance of American expansionist ambitions. Black Hawk's defeat meant Americans had made interaction with Natives safe to the point of allowing for some "sexualized rhetoric circulated in newspapers," this writing hinting at miscegenation all the while denouncing Native savagery. This message "further 'defeated'" the "defeated" Natives in the just concluded conflict and throughout the West. It was a clever connotation, signaling to settlers that the middle ground was no longer a necessary precursor to expansion west.[19]

The Seminole War

The Removal mandate soon reached far to Florida, where the Seminoles had survived the ambitious projects of Andrew Jackson. It was a surprising outcome. When the fighting began in earnest, no unified resistance surfaced. A few celebrated figures led bands against Americans, but others desisted producing a haphazard outbreak of violence. This was true of the earliest confrontations when Jackson directed the effort to tame the Florida frontier in 1817. Factionalism remained a crucial failure plaguing Native resistance in

1835 and when the last spasm was over in 1858, those Natives still fighting reflected the remnants of hopelessly divided peoples. It could not be otherwise; only opposition to American expansion unified these kinships and tribes populating the area.

The southern border fluctuated with a rich cast of characters of not always clearly defined origin. The great tribes in the south, the Choctaw, Cherokee, Chickasaw, and Creek, were not unified in any way, exacerbating the fragmentation of a region that already sustained cultures no longer adhering to the simple delineation of Native. The Creeks, perhaps the most divided, were split into two groups, upper and lower. As the American tide came south, many Creeks fled into Florida. There, they teamed with other dissidents in the region including Blacks to form a unique concentration of those displaced by American expansion. During the 1700s, these former slaves and displaced Natives became yet another group of people inhabiting Florida: the Seminoles. The Seminoles bore this reality as a historical problem, a longstanding need to exist in the untamed refuge that had been Florida since Spanish times. In fact, the word "Seminole" merely referred to a beleaguered people of diffuse origins and one galvanized by local events. The name was a simplification. Spaniards in the region labeled the new arrivals "Cimarrones" meaning "wild ones" or "runaways," overlooking the presence of aboriginal peoples in Florida. The Spanish did notice the fragmented roots and the fierce independence of these Seminoles and were more or less content to leave them alone.[20]

The Americans did not ignore them. Jackson had landed an early blow in 1817, launching a punitive raid into Spanish Florida. The Seminoles, Creeks, and escaped slaves had been unable to stop him, but Jackson's army was too small to accomplish anything more than inflame tensions. Jackson could do a lot more as president, and by backing Removal, he fostered another round of conflict in Florida.

The most charismatic leader opposing the Americans, Osceola, could not even call himself a chief. Held against his will by federal authorities before the fighting began in earnest in December 1835, Osceola's short time as a prisoner cemented his anger and his determination to wage a war against Americans. Once released, Osceola found some support but by no means a large backing. His followers seldom numbered more than a few hundred. A marginal figure in terms of command in the field, Osceola officially ignited the conflict anew because his presence made it dangerous for Natives to contemplate measures other than fighting. Osceola himself executed a Seminole chief espousing acceptance of the American terms of Removal. So when the fighting began at the end of December 1835, a clash that had been building for years had a loci, if not a center, a man capable of inciting violence and, therefore, conflict, but one hardly capable of finishing what he had started.

Divisions within the Seminole resistance grew from another source. Escaped slaves had sought refuge in the Florida territory for some time. Some of these fugitives had married into Seminole tribes or lived on their own so

Osceola of Florida, a Seminole warrior (Library of Congress).

that by the 1830s, some 250 freed Blacks could be added to the mix of peoples in Florida. American aggression forced Blacks and Seminoles closer together, but it was not always a harmonious union.[21] Blacks feared a return to slavery if Removal became a reality and wanted the Seminoles in place and hostile to Americans to ensure some support for their survival. This view strongly shaped their role in fomenting resistance. Black interpreter Abraham is the most famous case in point. Many believe he distorted the conditions of Removal to the Seminoles so that the Seminoles would continue fighting. Men such as Abraham may have taken the risk that a conflict could be won by recalcitrant Seminoles waging a long guerrilla war. However, when the U.S. Army guaranteed former slaves safe passage to the Indian Country, a number of these people—Abraham among them—reversed themselves and pushed for a cessation of the fighting. Should this be so, the Second Seminole War was as much of a "Negro war" as it was an "Indian war," as General Thomas Sidney Jesup declared when he took command in December 1836.[22] This label made it clear that any conflict was sure to make settlers fear an increased resistance among former slaves.

While Blacks joined Seminole war parties in these struggles, the front they formed was imperfect in composition and purpose. In fact, using Black people as slaves persisted as a norm among the Seminoles, as did private land ownership, commercial agriculture, and grazing cattle, which was the more widespread practice. Labor was as much a need as it was for Americans, and while slavery in Seminole culture did not amount to the harsh practice of permanent servitude as Americans defined it, slavery still spoke to the subservient stature of Blacks. Osceola famously captured this tone before the fighting broke out by denouncing Americans who refused to sell him gunpowder as trying to "make me black," i.e., a slave.[23] Yet the caustic reference hardly reflected the reality of about 500 Blacks who enjoyed some autonomy under Seminole control, who were armed, and who would prove more than willing to fight. That modest number represented a greater threat in terms of their example possibly inciting a large percentage of the other 4,000 slaves in the area to revolt, a problem all the more tangible given that only a few hundred Americans kept them in check.

A slave revolt was obviously a potential danger to settler aspirations in Florida. When the fighting started, 400 of the 4,000 enslaved Blacks did join the 250 to 500 "Negro Seminoles," other Seminole slaves, some freed men, and 1,400 Natives openly resisting Removal. Thus, comparatively few slaves joined the Seminole resistance and a large number of those who did join quit the fight fairly early on, even though this meant a return to servitude. The hardships of resistance often paled in comparison to life as a slave, including separation from family members who may not have escaped. The Seminole call for resistance proved shallower then might have been believed. Even when pressed for the survival of their way of life, Seminole resistance did not rally the many groups to a common cause. Rather, the movement reflected the internal contradictions. The calamity facing both Seminoles and Blacks if Americans controlled Florida did not produce a unified defense on their part but instead led to more fragmentation. It was an irony that pointed to a middle ground in the far reaches of the Florida territory, one again marked by violence among competing groups rather than opposing sides. This tension served American expansion; the Americans extinguished that interplay in Florida by promising a Native sanctuary in the Indian Country.

Other things suggested the difficulty of subduing the Seminoles. The terrain was problematic. Too much of that territory lay covered in swamp and dense foliage allowing concealment and, more significantly, giving the Seminoles a chance to escape if a battle went awry. The difficulty of detection and pursuit meant an army trying to defeat a foe in such terrian faced a daunting task. For this reason, the divisions besetting those Natives opposing Removal became an attribute. Their raiding parties enjoyed the advantage of being able to live—survive—in that land since their small numbers eased supply requirements, made evasion possible, and placed the onus of winning the conflict on the attacking force. This burden greatly impacted American efforts. The Seminoles mounted the only successful defense against the Americans in North America, and the terrian that they stood and fought on explained a great deal of this outcome.

Geography greatly factored into the causes of this new round of conflict in the wake of Jackson's Removal Policy. The Seminoles agreed to move to a reservation in the center of the Panhandle. This concession had been magnanimous in the extreme due to the fact that the land they were to occupy was poor in quality, mostly swamps and marshes. Little of this ground could be used for farming or even ranching, the Seminoles' preferred means of subsistence. To compound this sacrifice inherent in their proposed volunteer isolation, they had given up more arable land that all parties understood would become the purview of Americans when that inevitable demographic onslaught came south. For these reasons, the Seminole reservation represented a move to forestall conflict, and they believed that their sacrifices were more than enough to merit being left alone. They were right in the specific acts taken, but not when confronting the Removal Policy. Here the Jackson Administration stood firm, demanding the entire tribe move west where it would be free of any possible interference by settlers. It was the familiar kindness rationale, if ingenuous in that settlement had not quite reached the Seminoles in Florida. More pressing was Jackson's determination not to allow an exception. To permit one tribe to remain in Florida invited resistance from others. Therefore, the U.S. government applied Removal to all Natives east of the Mississippi River including the Seminoles.

What followed was a Seminole refusal of the Removal decree, repeatedly so, and then a willingness on their part to ensure incidents along the reservation border ignited a war. One could say Seminole belligerence fostered the violence and the war, except for the Removal Policy. American arguments in favor of this policy as a means of ensuring Native survival by removing them before they faced obliteration at the hands of settlers made little sense in Florida. Americans did not desire or attempt to seize the inhospitable terrain that comprised the reservation. Consequently, military action here was unnecessary in the service of the supposed humanitarian end of Removal. Seminole obstinacy cast an uneasy light on that policy as undertaken on behalf of saving them. Natives sensed the policy's highhandedness and invited war to come.

Americans sought a quick end to the violence as U.S. troop columns fanned out to box-in the reservation. Military leaders assumed that this show of force would subdue the Natives without much need for fighting. It was a naïve expectation. Instead, the military action helped foster resistance when the war opened with a Seminole success. In December 1835, a chief named Micanopy led a few hundred warriors who annihilated a column of U.S. soldiers under the command of Major Francis L. Dade, the troops marching from Fort Brooke in the Tampa Bay area in the north to reinforce Fort King in the south and located in the heart of the Seminole reservation. Micanopy, in fact, rose from the brush and fired the first shot, which killed Dade instantly. In a few hours, the ambushers overcame the rest of the Americans.

The destruction of Dade's command of 108 men galvanized the United States into action. A subsequent U.S. offensive unfolded but floundered at the end of December in the expanse of Florida. A Seminole war party trapped another American column in the wilds there; this one was marching south from Fort Defiance and, after crossing the Withlacoochee River, fell into an ambush. The soldiers survived annihilation, and then withdrew in humiliation. Newly arrived General Winfield Scott tried to overcome these failures in the new year. Starting in March 1836, Scott deployed his army in a three-pronged attack, which was designed again to box in the Seminoles and force them to make a stand in the swamps near the Withlacoochee. Scott reasoned that once he established military control over the middle portion of the territory, the war would end. Predictably, Scott's grand military plans netted little in return. His advancing columns converged in the Tampa Bay area, but the Seminoles eluded capture. The war dragged on, and blame could be heaped on the U.S. Army. It was led by men wielding military force as the sole means of enforcing Removal, an overt compromise of a policy intended to preserve those slated for relocation. The soldiers struggled to overcome the Seminoles, and Natives had a chance since the fight would boil down to a guerrilla war where terrain proved decisive. The swamps where the Natives made their stand greatly neutralized superior American numbers. At a high point a 7,500-man army could not eliminate no more than 2,000 warriors and Blacks and the struggle persisted, resulting in some four years of bloodshed.

General Jesup assumed command a year after the renewal of conflict in Florida. Not much had changed. Sporadic violence had claimed a few Seminole leaders, and Jesup managed to get peace in place by March 6, 1837. It did not hold. The Americans then captured Osceola, although they did so with deception, inviting him to a peace conference and then incarcerating him. Jesup felt justified in blaming Osceola for betraying the peace. The general now put his soldiers to the task of winning this war when he sent seven columns in pursuit of the Seminole defenders. Should the enemy fight, so would he; should they retreat, he would pursue. This strictly military solution ground forward and achieved some results. Military units managed to apprehend a number of Seminoles, including the aged King Philip and his son Coacoochee. This was progress. Better still, King Philip had relied on an old Black man named John Caesar to organize resistance. Caesar died fighting in January 1837, and when the Army captured a number of other Black Seminoles, resistance appeared to sputter.

This military approach had unintended consequences, however. For example, King Philip had tried to remain neutral, but the American offensive had encouraged him to resist. Soon, Jesup's tactics provoked a desperate Seminole response in that the remaining Seminole leaders united, which spurred on another round of fighting. This came in extraordinary fashion. Coacoochee escaped from Fort Marion, an American prison in St. Augustine. He then rallied a number of Seminoles to continue fighting. He was needed, since King Philip elected to remain in jail, citing old age. Osceola also remained behind as he languished with illness. This great symbol of Seminole resistance died in captivity a short time later. Coacoochee teamed with some new leaders, including Sam Jones and Alligator, individuals still looking to hold out. Together, they fought a pitched battle on Christmas day in 1837, as 800 U.S. soldiers and volunteers led by Colonel Zachary Taylor assaulted 400 Seminoles. The Battle of Lake Okeechobee was the largest to date, but it also ended in stalemate since the Natives escaped. This war seemingly did not have an end and the Americans grew increasingly tired of the struggle. Jesup pushed south. In a startling turn-around for someone who had a number of months earlier advised the War Department that the war "must necessarily be one of extermination," Jesup now recommended to Washington that since Americans did not need the land for settlement, the war should cease and the Seminoles be allowed to remain in place.[24] The U.S. government overruled Jesup and ordered him to enforce Removal without waiting "until the Seminoles were pressed upon by the white population."[25] The U.S. government directed that military force stop this resistance. Anything else was dishonorable, a waste of the blood and treasure expended to this point.

Fortunately for those ordering the war to continue, the Seminoles were exhausted as well. Overwhelmed and outlasted, a number of Seminoles surrendered and relocated west of the Mississippi. Peace was established again in May 1839, as the ranking general of the U.S. Army there, Alexander Macomb, agreed to allow the Seminoles a reservation in south Florida. However, this second peace ended with another massacre, as Seminoles ambushed a detachment guarding a storehouse. Scattered settlers in reach of the Seminoles were not free from attack either, and they retaliated at every opportunity. The constant violence meant hostilities continued long after 1839, sputtering on and finally ending in 1842. In this war, the cost in lives and money steadily grew, as did the loss of American credibility. There was no honor in this long, ugly, and highly publicized Indian War that became one of the costliest in American history: 1,500 U.S. military personnel killed and $40 million dollars spent in seven years. The only redeemable feature was the American conviction that a sanctuary awaited Natives forcibly removed from Florida. The promise that Indian Country would redeem American honor proved the main justification for the war and for its continuance.

More fighting soon exposed this delusion. Settlers did indeed come to Florida in increasing numbers and the inevitable tensions arose. The remaining small group of Seminoles, pressed by increasing American expansion and clinging to a base existence in the south, refused to retreat further and lashed out at settlers in 1855 in the southern and southwestern portion of what was now a state. A single chief led the resistance, which amounted to a third war in this troubled land. While Chief Billy Bowlegs mustered no more than 100 warriors, even this force produced enough tension and worry to draw a major American response. Soon federal troops and state militia were in the swamps attempting to ferret out Seminoles, although not without significant disagreement. Federal authorities were willing to leave these renegades alone; keeping the area quiet was the priority. More violence was unlikely given their small numbers and relative isolation in this remote part of the state. Chasing them into the swamps would only lead to more trouble. State officials thought otherwise. These hostiles were too great a threat to ignore, as the recent sporadic attacks indicated. Florida's government officials ordered a manhunt. This measure proved only somewhat effective. Patrols discovered a few villages and destroyed them. Fighting broke out and a handful of men died during some skirmishing. Anxious to end the struggle and ongoing headache, the state offered Seminoles increased compensation for Removal. Then some Natives already inhabiting the Indian Country visited the region to plead with the last remnant of Seminoles to relocate.

These efforts slowly produced results but not before the civilian call for Removal equated to demands of extermination. An editor of a local paper shrieked, "What has been done to remove or exterminate the Seminoles. We answer nothing!"[26] It was not clear if locals blamed the volunteers more than the Regulars for this failure. Neither was it clear whether the efforts had failed. A little over two years later this war ended as well, and a pitiful number of Seminoles agreed to relocate. A few, close to 150 or so, refused and remained in Florida. In this sense, the Natives had won the war, but the cost of victory minimized the triumph. At best, a guerrilla war of over thirty years had netted a painful stalemate, nothing more. This result was dubious to say the least. The Seminoles enjoyed but a slender toehold, reduced to inhabiting a shell of what had once been their domain in Florida. Yet, this end game was the best military "success" of Natives in their war against expansion to this point and, as it turned out, in the entire 300-year history of conflict that defined this struggle.

End of the War

The hopelessness characterizing the final resistance in Florida signified what had overtaken all of trans–Appalachia. The Army, frequently joined by civilians, brought to heel those Natives still fighting and expelled them west of the Mississippi River. In so doing, Americans did not see a largess from excessive power, but a reprieve extended to beleaguered peoples struggling to find their way in the new creation of the United States. That Native failure meant Removal ensured their survival so Natives could endure and slowly become American in a sanctuary west of the Mississippi. Indian Country was a hearts and minds promise satisfying Americans and supposedly mollifying Natives. The costs were enormous given the wars and bloodshed that followed the enforcement of the Removal Policy. If these costs were unavoidable, as Americans insisted was the case, the magnanimity of the gesture depended on posterity, and this augured poorly for Natives. The United States represented a work still in progress as Americans looked beyond the Mississippi River to a new, emerging region. The new nation's recent success lent credence to allowing a greater power to rise, an American behemoth that came clearly into view as the open plains further west appeared within reach of settlement. With the full appreciation of this goal, this Empire of Liberty, Native destruction was assured and would come next over a long period of time, rendering hearts and minds an empty gesture.

Search and Destroy

Rangers, Militia, Volunteers and the "First Way of War"

Texas Ranger "Rip" Ford stepped forward to investigate the body of the fallen warrior. He kicked the corpse, shaking the famous Spanish coat of mail strapped across the upper torso. Comanche Chief Iron Jacket was dead, and Ford looked up to find some appreciation in the moment. He gathered his thoughts, and as he did so, he saw some of the Natives allied with his Rangers mounting their horses and celebrating this victory as well. The numerous dead bodies about the camp did speak to a success, but Ford found the separation between Native friends and foes to be slight. When would he turn on these allies, he wondered? Ford then cast his eyes on the assembled Texans, a montage of men in varying dress, some awaiting orders, others plundering the camp for spoils. At that moment in 1858, Ford understood that his Rangers stood somewhere between soldier and mercenary, between hero and villain, between the civilized and the savage. Ford was in the middle of Texas, a state asking many of these same questions of itself.

The Arizona Territory took a similar measure when a group of miners looked up in surprise as the Army detachment filed into their camp. The man at their head, Colonel Joseph West, appeared disinterested in his surroundings until a special sight caught his eye. Tied to a wagon stood a very large man; the officer immediately recognized that man as Mangas Colorados, an Apache chief. Now West moved with alacrity, dismounting, issuing orders to tie up the horses, and asking to speak with the leader of these miners. They demurred, and West saw his chance. He ordered his men to take charge of the prisoner and prepare to stay for the night. A short time later, a few of the miners told him how they had lured that man into camp and now held him captive as insurance against Apache attacks. West approved of the capture, but cared little about its intended purpose. Mangas was to bother no one again. By morning, the great chief was dead, killed while trying to escape. At least, that was the story told in 1863. Who killed him, civilians or Army personnel, and why, remained a muddled story then and thereafter. The same question could be asked any number of times in Arizona, elsewhere across the West, and throughout the settled nation, with few clear answers.

One certainty was that the frontier at this point meant an American push west, less north or south. This single axis of advance ensured that Native tribes had fewer opportunities to team with European powers to stop a remorseless American expansionism. This new reality signaled the beginning of the end of the remaining Native resistance on the North American continent. As the war context against outside powers faded, the overt drive of Americans to consolidate gains beyond the self-appointed geographic barrier of the Mississippi became a call for the "first way of war." Soon the punitive aim of taking the battle to the enemy's homeland by burning crops and villages to wear down Native resistance (in effect, the targeting of women and children by denying them safe harbor), extended beyond the fading memory of the struggle with England. Americans used this approach as a stepping stone to harsher measures designed to settle the remainder of the continent. Natives, in what was now the West, became subject to much more aggressive American attacks that consistently looked to involve noncombatants in a war, and this war was led by civilians.[1]

The Expanding War

The Native tendency to seek accommodation with the European and American arrivals produced a haphazard resistance that surfaced immediately after contact and persisted until the end of this long period of conflict. As a result of the Indian way of war, eastern Natives never mounted a war that sought the eradication of settlers even when the indigenous peoples were fighting for their survival. The conciliatory approach to European arrival and American expansion among competing tribes could be said to apply to Natives located throughout the continent. This thinking soon became a crucial weakness since the Native foe benefited from the opposite of this progression. Expansion engaged settlers on a haphazard basis just as much as Natives, but ironically, each step inland contributed to forcing those contacted to capitulate. This ongoing success soon impacted the West, that is, the territory beyond the Mississippi River. Yet, the American push forward here had little to do with heroic frontiersmen exploring the vastness of an uncharted wilderness and much to do with an ugly hammer. Civilians led in this expansion and savagely so. If the former had opened the frontier, settlers would now close it. What came next rested squarely on rangers, militiamen, and volunteers who increasingly waged a war of extermination against Native Americans. Search and destroy had found its place in the American counterinsurgency effort.

The American success in greatly limiting England's support of Native resistance and in always encouraging the onrushing hordes of settlers, especially when emboldened by a politically defiant President Jackson, eclipsed Native fortunes to such an extent that by the late 1830s, no significant resistance was left east of the Mississippi River. Once the Americans had settled the land in trans–Appalachia, they looked to expand beyond that region. This objective rested on a number of factors including the international setting that presaged a limit to American ambitions. Mexico stood in the path of expansion south, and in the Pacific Northwest, England and even Russia could claim territorial rights and expressed a wish to defend these rights as a matter of economic gain. None of these powers proved able to stand up to American advances, although Mexico fought a series of wars, first against American settlers, and then against the United States, before relinquishing its claims. All the while, Americans also met and defeated the multitude of Natives in the new territory, again proving their ability to isolate the main target from outside support. Regardless of this largely diplomatic success of separating enemies, a military resolve surfaced as well. It came from civilians striking Natives and doing so in extraordinary fashion, a path so marred by violence as to call into question the morality supposedly undergirding an American expansion west. This idea of prophesying a validation, if not redemption, of the American soul was in jeopardy and so too was the desired preservation of Native Americans. This high-minded idealism fell short as that American clamor masked the hypocrisy always embedded in the goal of establishing an Empire of Liberty.

The lofty American expectations followed the nation everywhere. As the United States prepared to bring Florida under its control in 1835, Texans mounted a rebellion against Mexico. When that war ended with Texan independence the following year, the new country inherited many challenges, including how to contend with its Native population. It would be a punitive effort, and Texan ambitions soon confronted the problem of fighting the Natives in the open. Withdrawal into the scrub and grassland provided this foe with an advantage. Those attacking or attacked could retreat if something went wrong. Terrain offered Natives ideal "guerrilla" territory for this reason, but this advantage did not stop American expansion. The main ingredient of Texan success was settlement. The confrontation in Texas highlighted the plight of all Natives confronting Americans across the plains, as civilians in increasing numbers eventually ended any Native "space" advantage.

Mexico as far back as 1821 initiated this process of conquest via demographic advantage in its effort to use settlement to overcome the problem of open space in its most northern territory. Mexican officials allowed American nationals to emigrate to Mexican soil in order to confront the threat from the Native tribes also living and raiding there. A lack of national power persisted both in terms of military assets and people—the Mexican population remained sparse in California, New Mexico, and Texas. Consequently, the Mexicans could not police their land effectively, allowing Native transgressions to go unpunished. So emboldened, Natives threatened to overrun Mexican settlement, or, at least, to blunt their growth—in either respect an alarming development to say the least. To help with this problem, Americans offered to migrate into Texan territory and assist the Mexican authorities. More inhabitants would curtail Native incursions south. The logic received sanction by the Mexican government, which ceded land grants, *empresario* contracts, to Stephen F. Austin and others starting in 1821. Therefore, in a demographic prescription, both intentionally and unintentionally, the Mexican government set in motion a process enabling the United States to digest a further portion of the American frontier.

The Mexican settlement policy compounded its demographic challenge in the north, since the accord between the new inhabitants and the Mexican government soon unraveled. Americans did assume Mexican citizenship, as had been the agreed upon condition to settlement in that country's territory, but the allegiance of these new occupants to Mexico was too often nominal. Americans flouted Mexican authority by simply disregarding state decrees mandating Catholicism and prohibiting slavery. Their refusal to convert to that faith and their widespread use of slaves, as well as their haughty if not openly caustic attitude and actions toward Mexican officials, all worked to undermine Mexican policy and Mexican relations with the growing American population in Texas. The long-term implications of the policy were only too clear within ten years. These immigrants had become disruptive in their own right, a fifth column on par with the Native threat in restricting Mexicans from settling in the area. Worse, this development could attract the active interest of the United States. Mexican officials eventually confronted this issue; they hoped to hold onto territory that could fall to a group they had invited into their midst. Thus, Mexico prohibited further American immigration in 1830.

Initially, only a sympathetic identification with the Americans living on Mexican land had brought together the United States and American immigrants in Mexico. However, the clamor for greater accord increased markedly and rapidly from within Mexican territory among those inhabitants who believed that the developed Texas landscape now was more American in orientation than Mexican, if for no other reason than the skin complexion of the majority of its inhabitants. As always, this racial card proved a simplistic rationale. Lurking behind race relations was the economic reality that impacted the region stretching from Florida in the southeast to the Nueces River in the southwest. The increasing agricultural production in Texas primarily came to an American locale, New Orleans, for export, depriving Mexico of tax revenue from this growing trade bonanza. The profits generated by the American colonials living in Mexico certainly registered with American authorities, but this favorable trade arrangement meant successive administrations could afford to show remarkable restraint and not act to absorb the American settlements in Texas. Rather, the resourceful efforts of the Americans there would force things to a head between the United States and Mexico. The Americans in Texas and a substantial Tejano population drew together to offer a rallying call against Mexican governance. In a fairly short period of time, privileged slaveholders and a small rancher elite pushed that territory closer to open rebellion, something that came to pass by 1836.

With the eruption of hostilities in that year—the stand of a small number of Texans at the Alamo being the most famous event—the American uprising was afoot. Given this development, the Mexican policy was a failure, of course, but in extraordinary fashion since the Native tribes were hardly mentioned. They had in fact been pushed to the sidelines, so in this respect, the Mexican policy had succeeded. The Comanche in particular soon found themselves spectators of a struggle very much deciding their fate. The Texan war for independence was determined by a clash of arms featuring Mexicans and, if Americans is too general a term, then certainly Texans and Tejanos. After the Battle of San Jacinto in April 1836, the Mexican commander General Antonio López de Santa Anna accepted defeat, bowing before this mixed resistance.

As had been the case before with Native reaction to European turned American expansion, neutrality surfaced as policy. Some lesser tribes fell victim to the growing American presence in Texas, but Comanche territory remained largely intact. The main American settlements in Texas grew to maturity at the periphery of this powerful tribe, a mutually imposed reality but one that eventually proved a harmful outcome for Natives.[2] Only in the larger context of Mexican-American relations did their bleak fate become clear. Texan independence foreshadowed the war to come between the United States and Mexico. Given Mexican inability to quell the American-led rebellion in their midst, hesitation characterized Mexican policy toward both the new country of Texas and the always dangerous United States: an avoidance of war was the clear aim. At the same time, resentment of assumed interference by the U.S. government in Texas remained paramount, a belief all the more readily believed because the United States set the southern boundary of Texas at the Rio Grande River, as far south as one could fathom. To appease Mexican honor, negotiations stalled. Ironically, by not seeking war, Mexico allowed itself to be pulled in that direction, and the American annexation of Texas in December 1845 was the final step to this progression.[3]

The United States had its own reasons for war. Territorial acquisition cured American dissension over slavery, or so it appeared to many in that country. Just as many feared the consequences of that very expansion. Acquiring more land threatened to deepen sectional divides as the nation struggled to keep a balance among newly absorbed territory needing to be declared free or slave. Here was evidence of a brittle American construct, but also a reason for war. Only a war against an outsider could unite foes at home by easing the tensions between the north and south because of the practice of slavery. This in fact happened. The Mexican American War starting in April 1846, was a firm rallying point for the United States in the base motive of blame for provocation dumped on Mexico, but also given the prospect for more land. War came after Mexican cavalry killed a number of U.S. soldiers in the disputed territory between the Rio Grande and the Nueces Rivers. Americans rallied together to rebuke a Mexican threat to the United States, and to greatly expand the size of the nation if the fighting went well. It was a tempting war given the possibilities.

The threat and the reward were not so much imagined by Americans as simplified with a focus on Mexico. The larger American aim from such a conflict meant continued expansion, as personified by the foremost agitator in this story, U.S. President James K. Polk. A war with Mexico and perhaps England promised to secure for Americans land stretching from a disputed line separating Canada and the United States all the way down to a contested border with Mexico. In the process of this struggle, Americans ultimately ended the long history of Mexican conflict with the Native populations of the southwest, a service this war of expansion (aggression) bestowed upon Mexico. If that peace also betrayed the transparent motive of a U.S. land grab, squelching this centuries-old problem of Natives raiding south underscored how detrimental the ongoing strife had been to Mexican interests. The war with these marauders was so harmful as to cripple the Mexican ability to resist the U.S. attack in 1845 to the point of sapping any possible guerrilla movement in the wake of the American advance.[4]

The American tendency to debate Polk's public expression of the American sentiment of expansion when he ran for president revealed the extreme danger now facing Native Americans as a consequence of this war. A vast amount of land became part of the United States, over 500,000 square miles that today comprises the states of Texas, Arizona, California, and others. However, with the addition of this expanse of land, the southwest territory of the United States became a U.S. military problem as a clash with the Comanche, Navaho and Apache now loomed. Much fighting could be expected, since the war with Mexico had created success but also had created a challenge. Subjugation of the Native populations became an American responsibility. This effort gained traction because the strategic reality had so worsened for Natives that their continued resistance was anti-climactic. Absorbed into the American behemoth, the Native populations in the West had no hope of stopping this conquest. Only the means of defeat remained to be determined.

Texas Rangers

In Texas, civilian irregulars were legitimized with the title of Ranger. Rangers brought the war to the Natives by guile and outright murder. This purpose resulted in Ranger units using their mobility to fill the gaps between Army forts. Texans reasoned such a ploy could provide sufficient security, and they assumed the offense by targeting Native settlements. However, Texas Ranger units demonstrated a willingness to go further than destroying towns and villages. Killing as many Natives as possible became their task, and rangers became an arm of Texan authority bent on the expulsion, if not extermination, of their Native population.

Charges of barbarity and treachery soon accentuated this conflict. For example, in 1836, Comanche warriors surprised the Parker homestead, killing several men and taking hostages that included women and children. This attack proved momentous because the issue of captives sparked more violence. In March 1840, settlers killed at least twelve chiefs that Texan officials had invited to San Antonio as part of a delegation to discuss peace. Their hosts refused to allow the chiefs to leave a building where they discussed terms since they believed the Natives had failed to bring in all of the captives they held. When these leaders realized they were trapped, they tried to force their way out. The "Council House Fight" cost eight Texans their lives; the entire party of 65 Natives perished or became captives.

Rather than being considered outside the norm, these clashes typified the conflict and rangers spurred on the wanton violence. A year before this inflammatory event in San Antonio, two ranger units of sixty men each achieved only limited successes, if that. In the first half of 1839, one group under Col. John Moore surprised a Comanche camp and attacked, but had to retreat before a Native counterstroke. A few months later, a ranger unit under Captain John Bird roamed the countryside seeking a fight with Natives, but found itself surprised by a large Comanche force. The unit barely held off the attack, and Bird was killed. However, persistence allowed the rangers to score a pair of victories in 1840. Just before the clash in San Antonio, Captain Ben McCulloch and a force of rangers ambushed and killed over eighty Comanche. Later that year, Moore resurfaced and led 90 rangers on an attack on a Comanche village in northwest Texas that killed a similar number.

With these punitive measures, rangers attempted to thwart Natives, primarily the Comanche, from moving south to raid in Mexico. Texan citizens usually suffered as well during these Native forays. Over the first part of the decade of the 1840s, rangers pushed these attackers north, reasonably shoring up the Texas border. They did the same along the volatile Mexican border, and in the process, Texans won for themselves an expansive land stretching from the Rio Grande River far to the south, reaching up to the Red River to the north, and extending across the endless plains west. However, the U.S. government had to pick up many of the pieces. The Army sheltered some Cherokee fleeing northeastern Texas after Texans expelled these survivors of the Removal Policy from what was now Texan soil. General Matthew Arbuckle received the Cherokee in his charge and rebuked the Texan government by declaring the Cherokee harmless.[5]

The enemies of Texas only multiplied as violence begot violence. Many Tejanos faced marginalization in society and at times lashed out, provoking incidents that threatened to plunge the region into anarchy. The activities of these marauders and the remaining Native bands brave enough to venture south soon drew the attention of rangers who patrolled the frontier where previously the Comanche had roamed with virtual impunity. Ranger duty became confronting the "outlaw breed of three races, the Indian Warrior, Mexican bandit, and American desperado," and to defeat these foes, rangers combined the fighting qualities of the three races. In targeting outlaws, perhaps rangers assumed some of that lawless quality themselves.[6]

The term "ranger" highlighted this very fact of ruthlessness leading to excesses because the Texas Rangers pursued a larger purpose than merely functioning as a frontier defensive force, albeit one frequently needed in this role. The Texas government called up units, but often did not pay them, since there was no money to fund a standing force let alone volunteers. To receive compensation, Texas Rangers shared in the spoils of war such as farm goods, livestock, horses, and mules. The economic incentive was clear: a harsh dispatch of violence to maximize profit. Few quibbled about the former, even if remaining silent on the latter. For example, when Mirabeau B. Lamar assumed the presidency of Texas from Sam Houston, he made that violent aim policy, declaring a war of extermination resulting in the "total extinction or total expulsion" of Natives from Texas.[7] Given that purpose, the title Ranger was a clever pronouncement of military coercion barely masking the intent— civilians leading ethnic cleansing, as Gary Clayton Anderson says in *The Conquest of Texas*.[8] As such, in specific terms, rangers represented the over-arching effort of Texans to achieve economic vitality at the expense of their Native population, either for themselves or on behalf of that nation's civilians. For this reason, these volunteers added to an already volatile mix within that region.

Little changed when Texan security ostensibly became the responsibility of the federal government in the mid–1840s. Once Texas became a state on December 29, 1845, federal authorities soon dispatched U.S. soldiers to the area to stop Native raids and, in this way, helped secure the newly won border. They reasoned rangers, now operating at the behest of the United States, were an unneeded expense and one to be avoided. General George Brooke, commander of the Army in U.S. territory west of the Mississippi River, took a cool reading of the disposition of these Texan volunteers, writing that the rangers' "natural hostility to Indians would be very apt to bring about what we wish to avoid—a general war [with Natives]."[9] The Army believed rangers were unneeded because these men looked to expunge Natives, not provide security, exacerbating tensions. Only extreme duress prompted Army officials to consider using rangers to better protect the frontier from war parties ranging in size from several hundred to some 700. They posed a considerable threat that the Army could not ignore. Neither could the Army deny that rangers took great zeal in engaging Natives in battle. Bowing to the hope that rangers could help shore up the frontier, Brooke federalized three companies in 1849 and one in 1850.

This was a rare occurrence. The U.S. government was all the more intransigent in calling upon rangers since that local force's successes con-trasted with Army failures. A double ring of forts marked a tenuous Texas frontier, one line starting at the Rio Grande and extending north to Fort Worth near the Red River, the other string of forts 200 miles further west and reaching from near the Washita River down to the Rio Grande. However, these posts and their small contingents of soldiers could not offer civilians sufficient protection. Natives moving south, or returning north after com-pleting a raid, simply bypassed these strong points. The porous defense meant the Army had to act offensively. This it could do only in limited fashion. A good portion of the troops were not mounted, and therefore could do little to interdict Native attacks. The Army did try. Robert E. Lee led one extended campaign in 1856. Colonel Lee's command traveled hundreds of miles without success. He found few raiders, an outcome not born of a poor effort.

Civilians looked to overcome what they considered the Army's failure. A few years after Lee's expedition, the Texas legislature commissioned rangers led by John Salmon Ford to stop Comanche attacks, and he enjoyed some success. Ford, or "Rip" as he preferred, surprised and destroyed a camp of Comanche under Iron Jacket in May 1858. A bitter fight claimed the life of this steadfast foe, famous for wearing a coat of Spanish mail. Iron Jacket did not survive the ranger assault, one led by a Native auxiliary force recruited from an area near the Brazos River in Texas. Surprisingly, in this instance, Texans expressed a sudden tolerance for their reputed foe, at least when functioning as allies. These warriors, in fact, enabled Ford to locate the Comanche far to the north of the Red River near the Antelope Hills, and he lavished praise upon them for this feat and for their fighting prowess.

The ranger advance was a key moment because this unit strayed far from assumed Texan territory. The effort resulted in a dubious military action, one sanctioned by rangers since it was designed to take the fight to "where their families are."[10] That punitive goal of striking Native encampments was the same goal set by Army commander General David Twiggs the year before in June 1857, revealing that the distance between ranger and Army personnel was not all that great. However, Twiggs could not act with impunity because a federal mandate restricted the Army's ability to launch punitive strikes across uncertain boundaries in the hinterlands of the prairie. This limitation allowed rangers to succeed while Army units stood on the defensive. Ford's victory at the Battle of Antelope Hills resonated primarily because of this grating contrast, a civilian ability and willingness to conduct the first way of war by attacking villages anywhere they could be found rather than primarily looking to intercept marauding war parties.

The Army tried to keep pace. After this significant ranger success came an Army attack at Rush Springs along the Washita River at the end of September 1858, one also devastating a Comanche village. The slaughter of nearly 100 Comanche, including women and children, meant active Army participation in the first way of war with unprecedented civilian excesses. However, the targeted settlement had been seeking merely to collect its promised annuity from U.S. authorities. In that sense the attack was unwarranted, another example of Americans lashing out in the name of ending border raids or, much less flattering, as a signature of racism: attacking any Natives was acceptable. On the other hand, the same could be said of the victims. The camp destroyed was that of Buffalo Hump, who had raided Texan settlements before and looked to do so again by striking the men of the south, implying a desire to target Texans since he considered them separate from U.S. citizens. Any perceived differences seldom mattered; Native attacks fell on settlers wherever found. In this war, assigning the distinction of noncombatant meant more in retrospect as a blaming tool than it did when seeking battle.

In Texas, the violence persisted, a result that came from the impact of settler and soldier alike. However, the rangers carried forth the Texan goal of eliminating the tribes in their state altogether, including those on reservations. There was no place for Natives in Texas. Previously, military officials had hoped that Natives would agree to stay on reservations once defeated, but the U.S. Army found the option of reservations taken from it in Texas. The militant stance of that state was so pronounced that a point of no return was reached after a settler murdered R.S. Neighbors, a former Army officer and a Texan, who was the federal Indian Agent entrusted with marking the reservations in Texas. That violence came in 1859 and had long-lasting consequences, in particular making it clear that rangers functioned as a vanguard on behalf of settlers.

This citizen-led charge left Texas mostly free of its Native population by 1860. This success had not taken two generations. Comanche raiding continued, incensed by the attacks on their villages, but when the Comanche sallied back into Texan territory, they did so in mostly small raiding parties. The war they waged there did not express a resurgent Comanchería. That edifice had peaked by 1850.[11] Now, their effort was merely a blissful reminder of an always tenuous sovereignty, one amorphous in nature leaving Natives unwilling to recognize that a few punitive strikes by a failing people were the last spasm of a

Sam Houston, president of the Republic of Texas, 1836–1838, 1841–1844 (Library of Congress).

dying state. The once dominant tribe in the southwest now stood alone and vulnerable. While in the future strife and conflict returned at times between Natives and settlers, the state of Texas had prevailed in the struggle and, in so doing, significantly contributed to the practice of a first way of war in the southwest.

This outcome resulted in a beleaguered state of mind for Texans, however, and spoke to the price of a "siege mentality." Nothing underscored this more than another ranger attack along the northwestern frontier of Texas in December 1860. Lawrence Sullivan Ross, at the behest of now Governor Sam Houston, looked to strike at Native raiding parties in the area. He destroyed a Comanche village at the Pease River, recovering Cynthia Ann Parker, taken long ago in a Native raid in 1836. That success brought things full circle, in a sense. Americans appeared to be ascendant on the open expanses of Texas. However, there had been plenty of ranger failures. Ross, in fact, acted to redress the folly of Middleton Johnson, a ranger also commissioned by Houston earlier that year to curb raiding parties along the northern frontier. Johnson found no Natives to attack, but he did manage to provoke the U.S. Army when he threatened a concentration of Natives under Army protection. Houston disbanded Johnson's unit, alarmed by the prospect of state and national authority clashing in Texas. In a small way, Texan adventurism had previewed the looming intra-state conflict. By the eve of the Civil War, rangers had assumed a legacy touted as an unmitigated success but so marked by violence as to leave a nostalgic tradition that both enshrined and denied this stain coming from endless war.

No matter the myth making, the reality was that rangers had served settlers well. The two had been indistinguishable up to 1860, and the conflation continued into the Civil War. With no federal troops protecting the frontier, the 1,000 or so rangers provided a needed defense against Natives and the increasing numbers of deserters forming bands to pillage in the northwest portion of the state. When it came to Natives, rangers looked to their old practices of taking the fight to the enemy. Additionally, since the Confederate government refused to fund the rangers, the hallmark of their roots showed forth again; they provided their own arms and horses and put a premium on loot. The goal of plunder was understood and came along with an additional motive of exemption from service in the Confederate Army. Many Texans valued time in the so-called "Frontier Regiment" for this chance to stay close to home. Yet the war still denuded Texas of manpower and the rangers of much of their potency. Inferior men produced a feeble defense and a great defeat, the worst in ranger history. At Dove Creek in early January 1865, some 110 rangers led by Captain Henry Fossett and over 200 militia confronted

700 Kickapoos heading south. A two-pronged ranger attack quickly unraveled, as first the militia and then the rangers met a steadfast Native defense and counterattack. After five hours, the Texans broke off the effort, leaving 26 dead and suffering just as many wounded. Only a handful of Natives died. It mattered little that Texans maintained then and now that Fossett's command did not deserve the title of "Ranger."

This was a defeat but only a temporary setback. Natives could not match the growing population of Texas, which produced settlements that simply denied the Natives their homeland. When the Civil War ended, any Native foray across Texas became more uncertain. Ironically, as the Native threat receded in Texas, rangers became endangered as well. Soon divisions arose within the state regarding the rangers' continued utility. The east-west divide within Texas made obvious the recalcitrance of the eastern half to continue funding an increasingly unneeded strike force. Western settlers still desired the services of rangers because these men and women remained leery of a Native threat, albeit random and now extremely intermittent, but still lingering in their consciousness.[12] As if a matter of self-preservation, the label of "Ranger," no matter if overtly attached to the first way of war, became a heroic label for volunteers who had protected the land by expunging a deadly nemesis.

These volunteers, the outgrowth of a militant population, soon became professionalized after the war. Ranger duties shifted away from combating Native incursions to safeguarding state territory by conducting law enforcement. Troubles with Natives, when these occurred, became the responsibility of the Army. However, the Army's problem quickly became that experienced by rangers, and that was how to achieve success. Texas was secure below the Red River. Above that geographic marker and reaching to the Platte River, on the Central Plains, the Army now had to figure out how to stop rampaging Natives, including those warriors pushed out of Texas. Not wishing to share ranger ambiguity in purpose and method, the Army struggled to find a solution short of practicing a first way of war.

The Rogue River War

Further north, soldiers tried to curb this reality of civilians leading a first way of war, but Natives perished at the hands of an aggressive civilian militia in Oregon and Washington nonetheless. While this territory did not come into American possession due to conflict with Mexico, settlement still arrived there rapidly as wagons heading west increased in numbers. Not surprisingly, tensions flared between civilians and Natives here as in the southwest. Now, in the Pacific Northwest, Jefferson's Empire of Liberty underwent repeated testing and failed miserably. As civilians defended themselves, any Native sanctuary became a battleground.

Prospector and settler encroachment on Native land meant a long list of incidents and, as to be expected, violence. Familiar incidents started this bloodbath, like when the Cayuse Natives who inhabited a plateau between the Cascades and Rockies, slew Doctor Marcus Whitman and thirteen other missionaries along the Walla Walla River in 1847. Whitman's limited success proselytizing among the Natives made him a tragic symbol of inevitable conflict. To ease tensions, Army troops arrived and established Fort Lane, inland from the coast and astride the Oregon-California trail. After some fighting, its numbers augmented by volunteers, the Army imposed a peace treaty in August 1853. Natives agreed to the Table Rock Reservation, avoiding removal to land east of the Cascades, to barren country not desired by coastal Natives any more than by settlers. Calm returned for a time, but the peace did not hold as to the north the Yakamas attacked settlers and further south in the Rogue River area, Natives also resisted American encroachment so that by 1855 two wars erupted at the same time.[13]

Despite extended contact with Europeans, few firearms had come into possession of these Natives, leaving them badly overmatched in terms of their ability to resist. Their vulnerability was acute. Sensing opportunity, some U.S. officials called for a war of extermination due to Native provocation, and volunteers soon looked to carry out this purpose. A first parry in October 1855 consisted of 115 men led by James Lupton. They attacked Native encampments near Fort Lane, killing 106 men, women and children. The early demonstration of the reservation system now faltered, since the volunteers proclaimed their targets to be only those Natives off the reservation and preparing to exact some barbarity against settlers. However, "good" and "bad" Natives did not reflect the targets of opportunity that governed civilian actions; the volunteers killed Natives anywhere they found them. The Army refused to support the volunteers, and managed to protect the reservation population to some extent. It was a temporary success. Resisting Natives moved down the Rouge River toward the coast, attracting the attention of numerous volunteer companies mobilized by locals looking for acclaim as "Indian" fighters, often to advance their political standing. The Army again attempted to oppose the civilian effort, forbidding what E.A. Schwartz, a leading authority on this conflict, labeled a "partisan" war against Natives.[14] The word is accurate in that it revealed civilian efforts to amplify scattered threats and some clashes into a general state of war. As the fighting gravitated to the coast, Regulars were inevitably drawn into a stand alongside the volunteers, producing the largest engagement of this war, the Battle of Hungry Hill at the end of October 1855. Close to 100 Natives perished over the course of several days after launching a series of futile attacks. A large number of Regulars and volunteers were wounded and 35 Americans were killed. The battle was not decisive, but the warriors took flight.

Soldiers looked to shelter the remnants of a fallen foe and did so despite incurring the wrath of civilians. A local paper called for Native extermination after the fighting reached the outskirts of Seattle. It wrote, "These inhuman butchers and bloody fiends must be met and conquered, vanquished—yes, EXTERMINATED."[15] Fulfillment of this harsh decree was within reach on the ground where the Natives were in desperate straits. The split between civilians and Regulars widened when the Oregon territorial legislature complained to President Franklin Pierce that the general in charge, John E. Wool, had not supported the volunteers in the fighting. Indian Agent Joel Palmer rebuked this charge when he openly labeled the volunteer war one of extermination and looked to salvage the reservation system along the coast. Wool agreed with the characterization of extermination, and he said that that practice prolonged the war, creating a struggle like that he had witnessed when in command of U.S. forces in Florida fighting the Seminoles. He now acted in this conflict to spare Natives, not help exterminate them, by ending what he called the volunteers' "private war."[16] Joseph Lane, previously governor of the Oregon Territory, then serving in the House of Representatives as a territorial delegate, contradicted this view and blamed the Natives for the violence. Palmer's push for a new Coast Reservation became difficult, mired in the fact that the first way of war had proven effective, if ugly. Volunteers launched devastating attacks on Native homes and accomplished much in a short period of time. Civilians and soldiers had not worked together, but in tandem they had exacted a fearsome toll. Tribes soon faced starvation, but surrender proved a dangerous prospect. Many volunteers killed prisoners. The remaining Natives willingly surrendered to the soldiers, and the war petered out in 1856.

The Army's role as a humanitarian presence in the growing conflict west of the Mississippi River, a role taking soldiers far to the north as well as requiring them to range deep to the southwest, did not survive the reoccurring violence. In the Pacific Northwest, Regulars defeated a last Yakama outbreak after some hard fighting in the spring and fall of 1858. A number of Natives had refused to move to Palmer's hard won Coast Reservation and looked to fight, although they stood little chance of success. The first clash in May witnessed approximately 1,000 Natives almost overwhelm a small command of 152 soldiers. The troopers escaped with 21 casualties. For the Natives, from this high point came a low. That Native success provoked another American offensive and the emboldened Natives challenged a much larger column of soldiers in September. The Natives attacked in the open and into the face of Army howitzers alongside long-range rifles that broke up the hopeless charge. This act of futility ended the battle and the war. The war

Joseph Lane of Oregon (Library of Congress).

concluded as it had begun in 1855, with a display of military might from the U.S. Army, underscoring the dangers the Natives had faced by choosing to confront the invaders. Yet the war had been swiftly won in the years encompassing these two clashes, as volunteers ruthlessly sought out Native settlements and killed any males they found and incarcerated the females and children. The demographic feat was such that of the 10,000 Natives in the region, scarcely 2,000 survived. It was a proven tactic, and it called attention to who prosecuted the war and why: civilians looking to settle the land. Even this result was unsatisfactory to the settlers. The Coast Reservation given to the surviving Natives would go, in upcoming years, to settlers as well, so that no such reservation existed by 1875. In this way, a military victory in 1858 overtly yielded to an economic enterprise thereafter.

The Arizona Territory

The renewed acts of violence in seemingly pacified areas such as the Oregon and Washington territories, contrasted with Texas and that state's ability to expunge its Native populations. This model soon found imitators in the southwest. Arizonians proved willing to equal the Texan practice of the decimation of their Native populations at the hands of civilian volunteers who were pursuing a first way of war. Early on, at least, it did not have to be that way. The Apache who roamed that area had not objected to Stephen Watts Kearny's army crossing Apache land during the Mexican American War. Both were fighting Mexicans. Neither did the Apache object to the stream of Americans surfacing among them after the 1850s, as long as the new arrivals did not impede their long established practice of raiding Mexican settlements. When finally stirred to action against the Americans, it was because a personal affront provoked a hostile reaction. Prospectors captured and tortured Mangas Colorados, a Chihenne Apache, in 1851. It was apparently a random act of violence, but one that could hardly have been more poorly chosen. Mangas, an unusually tall, large Apache and therefore one who commanded great respect, also had proved his abilities in war. Now, his ill treatment at the hands of these miners set him and a large conglomeration of Apache on a path of revenge against miners specifically and Americans in general.

Cochise, the famous Chiricahua Apache leader, had endured his own humiliation at the hands of the Americans. Cochise escaped capture in February 1861 at Apache Pass in the mountains of what is today southeastern Arizona, cutting his way through a tent where the 60 men under the command of Lieutenant George N. Bascom held Cochise prisoner after requesting a parley with him. Once Cochise fled, Bascom followed orders and executed members of Cochise's family, his younger brother and two nephews, to punish Cochise for failing to deliver a captive assumed to be in his possession. Bascom failed to believe Cochise when he told him that he held no such captive. Stunned by Bascom's action, Cochise killed a few prisoners he had captured and hoped to use the rest to bargain for the release of his family. He left the area with a lasting hatred of Americans.

After the "Bascom Affair," the war between the Apache and the Americans began. Some experts argue that the American evacuation of forts as Regulars went east to wage the Civil War emboldened the Apache more than these personal affronts. This apparent weakness understandably confused Natives who were not aware of the dynamic of the American civil conflict. An end of the intrusion was welcomed, a return of the intruders not expected. By the early 1860s, the Apache had declared war on the American presence in the southwest. A formidable alliance had emerged since Mangas had married his daughter to Cochise. That Chiricahuan now pursued what he called a war of extermination.[17] Although twenty or more years separated him from Mangas, these two men worked well together leading a force some put at 700 Apache, likely an inflated number. Whatever the assembled strength, they threatened both the New Mexico and Arizona settlements with destruction. The mining camp at Pinos Altos held on despite an all out attack. Tucson faced elimination when reduced to but 200 brave souls clinging to existence.[18] The Apache offensive faltered when a war party was unable to overcome a detachment of 68 men from a volunteer unit coming from California and traveling along the Butterfield stage road east toward Apache Pass in July 1862. Two howitzers allowed the soldiers to hold a superior number of Natives at bay. These guns inflicted much harm, killing over 60 Apache warriors, an unprecedented number. Mangas, also present at this battle, received a wound that forced him from the battlefield. The Apache war of extermination had been short-lived.

Apache fortunes worsened when a party of miners and soldiers gunned down Mangas in January 1863. Miners lured him to their camp to discuss a truce and then took him prisoner and held him hostage to ensure his Apache followers would not assault the prospectors. However, a detachment of Army personnel joined them, and Mangas did not last the night. The soldiers asserted they killed him when he tried to escape; the miners said the Army commander, Colonel Joseph R. West, ordered his troops to shoot him.[19] The contrasting accounts could not hide the fact that this important leader was dead, and that an incident involving volunteers and soldiers acting in unison, if in obscurity, characterized American-Apache relations. It was a pattern that would continue in the southwest over the next few years and leave the Apache on the defensive.

Further north within the Arizona Territory, another group of Apache faced desperate straits at the hands of a resourceful Army leader, Lieutenant Colonel George Crook. Charged to overcome the Tonto Natives in the White Mountains in 1871, Crook made sure to have Apache scouts available in large numbers for obvious reasons: they could recognize subtleties in the terrain to track other Apache, endure much hardship on the trail, and predict the next moves of their brethren, all steps allowing the Army to maintain pursuit. More than this, Crook discarded baggage trains in favor of mules and forced his men to live off the land to a great extent, to become like the foe they pursued. Crook's innovation peaked when he sent mixed armed parties of Apache and soldiers after renegade Apache, the Apache scouts often outnumbering the Regulars. Here was a practice all but admitting the Army's inability to win a guerrilla war in the rugged southwest; the Apache had to defeat other Apache.

The Apache in the Tonto Basin soon surrendered given Crook's relentless hunt, which traversed hundreds of miles in the span of five months. This success soothed whatever consternation within Army ranks greeted Crook's tactics since they underscored Army shortcomings. A closer look offered more good news but again for reasons that were unpalatable to either Crook or the Army. His tactics revealed the campaign Crook waged against the Apache as no more than a veneer of glory covering inglorious times. By this point, the Natives were in trouble, their destruction ensured by the press of American civilization, aided by successful punitive, military strikes. Crook's achievements were the exception, not the norm, and his use of Native scouts underscored this reality. By relying on scouts the way he did, Crook admitted that Regulars could not become Apache enough to completely end the resistance. However, in the broad picture, this did not matter because Native scouts had become part of the American machinery of conquest which allowed this, assumed unique "Indian" identity to surface only because it served American ends. The converse was just as true; Native scouts had not become American. Rather, they excelled at the guerrilla component of the Indian way of war one final time and, as was the case before, sped their kind to oblivion.

Perhaps this insight was Crook's true genius, recognizing and capitalizing upon Native participation in the onrushing tide of settlement. If so, he should be commended for it. Instead, he allowed this long-range thinking to be obscured in continuing the hunt. Cochise remained a coveted target, and with Crook fresh off his success against the Tonto Natives, he relished the opportunity to chase that man. However, good fortune spared Cochise the predictable fate of being hunted down and killed or captured. General Oliver Otis Howard, the senior officer in the territory, granted Cochise the right of remaining in his cherished homeland and on a reservation overseen by an American who had befriended the chief. Having fallen ill, Cochise died in 1874, but he had lived out the remainder of his days in peace, an ironic fate befalling the most steadfast opponent of the settlement. This limited parley spoke to both the enmity and villainy now dumped on his person by Americans. Cochise had secured this peace with acts of violence, and though he claimed he only defended his own lands, settlers never forgave him for what they perceived as an Army failing. Cochise's good fortune, never a victory in American eyes, latently spurred on more punitive actions against the Apache, ones largely undertaken by volunteers.

At their height, the Apache numbered maybe 8,000 in total, but a decentralized creed was never more ingrained in a people. As a result, men such as Mangas and Cochise led mere pockets of resistance. If factionalism was a weakness in the face of the invader, it offered one strength. With the demise of these men, other leaders surfaced and continued this war exactly as it had begun, one marked by raids and ugly reprisals by all involved, but no visible change of the status quo. The American settlements survived, even if enduring a tenuous existence. The future state of Arizona languished in uncertainty stemming from an identity rallying around violence confusing indifference and crisis. Few souls wanted to be there. General William Sherman grew so exasperated with persistent Native violence that he suggested abandoning the territory altogether in 1871: "We had one war with Mexico to take Arizona, and we should have another to make her take it back."[20] National territorial cohesiveness, if no other reason, suggested otherwise. Buoyed up by a mini-silver rush, Arizona gained a reprieve and its citizens an offensive disposition. It was a far cry from what might be called a "siege mentality" gripping the few hundred souls clustered around sparse outposts and holding on to a hope for a better life, a reality that described the territory up to 1860.

Only a backwater for western expansion, those who remained there mustered a purpose in targeting Natives for retribution, and numerous violent acts followed that were almost always led by civilians. Examples included a rancher near Prescott named King S. Woolsey who, in January 1864, arranged an ambush of Apache. After inviting a number of Apache into his camp, he ordered his thirty men to open fire on his unsuspecting guests killing all of them. In this way, Woolsey made good on his boast of fighting "on a broad platform of extermination."[21] Others dealt out similar harsh treatment. In one case, a "citizen" army from Tucson in April 1871, composed of 50 Americans and 100 Papagos, attacked a reservation and killed 108 Apache, only eight of them men. Those responsible for the Camp Grant Massacre stood trial, but a local jury exonerated them.[22] Of course, these brigands had colorful antecedents, such as those involved in the scalping program the Mexican government ran. It drew Anglos hunting Apache for 1,000 pesos a scalp. Only when these marauders failed to distinguish Mexican from Apache hair, and therefore murdered Mexican citizens as well as Natives, did the Mexican government disallow Americans from collecting the bounty. However, the threshold of violence was extreme, hardly encouraging the Apache to make peace. Though weakened, they remained a great menace to the settlement and were increasingly willing to inflict depravities of their own, such as mutilations of the dead and the torture of captives. As the war unfolded in the 1870s, it was hard to find an opening to end the violence.

Too late to be considered leading a national movement, instead Arizonians embraced a Texan mindset of extermination. Parties of volunteers sought out Apache camps, and Natives perished in bands of twenty or thirty. After 1870, Americans could roam most of the territory almost at will. These citizens could claim success, such as it was. Army officials offered their own view. One officer remarked that settlers in southern Arizona were "a vicious renegade population of Texan Union haters" who murdered Natives and provoked conflict. Their main motive for the attacks was not self-defense but to keep the Army present in large numbers so as to make money off of the soldiers.[23] If so, the civilian initiative of volunteers hunting Apache had produced an unintended result. Daniel E. Conner, one of the prospectors who had witnessed Mangas' murder, remarked how Arizona in its early days had achieved a "pure democracy" given a lack of government oversight.[24] Now the government acted in force, attempting to end what it perceived as lawlessness and chaos. The Army reshuffled command in the region it now considered that "chronic sore of Arizona."[25]

Still, the wanton attacks produced results. Surviving Natives stood chastised upon reservations facing hardship and illness. Others took refuge in mountainous strongholds leaving settlers alone. However, the American successes also produced recalcitrant Natives so that the lone distinction Arizonians could claim in the long post-Civil War plains conflict was that the territory still faced outbreaks of violence into the 1880s. Geronimo was the most famous name of a host of Apache who could claim to have been bullied into a pointless war—this futility was still preferable to life on the reservation. Even Crook, who vacillated when it came to reflecting on the fate of Natives, at times hardened to their plight, at other times sympathetic, reserved his greatest outpouring of dismay at the treatment of Natives when it came to the Apache: "I think the Apache is painted in darker colors than he deserves and that his villainies arise more from a misconception of facts than from his being worse than other Indians." Crook had built up a respect for his longtime foe and told graduates of West Point that "we are too culpable as a nation, for the existing condition of affairs."[26] If so, even that tempered sentiment did not seep into the Arizonian consciousness. The volunteers assumed no responsibility for the continued resistance. Natives off the reservation posed a danger to good citizens; those on that land could be targeted as well since these Natives merely used the reservation to bide time before returning to the warpath. Thus it was that a community at one time huddled in Tucson praying for mere survival boasted of a reach far to the north of the territory. In this way Arizonians shouldered a load in holding Natives in check. It was more than this. If never original, Arizonan volunteers had served one paradigm well: a defining element of an offensive that was most effective when civilians took the lead in the increasingly awful practice of a first way of war.

The Civilian Scourge

As settlers moved west, the stakes were rising in terms of what could be gained and the costs thereof. If the frontiersmen opening the west had found force a necessary act of self-defense given their activities, rangers, militiamen, and volunteers could look to no such excuse and appeared at times to enjoy the violence left in their wake. They often sought it out. Those that emerged in Texas after 1836 attempted from first to last to end the Native threat with military force bordering on criminal activity. Consequently, raiding, murder, and retribution visited this frontier and exacerbated tensions between Americans and Natives. The methods chosen produced the desired carnage, even if this search and destroy legacy is replaced in popular imagination by the more celebrated American exploits of the Texas Rangers and of the many steadfast Americans braving the odds to settle the West. This jubilation drowns out the element of citizen militia practicing the first way of war in the southwest and the Pacific Northwest. It was a step the U.S. Army often hesitated to take and, at times, opposed. However, the Army soon yielded to that impulse, allowing civilian unrest to spark military conquest. In this endeavor, civilians had led the way, but together with Regulars the act of settlement became a very effective counterinsurgency method of search and destroy.

Pacification

Soldiers and the Pursuit of "Total War"

The pace slowed as the horses tired. The long, thin line of cavalry maintained formation but soon broke off the pursuit. The soldiers heard only a few echoes as war-whoops faded into the emptiness of the prairie. A bugle sounded recall, and Colonel Edwin Sumner drew to the front of his troopers now closing ranks. He returned his saber to its scabbard and the others did the same. It had been a glorious charge, except for the reckoning that now took place. Perhaps a few Cheyenne warriors had been killed, but no more. Sumner could not be sure. He soon learned he had lost two men, not a grievous loss, but painful because all involved knew they had gained little in return for their efforts. This battle in 1857 began with a burst of bravery, but now ended without a test of arms, without acclaim, and without victory. It was a typical outcome the Army would have to change.

They struggled to do so. A decade later in 1867, General Winfield Scott Hancock looked for some high ground to escape the smoke now filling the valley. He settled on a mound off to his left, and he settled for not much of a view at all. It mattered little. Hancock's sweeping offensive had alarmed his foe and chased them off, but it had not brought them to battle as planned. Hancock's lone exploit was burning some Native dwellings, and he now considered killing a large herd of captured ponies. It was a poor exchange, animals instead of a host of dead Natives or, better still, a penitent assemblage of chiefs asking for peace. In frustration, Hancock gave the order to kill the horses, not realizing that in so doing, he had delivered a grave blow by targeting the means of Native existence. Later, Hancock turned his attention to launching a new attack, a new offensive, a new chase about the plains. Somehow he had to kill Natives in order to turn these village attacks into a victory. In this effort, the U.S. Army hoped for a triumphant end, but in this pursuit, it earned accusations of committing massacres.

The controversy in that outcome dogged the soldiers and exonerated the main perpetrators of the violence, civilians. Limited results in punitive attacks forced Army recognition of its shortcomings on this plains battlefield. In response, experimentation with civilian elements brought success via tactics falling well short of military strictures. Various methods replaced Army belief in an honorable fight with a vindictiveness soon justified by a declaration of total war. Yet, to enact this decree, civilians took the lead, although only after formal incorporation into Army ranks. Here was an unusual compromise of professional integrity and mission, and an invitation of criticism if plans went awry. To follow the more civilian means of attack with a mantle of Army propriety ensured that the violent struggle on the plains again pulled noncombatants into the fray, an outcome turning bloodshed into recrimination, not success. The Army was a long way from victory.

War on the Plains

Civilian success in pursuing settlement had meant a blight upon American honor but a validation of military tactics. The U.S. Army had been slow to accept this truism and capitalize upon the lawless nature of this war. Even after defeating Mexico, Army actions amounted to little more than exploration in terms of assisting settlers moving west, and this posture meant a limited American military presence in the region. The Civil War increased the Army's efforts to protect the growing number of these intrepid pioneers. Not surprisingly, the next stage of the conquest of the west fell to that instrument of the U.S. government. Once reinforced by volunteers, the Army followed the civilian lead of striking Native settlements as a means of subduing tribes in the Central Plains that, at its greatest expanse, reached from the Rio Grande River in the south to the Platte River in the north. A bleak fate lay in store for these Natives because of the American strategic ascendancy. Isolated and facing a contraction of their lands, warriors mounted a desperate and, at times, heroic resistance, but one hopeless in the face of the military arm of the American counterinsurgency effort. Unleashing the U.S. Army after 1865 meant a confused purpose as Regulars took their place in the saga unfolding in the American interior, amounting to a rather ineffective pacification effort that lost its benign focus and became a punitive mission stemming from a reluctant acceptance of a first way of war.

That blow landed on a formidable enemy. After wresting a good part of Mexico's northern territory away from that nation, the United States inherited the problem of dictating terms to the Comanche, the Navajo, and the

Apache in the southwest. These Natives enjoyed a well-deserved reputation earned at the expense of both the Spanish and the Mexicans. The civilian inroads on the part of Americans in Texas and later in the Arizona Territory blunted this Native power to a great extent but did not eliminate it entirely. Civilians did achieve that outcome in the Pacific Northwest during the Rouge River War. However, to the north and far inland from the Pacific Coast lay an even more dangerous opponent, the Sioux. The most powerful tribe remaining in terms of numbers and one relishing a warlike creed, the Sioux also enjoyed a large claim of land established due to previous victories over neighboring peoples. Other Natives contested American control of what was now the center of the advance west. On the plains lay fearsome tribes, such as the Cheyenne, Arapaho, and Kiowa. Like the Sioux, these Natives embraced a martial spirit and often joined together when raiding on the vast prairie.

The Army made a genuine attempt to manage interactions between the settlers and Natives. For example, the U.S. Army's peace mission at the newly established Fort Laramie at the confluence of the Laramie and North Platte Rivers in 1851 looked to do just that. The Army delegation of no more than 270 soldiers invited the plains tribes to a conference that by September 1851 had attracted some 10,000 Natives. Given the disparity in numbers, the lack of violence between Americans and Natives was pronounced, as was the lack of violence among Natives. Never before had such a large number of tribes assembled in the "great American West," as Crow joined Sioux and Cheyenne as well as Shoshones and many others.[1] This parley unfolded without incident, the Treaty of Laramie assuring its signatures that the Army would keep the now clearly delineated Native land free of settlers, an accord that promised to head off tensions on the plains.

The same could be said of a diplomatic effort looking to make peace with the Navajo in 1855. Only a small military escort accompanied the governor of the Territory of New Mexico, David Meriwether, as he visited a camp at Laguna Negra on the eastern fringe of Navajo territory. Over 1,000 Natives attended and, at times, threatened the small delegation, but violence never erupted. After five days, Meriwether emerged holding a treaty with 27 signatures and terms indicating the Natives had just relinquished over half their territory.[2] The Navajo never abided by the treaty, and conflict arose as a result, but these efforts emphasized that officials hoped to avoid a clash with Natives by securing safe overland passage for settlers.

No matter the recent American successes at negotiation, or perhaps because of them, the plains tribes did not remain quiescent. As settlers increased in numbers, tensions arose, and the Sioux challenged the Army presence. Soon a crisis emerged when, in mid–August 1854, Sioux warriors annihilated an Army detachment of thirty men sallying from Fort Laramie under the command of Lieutenant John Grattan. The Sioux easily overwhelmed this pitifully small column attempting to apprehend those Natives responsible for killing a settler's cow. This Native success provoked an Army response to the "Grattan massacre." A year later, General William S. Harney emerged from nearby Fort Kearny with a considerably larger column of several hundred men and wiped out a village in early September 1855. Mostly women and children perished, an attack savage enough to force the Oglala Sioux to sign a peace treaty. It was not a unanimous decision among the Sioux, and more violence loomed in the future.[3]

The Army repeated this type of attack often over the next twenty or so years, but at this time, for Regulars to target a village, was a rare occurrence. Soldiers made a genuine attempt to remain apart from the various types of volunteers who often took matters too far in a violent direction by striking Native encampments and killing everyone there. Only after a long internal struggle did the Army yield to this punitive civilian thrust and wage a first way of war. Harney helped moved things along in this direction.[4] More than this, his strike revealed that the Army's ideal was confused, since smashing villages proved a choice of circumstance. The main effort was to draw the enemy into battle, something that would prove nearly impossible to do.

The Natives recognized the folly of making such a stand that so clearly favored the Army. The Cheyenne tested this fate in August 1857, when a war party met Colonel Sumner and six companies of the First Cavalry on the open plains. The soldiers hoped to avenge a killing from the previous summer. As the battle lines approached one another, Sumner grew excited at the prospect of a fight and ordered a charge. The startled Natives fled. The troopers took possession of an abandoned camp, but slew only a few warriors. Despite having suffered just two killed themselves, the Army could not claim a great victory. The Cheyenne appeared cowed, but the transitory nature of this outcome was as apparent.

These clashes proved the exception since Natives wisely avoided such confrontations. Consequently, the Army seldom faced Natives in battle. When fighting did occur, skirmishes and ambushes were the norm. The small size of the Army explains this outcome at least in part. At a low point, there were some 7,000 soldiers manning 79 posts in the trans–Mississippi west, and this number was enough only to guard key steps along the way.[5] The Army did not have large numbers of troops at its disposal and this factor limited options. Dispersed in a series of forts spanning the width and length of the continent, the Army seldom assembled a great force for offensive operations. It did not have to muster large numbers since the Natives did not present big concentrations as targets. They remained dispersed in their own right, a roving culture emphasizing this tendency in search of food, shelter, and survival. In this respect, American dispositions were well-suited to confront their foe and engage in frequent skirmishing. Yet the Natives enjoyed the advantage of mobility and operated in terrain that allowed them to evade contact, a feat that challenged the troopers in many ways.

The fighting quality of the warrior and the U.S. soldier receives enough attention in the literature to make several observations that reinforce this outlook.[6] Undoubtedly soldiers enjoyed advantages over their Native counterparts due to a trooper's professionalization, no matter how limited or incomplete this may have been. In this regard, a chain of command served as a soldier's greatest asset. This structure compelled the solider to appear on the field of battle. Natives lacked this discipline. Chiefs exerted a personal magnetism that hopefully carried over to the battlefield, but it did not always do so. Warriors were free to come and go, so the Natives could not be certain of their numbers or their execution of a plan of battle. This failure of leadership rebounded in retreat; Natives were completely unable to sustain a defense when necessary. The contrast was striking. The last stands or successful weathering of sieges are frequent in Army history when confronting Natives. There are few such Native examples.

This leadership advantage was surprising because on an individual basis, the warrior proved superior to Army personnel who left much to be desired. Even motivated officers too often found frontier life boring and uneventful with the added frustration that a posting in that desolate land too often limited career advancement. Their understandable reticence to serve in the West rebounded in the enlisted ranks, and desertion was a constant issue. For the Army, mounting an effective fighting force was problematic in the extreme and, even if accomplished, involved risks on the battlefield because it was not clear how troops would respond to orders. In contrast, among Natives a focus on individualism bred a natural warrior because of a lifelong devotion to hunting and outdoor survival. Weapons did not restore a balance or always push things in favor of Americans. Supplied from forts and outposts, once the Natives made acquiring guns a priority, they more often than not outgunned their counterparts. The repeating rifle, coveted by the plains tribes, seldom came into the hands of soldiers; they relied on the steady, but unspectacular, carbine. The same could be said of transportation. On the plains where it mattered most, the Natives relied on ponies, steeds that reflected the qualities of their riders. They were bred for endurance and, while smaller than cavalry horses, better suited to the prairie since they required less fodder. In so many ways the U.S. soldier had met his match: a hardened, mobile warrior operating on terrain with few natural features other than open space enabling the warrior to refuse battle whenever desired.

Fortunately for the Army, as expansion west gained momentum, it did not have to pursue a military defeat of the Natives, which would be hard to deliver. Soldiers initially found themselves serving as a constabulary presence featuring law and order. The Civil War interrupted this mission to protect settlers, creating an opportunity for civilians to assert themselves in the war against the Natives. Both the North and South needed soldiers for operations in the east and therefore the belligerents pulled their Regulars from the far West. Civilians had to fill the void, and they eagerly did so. These volunteers increasingly dominated the fighting that erupted across the plains. Because of this change, a focus on combat emerged after all. This tragic outcome leading to much loss of life spoke to a great irony considering the often frayed interaction between military and civilian authorities, resulting from recurrent Army efforts to mitigate the impact of settlement on Native populations.

The civilian mandate emerged in the first few years of the war. For example, in Minnesota in 1862, a number of eastern Dakota Sioux living on reservations, but facing increasing hardship, lashed out at settlements and killed over 400 Americans. Although the American population remained preponderant, the Dakota strike, consisting of over 800 warriors, engendered destruction not seen since the final wars east of the Mississippi. With the Civil War in its second year, and since the 900 soldiers usually stationed there were no longer available after the Union high command had ordered them east, 600 untested civilians attempted to end the threat. This they did successfully, quickly confining the Natives to their reservation in just over a month so that which erupted in mid–August petered out by late September 1862. It was the usual flare-up of violence, followed by a swift American response. In this case, the volunteers pursued legal ramifications as well, and some 300 Sioux were sentenced to hang. President Abraham Lincoln reduced that total to 38.

That tally proved a modest number compared to those dying in an attack by volunteers in January 1863 in the Utah territory that left over 200 Natives dead. General Patrick E. Connor's "California volunteers" bore down on a village of rampaging Shoshonis, creating a bloodbath but little controversy. After what came to be known as the Bear Creek Massacre, the Army promoted Connor and, in so doing, tacitly endorsed the first way of war.

Whatever successes could be attributed to volunteers in Minnesota and in the Utah territory, the accomplishments did not stop the Union Army from taking over the campaign to end Sioux resistance. In the wake of this violence came one of the largest U.S. Army offensives ever undertaken on the plains as 6,000 soldiers set out to pacify the Sioux. General U.S. Grant ordered Major General John Pope, a failed commander in the eastern theater of war now relegated to duty facing Natives, to take charge of the Minnesota frontier. Pope planned a two-pronged attack, and his sweeping encirclement soon met the enemy. General Henry H. Sibley headed northwest from Fort Ridgely on the Minnesota River into the Dakota Territory and managed to disperse a Native concentration and push them south into the arms of General Alfred Sully, who was advancing from Sioux City alongside the Missouri River. Sully engaged the Natives in serious fighting at the Battle of Whitestone Hill in September 1863, where he attacked a village home to at least 950 braves. Sully just managed to relieve his hard-pressed advance guard in time to force the Sioux into a series of ravines where they mounted a desperate defense. Over 100 Natives died, as did twenty troopers. The warriors slowly retreated but a shortage of supplies limited further Army pursuit. With Sully's indifferent results, Pope's grand offensive came to an end.

Another campaign the following year spoke to the limits of success in 1863. A two-pronged advance again went forward in the Dakota Territory, and Sully, as he had the year before, meted out similar punishment in July 1864 when his reinforced command of 2,200 troopers met a Sioux force arrayed against a river and totaling 1,700. In the front of the village some rough ground sheltered many defenders as the remainder massed on the flanks of the advancing soldiers. Troopers engaged the Sioux horsemen in close combat, and a howitzer battery killed many Natives taking shelter at the forefront of the village. Soon, the Sioux accepted defeat and attempted to evacuate their village. This was done successfully as darkness thwarted Sully from further prosecuting the battle. For the Army, the Battle of Killdeer Mountain had been successful in that only five soldiers had been killed, and over 100 of the defenders had been slain. Yet, it was at best only a partial victory, since the majority of Natives had escaped. Sully pushed on to the Yellowstone River, which he reached in early August. However, Sully broke off the pursuit because he was puzzled as to how to achieve a more complete success with further military operations.

Kit Carson

These great Army offensives produced few results, leaving senior officers with questions of how to win the Plains war. The Civil War would helped the Army to clarify what it sought to accomplish when looking to engage Natives in battle. During that war, both the Union and the Confederacy launched military strikes seeking the annihilation of Natives. The harshness of this aim was particularly pronounced in the Southwest, as both governments sanctioned the killing of all Apache adult males and the capture of women and children. Jefferson Davis, president of the Confederacy, later rescinded the order; Lincoln did not.[7] Any mitigation of the American disposition toward Natives was short-lived, however, since Natives were unable to resist a push led by civilian volunteers. While the Civil War disrupted military operations against Natives in the West, it also shifted the fighting to a more expedient footing, since that war saw citizen soldiers formally inducted into the armed forces of the North and South lead the attack and appear increasingly willing to ignore restraints previously adhered to by Regulars.

Union forces of this make-up achieved the greatest feat of arms when Christopher Houston "Kit" Carson, mountain man now turned army general, used volunteers to force the entire Navajo nation to move to a reservation. Here was an unexpected outcome given the Navajo's great numbers, some 12,000 strong, and a willingness to engage the Union forces directly. At one point, 1,000 warriors placed Fort Defiance under siege in April 1860. Despite its location in the hinterlands of the Arizona Territory, like most western posts, there was no stockade. However, the garrison was sufficient to prevent its capture or significant loss, and the fort held with little resolved. Navajo temerity in fielding such a force was never again repeated; it simply was too difficult to mass in such numbers. When U.S. Army personnel chased Navajo warriors, the Natives simply avoided a pitched battle. There was no end in sight to the pattern of raiding and ambush that characterized the fighting.

Mountain man Kit Carson (Library of Congress).

The last attempt to fight a battle prior to the Army's decision to unleash Carson was led by Major Edward Canby in 1860–61. The offensive typified Army frustration of campaigning without result; a few Natives were captured, some livestock and huts destroyed, but no key success came from this effort. The Navajo tendency to surrender, but only temporarily, compounded the Army's difficulties. Once securing a reprieve from the fighting, the Navajo resumed raiding when it suited them, a practice they had undertaken since their first contacts with Americans in 1846. Their aim was not so much a disregard of American rule as it was a continuation of an ancient practice: raiding south into Mexico. American demands that these attacks stop meant their direct involvement in a seemingly interminable conflict. Raiding, to Southwestern Natives, represented a way of life, and it was one of relishing warfare.[8]

Things changed drastically when the Civil War erupted, and Brigadier General James Henry Carleton assumed command of a "California column" of volunteers. It was advance elements from this unit that bloodied both Mangas and Cochise in July 1862 at Apache pass. Once Carleton had helped chase Confederates from Arizona and New Mexico by the end of that year, he then looked to end the troubles with Natives altogether. A warning demanding good behavior did not stop the raiding, so in April 1863, Carleton took other measures.

First the general struck the Apache. American patrols fanned out from Fort Stanton and covered an extensive area of the New Mexico territory. Soon many Mescaleros Apache favored life on the Bosque Redondo reservation to being hunted in the mountainous wilds. Then Carleton sent Carson and 700 men to take the war to the Navajo. Carson commenced his military operations in July 1863, and he honed his battle tactics to scorched earth efforts alone. Stored food supplies, crops, shelter, and cattle all became desired targets, pursued in fair weather and in the winter months. It was effective immediately, and the effort peaked in six months when Carson led a portion of his volunteers totaling 375 men into the Navajo stronghold of the Canyon de Chelly in January 1864. No American invaders had dared enter the canyon for fear of ambush and for not being in a position to do so. Carson now boldly advanced. He encountered almost no opposition and destroyed fields, damaged dwellings, and confiscated livestock, targeting anything that could be of use to the Natives. After this punishment, the Navajo surrendered *en masse* having had enough of this kind of war. Carson had earned a crowning achievement, and the tally of only 78 Navajo killed made clear the true source of the victory—the Navajo had been defeated psychologically. This was not genocide in substance but in mind, the end of a way of life more than that of a people.

The "Long Walk" to the declared reservation ground of the Bosque Redondo rekindled charges of genocide. On this Navajo "Trail of Tears," 336 people died and several hundred others either escaped or simply went unaccounted for at the destination camp. Hardship, misery, sexual assault at the hands of the military escort, and all sorts of deprivation surfaced during the ordeal. Now, the Navajo had to rediscover themselves and adapt to a new way of life on the reservation. After several years of suffering in this inhospitable land, the Navajo returned home with the blessing of the United States. The U.S. government had relented, but the Navajo never again assumed a warlike posture. Here lay the end of a culture. In this respect, Carson's tactics and the harsh results may well have paid off, as this mountain man at the head of volunteers probably spared several thousand more Navajo from death at the hands of Carleton and his civilian army. Yet the fate of the Navajo symbolized the conflicting motives of the perpetrators of these events. Both Carson and Carleton expressed sympathy for the Natives as well as animosity. Carleton's infamous order to exterminate all males and Carson's too eager execution of that order now confronted the reality of feeding the over 11,000 Navajo who had surrendered. Carson's military success exemplified the proceeds of the first way of war, but also the effort to then mitigate the consequences. The outcome of human suffering was not new, and it continued with civilian volunteers at the apex of the effort to overcome Native resistance in the West.

The Sand Creek Massacre

Military expediency also produced an unwanted byproduct from what success had been achieved. Too often these hybrid forces of Regulars and volunteers felt unrestrained by martial law when facing Natives and eagerly tested the limits of the conflict. Soon, there were no such limits. This condition became clear on the Central Plains as Colorado's militia committed the worst excess, massacring at least 150 Cheyenne and Arapaho in November 1864 at Sand Creek, a camp along the Arkansas River near the Army outpost of Fort Lyon. The volunteers boasted killing 500 Natives. Although this number was inflated, this attack, was so odious due to the peaceful disposition of the Natives. Chief Black Kettle watched over this group of southern Cheyenne and a few Arapaho that numbered probably close to 300, the majority being women and children who were bracing for a long, hard winter. They had drawn near the Army post in the Colorado territory to enjoy the protection of U.S. forces. However, Colonel John M. Chivington, a politically ambitious and self-righteous man, was determined to end Native raids and disturbances once and for all.

These circumstances were tangible enough on the Central Plains to provoke heightened Army activity. By mid–1864, in the wake of the Dakota uprising, the Army offensives meant that an increased military presence came west in order to punish the Cheyenne and Arapaho disturbances. When added to Carson's push up from the south, the Colorado territory paid the price for this military sweep as Natives on the Central Plains lashed out at enemies anywhere they found them. The alarmed governor of the Colorado territory, John Evans, ordered all Cheyenne and Arapaho to come to Fort Lyon or face a war of extermination.[9] It was rhetoric devoid of actuality in terms of Native compliance or military enforcement. Yet, a series of events resulted from this decree, which offered protection but also sought Native punishment, since Black Kettle and several other chiefs did in fact accept the offer. The difficulty of sorting "good" from "bad" Indians soon became tragically clear.

The attack at Sand Creek exposed the internal combustion of the volunteers. Major Edward Wynkoop, a Regular, had persuaded Black Kettle to stay near the post, and Wynkoop had succeeded after meeting with the chief in person. Before that interview, Wnykoop had held Natives in low repute, seeing them as distrustful and dangerous, a view in line with the majority of volunteers. However, Wynkoop's interactions with Black Kettle redeemed the Cheyenne in his eyes. He then sought accord, leading the chief and a few others to Denver to meet with Governor Evans in late September. Here came the offer of government protection for all Natives refusing to go on the warpath. Evans extended the offer reluctantly since it collided with his desire to use force; he already had petitioned the federal government to fund a third regiment of volunteers to combat Native attacks. This was Chivington's unit, commissioned in August 1864, and now operating near the South Platte River. A chance for peace caught the governor off-guard as it had Wynkoop. Still, both of these men, reluctantly or otherwise, may have contained the more violent impulses of the volunteer units but for the alarmist and vengeful outlook of the population of Colorado. Enlisted for only 100 days, the "Third" appeared likely to complete its time with no Native contact. The public heaped scorn on the unit with the derisive nickname, the "Bloodless Third." Chivington wished to erase that stain at Sand Creek, and so this attack went forward, Chivington leading the assault in a very real way to assuage public sentiment, something his command embodied in mission and personnel.

Chivington's 700 volunteers struck at dawn on November 29, 1864, advancing along two avenues and pushing the Natives against the river. Black

Kettle stood defiantly alongside the American flag in the center of the camp, as well as next to a white flag, but it mattered little. He fled as the slaughter became widespread. Black Kettle survived the "battle." Most of his people did not. By mid-day, nine soldiers had died, as well as numerous Natives, mostly women and children, but also a few braves.

When this pointless slaughter became public, the Army investigated and denounced the assault. Despite the condemnation, Chivington never apologized for attacking a friendly village. His crusading zeal amounted to a mission to exterminate Natives since they had done the same to Americans. In Chivington's eyes, any man who sympathized with Indians was villainous. For this reason, almost any Natives would do as targets. In so arguing, Chivington had fulfilled the convictions of the western public to a great extent. His unit, now saluted by an unrepentant public as the "Blood Thirdsters," received a parade in the streets of Denver.[10] Native depredations had been real enough as the increasing number of settlers moving west provoked attacks across the plains. However, Chivington had targeted a village deserving better treatment. Besides Black Kettle, several other chiefs were present at Sand Creek, a concentration that indicated they supported peaceful coexistence with Americans. While these chiefs were not always able to control their young men from striking the travelers, in seeking U.S. government protection, these chiefs were trying to send a strong message of peace to their warriors. A number of these leaders perished at Sand Creek, leaving the recalcitrant Dog Soldiers (Cheyenne warriors dedicated to resisting American encroachment through armed resistance), vindicated and actively seeking revenge.

The Army vilified Chivington. Before the attack, several officers had protested that to strike would be "murder" and a "disgrace to the United States uniform." Others declared Black Kettle and his followers "prisoners of war," a condition that protected them from attack for that reason.[11] Wynkoop fumed from a distance, having been reassigned just prior to the attack. Subsequent inquiries condemned the attack as disgraceful, but since the colonel was out of the Army by the time retribution could be served, he was beyond prosecution, leaving the findings as no more than hand wringing after the fact.

To many, all this investigation was more Washington machinations. In the West, this unrepentant man became a hero of sorts, best seen in Denver in July 1865, eight months or so after the massacre. When Senator James R. Doolittle of Wisconsin, a leading peace advocate, stood before a packed opera house and spoke of a tolerant policy toward Natives, the crowd greeted him with calls of "exterminate them."[12] But Chivington's biggest critic was his second in command, Major Scott J. Anthony, who argued that Chivington had failed because he had not done more. It was one thing to start a war by striking a peaceful village, but it was another to end it altogether. With such a large force at his disposal, Chivington, in Anthony's estimation, could have continued up the river and decimated more Native encampments. When that did not occur, Chivington left the entire area vulnerable to Native vengeance.[13]

Over the following two months, war parties killed over fifty settlers, prospectors, and soldiers. The Army clung to form. Another effort by Pope came in the summer of 1865 as he moved north to curb the Sioux, but his two-pronged attack failed to bring the Natives to battle. The Sioux merely evaded their pursuers. Sully continued moving north up the Missouri River and almost had a pitched fight when a soon-to-be famous chief named Sitting Bull emerged and rallied the Sioux defenders to make a stand. No matter, that engagement at Fort Rice was but a skirmish as the Natives kept a respectful distance. For Sully, his advance, this act of war, defeated even his limited purpose of initiating peace talks. The expectation was that the threat of military force would compel Native submission. Instead, the Army columns chased Natives away. By September, only General Connor was still advancing, reaching north to the recently established Bozeman Trail an offshoot of the Oregon Trail and heading north into unorganized territory, i.e., Sioux territory. Connor, pushing hard as always, issued orders to "kill every male Indian over twelve years of age."[14] He found an Arapaho concentration but did little damage, and then he retreated to safety.[15] Consequently, the Army offensive meant little. Yet the war sputtered to an end. The Natives refused battle, and the Army looked to suspend what it saw as expensive and ultimately inconclusive military operations. In this way, a peace came to the Northern Plains as decreed in a treaty signed in October 1865.

To the south also came an equilibrium of sorts, although one favoring Americans. In widespread raiding, the Comanche killed a handful of settlers, slew a few Union and Confederate soldiers, and took a number of civilians captive. The limited forays back into territory they already had lost meant little. These tribes and others merely faced a number of harsh counterattacks conducted by volunteers and a renewed American effort to "secure the peace" in the West. By the end of 1864, the activity of the Comanche and that of other tribes such as the Kiowas, had been enough to draw the attention of Kit Carson at the head of a punitive column 400 strong and operating in the Texas panhandle.

Carson, worn out by the incessant campaigning and feeling remorse over the plight of the Navajo, had demurred about accepting the assignment. Carleton insisted. Carson acquiesced, and his attack in early November funneled a number of hostile warriors together. Carson advanced further before having to make a stand in the ruins of an adobe structure. Here Carson suffered a few casualties, claimed to have inflicted 100, and then quickly retreated when confronted by 1,000 Comanche and Kiowa warriors. Carson's supposed victory at the Battle of Adobe Walls provides another measure of the confused state of the war across the plains. The Army could not usually match civilian triumphs, or, if it did, it regretted the seemingly inevitable charge of massacre. Yet, the Army usually had little to show from battle, as Carson's recent fight exemplified. This battle, if not a success, at least provided relief. Not defeated but not triumphant, Carson at last retired from leading military efforts to break Native resistance. Others replaced him and attempted to erase the ambiguity inherent in winning the war on the plains.

The Battle of Adobe Walls also provided something of a demonstration of the transitory nature of American weakness by exhibiting its latent power. A civilizational push via increasing settlement loomed large in the near future. When that came, the treaties signed in the fall of 1865, not surprisingly, collapsed after providing only a brief lull in the fighting. At this time, a Sioux chief, Red Cloud, adopted a defiant stand to American incursions via the Bozeman Trail, a path taking prospectors into the Bighorn Mountains and into the heart of Sioux territory. Red Cloud then marked his threats with success in what became known as the Fetterman Massacre. Captain William J. Fetterman led 79 U.S. soldiers and two civilians on a strike against Sioux warriors who were menacing his post in December 1866. This foolhardy officer emerged from the protection of Fort Phil Kearny and its 400-man garrison, confident his command could defeat any force he encountered. "With eighty men I could ride through the entire Sioux nation," he reputedly said.[16] Not far from the fort, his entire column was ambushed by hundreds of Sioux. The troops quickly divided into three groups and mounted a defense that lasted less than an hour, the warriors boasting that not even a dog accompanying the soldiers escaped harm.[17] The Natives saw this as a great victory and one that represented a blow leading to the end of hostilities. Americans decried it as a massacre; Sherman sought to "act with vindictive earnestness against the Sioux even to their extermination, men, women, and children."[18] The general demanded further attacks to avenge this outrage and to end the conflict in the north against the Sioux. This resolve meant the war went on as the Army looked for a way to end the conflict in the north against the Sioux.

Further attacks would have to wait. At the insistence of the Peace Commission, a mostly civilian federal body attempting to curtail the violence between Americans and Natives, the Army tried diplomacy. It invited Red Cloud to a meeting to discuss the latest round of violence, but the chief would only accept the offer if the soldiers destroyed their forts in Sioux territory.

In response, the Army planned its next offensive, but it did so in the face of a strong headwind arising in the East since the Indian Bureau of the Department of the Interior favored making peace with the Natives. This opposition climaxed in 1867 with the release of a report by Senator Doolittle. Initiated in the wake of Sand Creek and surfacing in the aftermath of the Fetterman Massacre, the Doolittle Report reviewed the history of American-Native contacts and blamed military provocations by civilians and Army personnel for the hostilities. This finding gave impetus to a Peace Policy. Now, a reservation process was to come into place and, with it, an aim of assimilation rather than attempted extermination. It was a renewed appeal to Jefferson's Empire of Liberty, only with the hope that this dream could come to pass.

This sudden call to peace underscored the Army's frustration out West. A frontier had come into focus, and it was one where Americans opposed Natives in a theater of operations. However, there was little middle ground on the Central Plains. There were opposing sides—soldiers versus Natives— yet no clarity as a result other than frequent violence. For the Army, the war and its aims, and the means of waging that war, were as confused as ever, and victory was not in sight. Moreover, a prolonged struggle was just as likely to sap Army strength as it was to wear down Native resistance. In an effort to avoid this development, the Army pursued a decisive battle. When unable to win such a battle, the Army tepidly moved toward a first way of war by allowing civilians to serve as the apex of the offensive. This gradual, albeit reluctant forfeiture of its role as a police force, spoke to a crisis of morality, one of decimating Natives or protecting civilians. The Army sensed the true current pushing the Natives to defeat, and that was the civilian tide of settlement. Spurring demographic change became the soldiers' *de facto* purpose, but they searched for a means of doing so short of Native extermination. The Army was only partly successful in curtailing this violent approach, but completely successful in aiding the ultimate end of Native destruction. It was an ugly war in many ways.[19]

Beecher Island

The Army continued to try to aid the settlement movement via overt military means. The question was where the next attack should fall. The Peace Commission set the table in this regard since that commission's immediate result was to give the Sioux a reprieve. With government officials actively consulting these Natives, Sherman calmed himself and postponed a planned strike to avenge the Fetterman disaster. Instead, he looked south and ordered

General Hancock to take 1,400 soldiers into Kansas to intimidate Native opposition there. In order to stop a war from occurring, Hancock was to demonstrate a willingness on the part of the United States to fight that war. Here the Army alone became a vehicle for the familiar duality of the United States advancing both peace and war. It proceeded with some justification for the Natives did the same. Tribes faced internal divisions of their own over whether or not to fight. This was particularly so on the Southern Plains. Cheyenne Chief Black Kettle spoke of peace, and so did a few others, but Cheyenne Dog Soldiers openly advocated war and menaced settlers. Kiowa Chiefs Lone Wolf and Kicking Bird also sought accommodation, but Kiowa Chief Satanta issued threats. In this confused situation on both sides, the region between the Platte and Arkansas Rivers, the key avenue funneling settlers west, became a pivotal battleground.

It did not take long for Hancock's advance in April 1867 to spark war, not peace. He moved forward and found a large Cheyenne concentration along the Pawnee Fork, an offshoot of the Arkansas River. These Natives agreed to meet with him, but then fled. Hancock took this act as purposeful evasion and a sign of war. In possession of an encampment without any Natives, Hancock hesitated to destroy the camp, but after a short deliberation, did so. U.S. soldiers burned what they could find in terms of shelter and supplies and killed a large pony herd. As a number of subordinates had warned him, this act meant war on the plains, and they were right. After hearing news of this attack, the Cheyenne and Sioux struck anyone they could find north of the Arkansas River. In response, Hancock ordered his forces to pursue them, and in June, a wild chase commenced as he sent his cavalry forward in several columns and attempted to bring these Natives to battle.

Hancock named George Armstrong Custer the key leader of the attack. Famous for his impetuosity during the Civil War, Custer's successes in that war earned him the temporary rank of general at 23 years of age. Now, Lieutenant Colonel Custer maintained that reputation on the Plains. Ranging far ahead of supporting troops and underestimating his enemy in terms of numbers and capabilities, Custer soon exposed his small command of 300 troopers to isolation. In fact, Custer almost met with disaster during this campaign, long before he did die at the Little Bighorn River. When his efforts ceased in mid–July, Custer entered Fort Wallace with an exhausted command that had traversed some 1,000 miles, but one that had not encountered any sizeable concentration of Natives. Having divorced themselves from the cumbersome supply wagons, an increase in mobility had given them only a temporary gain. In just a matter of weeks, with supplies depleted and the troops worn out by the incessant marches, the soldiers were vulnerable to attack and forced to retire.

In truth, Custer and the 7th Cavalry were fortunate to have survived. Had they confronted a concentration of Natives, the outcome would have been uncertain. The boy general revealed a remarkable good fortune at the time, even if later on he showed a remarkable inability to learn from his mistakes. The same could be said of Hancock, at least in terms of learning from mistakes. This general did not merely accept failure: the inability to engage significant numbers of Natives who abandoned their camps and villages as he approached at the head of a large, slow-moving force. Custer led a much more nimble force in pursuit, an action that netted no tangible gain either. To Hancock, the fault lay with Custer. Custer also invited the label of scapegoat. Having dealt harshly with deserters while on the march and having left Fort Wallace to try to rendezvous with his wife at the end of the march, Custer faced a court-martial ending with his suspension from command. Because of Custer's behavior, Hancock appeared vindicated. Yet there could be no mistaking that this round of the conflict on the plains had ushered in a desperate military action where the U.S. Army struggled to avoid the taint of defeat.

The Army appeared caught in a dilemma. Regulars could only operate on the prairie with a cumbersome supply train and could not force the Natives to accept battle. If some success had been had in the north in the Dakotas, the effort produced almost no comparable result on the Central Plains or to the south. To strike with smaller, more mobile forces did not necessarily guarantee a battle, but should one occur, these battalion-level commands invited a successful Native counterstroke. Custer mulled over his role in the past offensive and drew momentous conclusions that directly impacted this problem. He believed Native settlements should be targeted by fast moving but stronger columns, avoiding the fruitless chase about the plains.[20] Of course, seeking Native settlements was already an Army practice, so the real issue was what should be done after finding these villages. Once engaged in this manner, it was uncertain what the outcome would be—either a parley, a surprise attack seeking elimination of the Native foe, or more often than might be expected, a desperate military action to avoid destruction at the hands of Native retaliation.

The most negative of these options came to pass in a few years at the Battle of the Little Bighorn. For now, the Army tried to employ civilians again. This effort came after the collapse of the Medicine Lodge Creek Treaty in October 1867. At that time, nearly every important chief had agreed to move to reservations, suggesting Hancock's offensive had not been fruitless. However, the advent of winter had dictated peace more so than the U.S. military threat. When spring came, warfare returned. Cheyenne warriors raided throughout the Kansas plains, attacking settlements and leaving fifteen civilians dead. The Comanche continued to raid south into Texas and did so from their newly established reservations. Additionally, Sioux warriors came south to support Cheyenne bands priming to attack settlers.

General Philip Sheridan replaced Hancock in March 1868 and sought a battle to end the strife altogether. The new commander of the Department of the Missouri found a battle a short time thereafter, but it took an unexpected turn. At the Battle of Beecher Island in mid–September 1868, a war party of several hundred Sioux, Northern Cheyenne, and Arapahoe isolated a reckless column of "scouts" functioning as an arm of the U.S. Army's war on the Cheyenne Dog Soldiers. The small Army strike force invited this danger. Sheridan's "rangers," as he labeled this unit totaling two military officers and 51 civilians, found themselves alone on the prairie but uncertain of what to do after the Native trail they were following simply disappeared. To advance meant perhaps finding a nearby village and forcing a battle, something the commanding officer, Major George Alexander Forsyth, did not relish for fear of facing superior numbers. To retreat invited the same risk for a different reason: they would be forced to stand in the open against a larger force.

Forsyth, a Regular officer hand-picked by General Sheridan for this command, did not know what to do. The Natives soon made his decision for him. In the early morning, as Forsyth prepared to move out in a direction still unknown to his men, he heard an alarming commotion and a terrifying utterance: "Oh heavens ... look at the Indians."[21] Before them, hundreds of Natives came racing toward their position. The Natives had indeed found his command and were closing in for the kill.

The Central Plains had again erupted in conflict, and this hybrid force took center stage. Forsyth called his men by still a different name, that of "frontiersmen." This was a surprising label or, at least,

Gen. George A. Forsyth (Library of Congress).

an ambiguous label at this point in the American-Native confrontation. Forsyth's use of the word "frontiersmen" was meant to describe his men as individuals who could survive the travails of prairie campaigning: long rides, meager food, and the nervous tension stemming from not knowing if or when they would encounter Natives. For the most part, this label was accurate. Being comfortable in the saddle and enjoying a high endurance level defined most of these frontiersmen, although several of this company lacked both the stamina, and experience for fighting with Natives. It was a measure of the Army's desperation that Sheridan turned to men like these to offer a "quick fix," as it were. The general was short of Regulars, so he looked to augment his command, and the Army was willing to experiment with civilians acting under proxy Army authority. Moreover, the Cheyenne had evaded Army patrols the previous year, and the newly arrived Sheridan embraced the notion that rangers could do better.[22] Also, Forsyth had served under Sheridan during the Civil War, and Sheridan reasoned that an experienced officer could lead these men and succeed where Army columns had failed. He would be both right and wrong in his estimation of Forsyth.

Doing "better" became dubious within a week as the headstrong Forsyth led his command in headlong pursuit of Natives at the end of August. More than a few of his company feared a confrontation with any warriors given the column's small size. Forsyth ignored the cautions and moved audaciously forward, then slowed his pace. It was too late, and his scouts soon collided with Natives rallying to defend their villages. Forced into a hasty retreat, Forsyth led his men into a river basin where they mounted a desperate defense on a sandbar in the middle of the Arikaree Fork of the Republican River. They repelled several charges, killing a prominent chief named Roman Nose. However, Forsyth's second in command, Lieutenant Frederick H. Beecher, the only other soldier with this group of scouts, had fallen during the first Native attack. Badly wounded, Beecher endured throughout that first day in great pain and died that night. When counting an increased number of wounded and a depletion of supplies and ammunition, the scouts were in desperate straits after just a few hours. Still, they held on. A few of them managed to escape and get help, and after a nine day siege, a relief column reached the beleaguered detachment and the Natives broke off their attack. When it was over, five Americans had been killed and another eighteen had been wounded. The Army estimated inflicting 100 Native casualties, a number certainly exaggerated, but no doubt the defenders felled an equal or greater number of the enemy as they themselves lost. The survivors commemorated their survival by naming the island they had defended after Beecher.

In spite of the heroics, the overall mission of using scouts as a concentrated body was discredited in the eyes of the Army. Sheridan discovered the folly of assuming "rangers" could wage war more effectively than Regulars on the plains. When it came to ensuring success through military arms, something greater than an engagement was needed and so too were numbers larger than a handful of men. In fact, when this confrontation was over, frontiersmen would not be deployed again as an independent command. Scouts would resurface, but the Army became the main military force contending with the Native threat. Its successes varied and highlighted the Army's struggle to get results. Forsyth's frontiersmen represented this reality best, a force at the center of a tempest somewhere between military officialdom and civilian excess.

As the drama unfolded at Beecher's Island, Sheridan's other offensive floundered. In the first week of September, he sent Sully with a large contingent of Regulars south of the Arkansas River in search of Natives. This strike accomplished nothing, and the command returned to Fort Dodge after ten days of campaigning. The repeated Army failures convinced Sheridan of the need for a winter offensive on the Southern Plains. The Natives would be essentially immobile at that time, and their villages would make inviting targets. Moreover, the Army could supply itself via wagons, turning what had been a disadvantage—a slow-moving baggage train—into an advantage. However, the winter was also a time when Natives did no raiding of their own, thus their outrages would be nonexistent, and a military strike perhaps less justifiable for this reason. Not so in Sheridan's mind nor Sherman's, for that matter. They had a long memory. Too many Native depredations had occurred to mandate a shift away from a punitive military effort in winter. This approach was rooted firmly in the recent experience of the Civil War, where "total war" had achieved victory in their eyes.[23] That practice now reached an apogee of sorts on the plains, as senior Army commanders ordered year-round attacks on villages, and lower echelon commanders once again set out in search of victory.

The trouble was determining which tribe to attack. The Cheyenne were a primary target, as were their Arapahoe allies. However, hostilities were now to range far to the south and approach the Red River. Here was a carry-over from Sully's summer campaign. The Army believed a push south would force warriors north of the Arkansas to come back south to defend their villages. This approach represented some sophisticated thinking beyond desperately plodding about the plains hoping to discover a village or to make contact with a raiding party, an act too often of futility as Sully's slow column had just made clear when it found no Natives to attack. However, this idea of attacking to force warriors to come south did not hold true in the winter months, since warriors would not be loose in the north but would be with their families to the south. This thinking blurred the Arkansas River as a point of defining military operations. It was clear that any Natives north and south of this river were a fair target, and there would be no holding back on the means of attack. Sheridan told a fellow officer that when engaging these southern Natives, "I want you to kill all you can."[24] Not sure his intent was getting across, Sheridan sought a determined commander for the job, and he wanted Custer. Grant, now Commanding General of the Army of the United States, and with Sherman concurring, approved Sheridan's plan and his demand for Custer, who arrived at the end of September and immediately began to ready the 7th Cavalry for its pending attack. The upcoming winter campaign began the Army's formal implementation of total war on the Western Plains, a policy that also began the Army's leading role in waging a first way of war.

Doom

Both civilians and U.S. Army personnel had provoked this confrontation on the Central Plains and it was hard to blame one more than the other for poisoning American and Native relations. In tandem, volunteers and the U.S. Army forces looked to make a difference and their attacks accelerated rapidly in the wake of the Civil War. Military action became the preferred option of the government to overcome Native resistance, but the results were mixed. In frustration, the Army often conducted operations unfolding outside of formal military channels. The attacks such as that at Sand Creek merely underscored this American imperative of using volunteers to test the first way of war. Calls for extermination compromised Army standing as a constabulary force searching for a means to mitigate conflict on the plains. Any sense of pacification shifted tone as a result. In this latest round of the drama, the military at last caught up to the public's mindset. This shift came in spite of Army efforts to mount attacks that stopped short of this result and sought out enemy warriors so as to engage them in a frontier battle. That some of this success unfolded in the Dakotas could not change the larger picture of frustration stemming from the Army's initial refusal to mount a first way of war. When this feature shone forth as the decisive factor, an ultimately unconscious line of attack obscured in a violent call to avenge Native outrages via total war. It was an ominous sign for the plight of Native Americans. However, once again, and at best, limited military success was redeemed by a far stronger current of pacification. For neither the volunteers nor Army personnel overcame Native resistance. Civilians won this war by settling the plains.

7

Sustaining
the Home Front
Settlement and the Triumph
of the "Peace Policy"

John C. Frémont, U.S. Army engineer, had no great affinity for Mormons, but he helped them find a place within the confines of an expanding United States. His exploration of the Great Salt Lake in 1843 helped a radical faction of Americans to gain a foothold there and inclusion within the understanding of "American." Just over a decade later, the U.S. government concluded that these Mormons were not American enough, and launched a military campaign to ensure federal authority over this radical sect. This effort stemmed from the often momentous consequences of Frémont's supposed peaceful act of exploration. He reached the Pacific Ocean via the Oregon Territory, but this exploit assured the exclusion of Natives from the American domain there. Frémont foolishly wandered into Californian space and defied Mexican authority, an act that meant U.S. territorial expansion at the expense of this nation, and so it was not that foolish after all. Frémont returned to the East and ended his adventures, but his travels instilled within large numbers of settlers an urge to head west and make this land answer to an American identity. Exploration had never been more consequential or politically charged.

Settlers accomplished this journey over and over again, and the land was made American. Frémont knew this to be the case in the act of naming the fauna he contacted, mapping the rivers and mountain peaks he crossed and climbed, and categorizing the animals he observed about the plains. Nomenclature was ownership, a process of discovery made good by an expedition favoring increased knowledge. It was the American way, an act of belligerence so often mistaken for poetic license. This ode prepared that generation for the arduous overland journey, convincing them of the legitimacy of seeking a new existence without having to accept what had come in

the past. The shared American experience of going west was fulfilling the
destiny of a nation. However, that act wrestled a great future from those
inhabiting these lands, the Natives. "American" marked legitimacy for those
who did not deserve it and stripped that legacy from those already ascribing
to that heritage.

The physical act of exploration required an equally important intellectual
act of obfuscation in order to efface the legalities in place protecting those
in possession of the land. Settlers pushed treaty-defined boundaries farther
west with each successive wave of American expansion. This process continued until linear parameters became obvious as feckless demarcations of a
failed attempt at exclusion. To consolidate the West, Americans confronted
the Native populations among them with no rationale for their expulsion.
Guarantees of co-existence now had to be made good via reservations. The
American aim to see that region as offering enough space for differing peoples
to coexist and as providing a resource for molding what was different into a
singular unit needed one more label upholding this ambiguity as a single
truth. Americans found this nomenclature in the annunciation of the Peace
Policy, a push to make reservations an unneeded entity given the conquest
of Indian Country. This fiction of homogeneity required a related ambiguity
since the separation between soldier and settler again blurred virtue and success, a demographic wave transgressing on the former even if delivering the
latter.

End of the Frontier

In North America, economic gain via land acquisition ensured that colonials and then Americans stayed in battle readiness against the Natives and
never tired of the war. However, settlement as territorial avarice was too ugly
to admit, so it was not the accomplishment they heralded. Instead, these pioneers masked their push west with a call to arms for other more noble reasons:
wars ensuring survival, wars advancing the benevolence of Removal, and
lastly, wars in fulfillment of Manifest Destiny. No matter, the stunning acts
of violence perpetuated in the name of necessity grated against the morals
of these settlers. Rationalizations were found, blasphemous exceptions made.
However, the contradiction was acute and impossible to ignore even if undertaken with a steady stream of self-righteousness. This hypocrisy meant that
Indian Country went from promising tribes sanctuary west of the Mississippi
to a justification allowing Americans to direct more punitive measures at
Natives. Soldiers were just plentiful enough to undergird this shift in emphasis

that enabled civilians to subdue the remainder of the Native populations in the West. In this way, expansionism provided a singular motive that sustained the home front for so long that settlers became the front line of this very lengthy counterinsurgency.

Treaties had settled the "frontier" in the minds of Americans—an ever-changing line moved west to the Mississippi River at the expense of Natives. When the geographical restraint of the Mississippi did not hold, treaties soon gave way to maxims expressing overt ideology. Manifest Destiny became the call of Americans in the 1840s, a desire to plant their civilization from the Mississippi to the Pacific Ocean, but being less clear—even purposely obscure—about the means. The currency was again primarily land, although the discovery of gold in California lent added weight to the geographical expansion. This economic reality was rhetorically muted, however. Manifest Destiny decreed that Americans had a god-given right to settle the West, as this region now became known. While this mantra invoked theology and race, its brazen call to establish American hegemony from coast to coast neglected the incentives of securing acreage and precious metals. As always, here lay the central motive of Americans, the true "ideology" leading to expansion. Still to be determined were the northern and southern limits of the new American colossus, but the economic objective was in reach.

Americans got their wish to extend the new nation from one sea to the other, an end that came only after their government employed its military in a campaign sanctioned by a public hoping to be free to enjoy the spoils it coveted. This expectation was met in fantastic fashion. When war came with Mexico in 1845, Americans rallied together to rebuke an exaggerated threat from the south. Dictating terms to Mexico defined an opportunity so unique as to be ordained by god: desire, defeat of rivals, and then settlement acting as a holy trinity of sorts. Accordingly, U.S. citizens assigned only altruistic reasons to the success of expanding west into their new domain. However, this ideological intent fostered strife more than prevented it, since Natives fell victim to a growing Anglo-Saxon belief in their racial superiority. With the defeat of Mexico, three racial groups had succumbed to American expansion: Mexicans now joined the ranks of Blacks and Natives. Since liberation brought exploitation and destruction, race became the tool to justify economic pursuit leading to the exclusion of others, rather than their salvation.[1] Only in the wake of this last war did Americans think in clear terms of continental expansion, as rationales of offering tutelage to uncivilized inhabitants accelerated a juggernaut focused on self-interest. Transitioning from east to west indeed meant a constant exploration of shifting lines—imaginary lines for the most part—with dire consequences for Natives. Now the ideal of a cast-off Native homeland somewhere on the open plains next to the new America was in great jeopardy. Frontiers were disappearing, and tribes no longer needed transformation but rather protection from being obliterated by settlers.

This malevolent aspect of settlement came to define the meaning of Indian Country, a debate initiated long before a crisis of consciousness over what Americans meant by Manifest Destiny. When the U.S. government had conceived of Indian Country west of the Mississippi River, here was a seemingly unique, benign approach. The stated mission was that removed tribes would exist independent of American influence and survive. This hands-off approach suggested sincerity on the part of Americans, but an old ambiguity in American consciousness laid bare the shallow promise of Indian Country. It soon became clear that Natives who were so empowered were not in possession of sovereign land. They occupied territory beholden to Americans when the latter were ready to act on the impulse of settlement. Because of this always present push, after the 1840s, Removal meant only assimilation was possible, and this became the main rationale for Indian Country. When given an opportunity, Natives could become a part of the United States over time. In this way, Indian Country went from being a sanctuary to a refuge granting its inhabitants a chance to be American. It is difficult to pinpoint how genuine either sentiment was. The entire idea of Indian Country was a justification for settlement of the East half of a continent, and then an invalidation of the West as beholden to that concept.

Trail blazing dictated this transition by canvassing huge parts of land and better defining Indian Country. A number of explorers now combed the area, sent by a government no longer concerned with overcoming frontiers but with settling the remainder of the nation. At issue was not just a determination of what that entailed in terms of geography, but the fate of the Native population within that expanse. The United States soon faced a reckoning sanctifying Manifest Destiny as the fulfillment of the promise of the Empire of Liberty, but as a prescription only for Americans. This outcome, inherent in the call of Manifest Destiny at its inception, ended the promise of the Indian Country sheltering Native Americans. In this way, ideology became the centerpiece of the American effort to settle the West, and that belief was bigger than a righteous indignation. Manifest Destiny was a thinly veiled drive for conquest, starting with military officers "exploring" the West at the bidding of a rapacious civilian population. From this rudimentary beginning came a more robust alliance between soldier and settler.

Exploring the West again meant opportunity for mountain men, but now overtly in the employment of the U.S. government. The best examples of these trappers turned government agents were those accompanying John C. Frémont, U.S. Army. Frémont became a key surveying force on behalf of the U.S. government in the early 1840s. A number of soldiers and these irregulars accompanied Frémont, men he recruited to help him lay claim to the West on behalf of the American nation. Through Frémont, the union of frontiersman and government policy became overt, frequent, and markedly advanced. In particular, he employed mountain man Kit Carson on expeditions spanning the years 1842–49. The junction was so frequent that Robert Utley, in his book on mountain men, *A Life Wild and Perilous*, could write of Frémont that he "embodied the spirit of Manifest Destiny," and of Carson that he had "donned the mantle of imperialist."[2]

Frémont's first expedition in 1842 proved a primer for the second one the following year. With his initial effort, this soldier had merely demonstrated the still adventurous nature of travel from the Platte to the Green River. It also earned him another opportunity, and a more grandiose task was in his sights the second time. Frémont now looked to mark the connection of the south pass to the Pacific Coast. In other words, he had made it only to Bridger's outpost the first time, and did so with Carson's help. While Frémont had learned a great deal, his larger contribution to opening the west remained to be realized.

Carson had come down from the mountains because the trapping no longer remained viable. Meeting Frémont on a boat ride up the Mississippi and on the way back to the mountains after tiring of civilization, Carson was impressed by the Army officer and willingly joined forces with him. Once again, explicit motives of economic survival stirred the mountain man to attach himself to the American columns exploring (claiming) the country. Carson, like Jim Bridger, had few choices that could sustain his interest in staying in the wilds of America. Fortunately for him and many others like him, his backwoods experience proved invaluable to men like Frémont. Carson was fortunate to have found Frémont and vice versa.

Carson joined the second Frémont expedition in 1843 as well. Even with an experienced mountain man in his company, Frémont's travels over the next year ran into difficulties that almost killed the entire group of thirty-nine men. Frémont's push to make his travels matter caused the crisis. He reached the Pacific Ocean, entering Fort Vancouver in November 1843, but not before deviating from his course and exploring the Great Salt Lake. Boating on this lake exhausted the men with him. The sojourn south had little purpose, and it appeared that Frémont had tackled the Great Salt Lake mainly to boast of having done something unique on the trail west to Oregon, a now fairly well-established path to the coast. He then had to double back to the north to make the crossing to the Pacific Ocean. He would engage in such a tangent again and once more create undue hardship. When it came time to head home, rather than marching east back over the Oregon Trail, Frémont went south and in the dead of winter. He looked to disprove the idea that a river joined California to the Rockies via a more southerly route. In the process of verifying that this topography did not exist, Frémont violated Mexican sovereignty, exposed his command to Native attack and did so by inviting the folly of traversing the Sierra Nevada Mountains in winter months. Yet, Frémont persevered, and by May 1844, he had returned to the East and soon enjoyed great acclaim. In some respects, it was well-earned. He had dispelled the hope of a river from the Rockies across the plains to the Sierras. This latter range Frémont established as a formidable obstacle in and of itself, a landmark that spoke to the difficulty of making the western crossing to California. Additionally, Frémont's group had canvassed huge sections of the West, scientifically documenting what they saw. Plants, fossils, landmarks, and the aboriginal inhabitants were all codified and the findings presented in reports to Congress.

When Frémont's travels were complete, these findings were consumed by an interested public willing to move west. For this reason, Frémont's expedition helped unleash a deluge of settlement. Here was the true payoff of Fremont's efforts from 1842 to 1845: he provided a calling card to opening the West.[3] The juncture of explorer and mountain men may have made clear the difficulties of moving west, but it also inspired such a movement. Any gratitude came less from a government that already looked to this end—that was the charge after all. Rather, the public accepted Frémont's challenge as it was: a willingness to endure his hardships and settle the nation. Frémont had made this adventure a national enterprise. In the process, he had set forth how to destroy the chief obstacle to this vision, not natural barriers, but Native Americans. He had, in effect, mapped the course of Indian Country, paving the way for its destruction. As this process accelerated in the years to come, the U.S. government declared that the Army acting on behalf of civilians functioned as an instrument of peace, protecting Americans and Natives alike. It would take years of fighting to make this declaration effective policy on the ground, and the results would not necessarily speak to having served Natives as well as settlers.

The Indian Territory

The Indian Territory stood directly in the path of the American ambition of reclassifying Indian Country as something amendable to settlement. This was the case because of Native successes. Many tribes took advantage of Removal to start over and make a new life in what would become the state of Oklahoma. By the time of the Civil War, some 100,000 had done so, and this activity included Natives from multiple regions. The Cherokee, in particular, had flourished since 1830, with increased agricultural production evidence of a great movement away from the Native lifestyle to embrace American culture. The redoubtable John Ross once again presided over this progress. Other tribes enjoyed success as well, and the Native fulfillment of Removal appeared genuine. It also suggested a separate status. Still regimented by tribe, accord among Native peoples came by proxy with the label of being inhabitants of the Indian Territory. However, these Natives discovered that this edifice did not safeguard their aspirations of sovereignty once American expansion came west.[4]

Natives formally occupying this reserve entered the Civil War in an effort to achieve a guarantee of sovereignty, and they enjoyed some leverage once the war started. The Union and Confederate reach west of the Mississippi was limited in terms of military assets, so these relocated Natives represented key allies to help bolster one side or the other. This meant that the tribes that had experienced Removal thirty years before, the Cherokee, Seminole, Creek, and others, now risked a repetition of their previous fate when colonials and Americans had coveted these Natives as allies but then discarded them once the wars against England ended. What appeared a good chance to take in 1861 soon proved otherwise.

The fighting settled nothing. Northern triumph in the western theater of the war came from a greater material preponderance established over an extended period of time. Until that point, Natives in the Indian Territory faced some hard choices. An early Confederate advance predicated on tribes there formally allying with the Confederacy led to a Northern withdrawal abandoning the Indian Territory. However, the alliance was not uniformly supported, particularly among the Creeks, Seminoles, and Cherokee, and many Natives now fled north. In December 1861, Confederate cavalry caught up to one of these retreating groups following the Creek chief Opothleyaholo and totaling close to 2,000. The Rebels dispersed this concentration in a swift attack that left the South firmly in control of the region. However, once Northern reinforcements came west, a Union offensive forced Southern retrenchment in the territory. The North cemented its ascendency in the area after Union forces won a victory at Pea Ridge in March 1862.

This Union success changed the conduct of the war in the Indian Territory. The conflict gravitated into a guerrilla war as raids, hit-and-run attacks, and ambushes became commonplace. This fighting exposed the Natives to calamity as a bitter, long war now ensued for control of the territory. The fighting took on dimensions intense enough to kill 7,000 Natives and leave the Indian Territory in ruins. When it was over, the depopulated tribes found their claims to land less tenable, which made it clear that sovereignty had never been a reality for the inhabitants of the Indian Territory. Rather, Natives had been consumed in a national struggle among Americans that did nothing to define Natives as a nation, but underscored their lack of viability as an entity other than on American-granted terms.[5]

A Union triumph also meant retribution for those having supported the Confederacy, and this acrimony served as another Union justification for destroying the integrity of the Indian Territory. The always present fissures in Native resistance had resurfaced during the war, and the Cherokee exemplified this negative outcome for having served in both the Confederate and Union armies. Not surprisingly, Ross led one faction, eventually siding with the Union after a torturous political odyssey. As war broke out and the Union surrendered the Indian Territory, Ross feared a rival gaining Confederate support and unseating him. After the early Rebel victory at Bull Run in July 1861, Ross bowed to mounting pressure to formally ally the Cherokee with the Confederacy in exchange for a Rebel guarantee of Cherokee territorial integrity. When Union forces overran the Indian Territory the following year, they captured Ross, and he soon became a symbol of Cherokee support for the North. His struggles during the conflict exemplified the choices facing Natives: continued allegiance to the United States, the nation that had so wronged the Native peoples and that may continue its assault on Cherokee land after the war between the states, or the hope that a Confederacy could emerge and would honor the territorial integrity of the Cherokee in the Indian Territory.

Ross could not prevent the reduction of Cherokee land in the aftermath of war, nor could his rival, Stand Watie, who led a faction of Cherokee siding with the Confederacy throughout the war. Watie enjoyed only a brief reign as the dominant figure of Cherokee affairs, assuming control once Ross departed and soldiering on after the Confederate collapse again exposed the Indian Territory to Union control. His continued resistance symbolized his effort to use the war to bolster Cherokee independence. Allegiance with the Confederacy was only a means to this end, and that end superseded all concerns. Watie expressed confidence that he could defend the Indian Territory even without Confederate support, a dubious assertion but one that expressed his own struggles to gain an ally to secure Cherokee independence. The United States had proven malicious and untrustworthy. It made no sense to ally with that nation. The Confederacy represented a new opportunity. It could well flounder, as in fact it did, but in the meantime, Cherokee resistance could gain arms and legitimacy by virtue of this war, and stand on its own in the aftermath of the conflict. It was a vision sharply divergent from that of Ross, who hoped for the preservation of Cherokee power after the war because of their belated support of the Union. Watie, however, refused to place his trust in a long-time foe, and he probably made the best use of the situation. Watie was the last Confederate commander to surrender, although his intransigence symbolized the lost cause of the Cherokee, not that of the Confederacy.[6]

The four-year fratricidal conflict among Americans that was the Civil War represented a poor return on Native efforts. The Indian Territory remained intact but much reduced. It became a marginal area for Native existence in terms of standard of living and, as stressed above, in terms of offering Natives a permanent refugee against settlers advancing westward. The Civil War confirmed that land as "conquered soil," and therefore as an American dependency, and exemplified the fate in store for the larger entity of Indian Country.[7] Here was a fatal blow to independent Native existence in the West on the basis of Removal, and perhaps the chief outgrowth of Manifest Destiny. Armed with a racial imperative requiring Natives to submit to instruction in civilization, and having discredited the sovereignty of the Indian Territory, Americans could proceed with settlement unimpeded by any restrictive understanding of Indian Country. It was a key moment, a transition that underscored how the Civil War had made the Natives in the Indian Territory ostensible allies to the Americans and brought disaster, a recurring theme of this confrontation.

Pioneers

Indian Country's benign outlook, the idea of neglect, could not survive that of settlement, a desire to control the West and the American cause after 1865. A sanctuary Americans granted to Natives was in stark contrast to the latent fears associated with Indian Country in the aftermath of the Civil War. Always having to set parameters around the American world and Native existence meant a people existing outside the American experience—no assimilation was desired—and therefore inevitably bringing a sinister connotation to Indian Country. Here was land that needed to be avoided, to be feared, and only entered when reclassified as open space inviting settlement. Explorers such as Frémont did that, feeding the ideological urge to move west in pursuit of the Empire of Liberty. Identifying spaces as free of Native control

"Westward Ho!" Men walk alongside covered wagons pulled by oxen (Library of Congress).

soon meant the same thing as claiming Indian Country, a needed step in order for Americans to renege on the guarantee of Removal. The term "settlement" now became a badge of honor in that it was meant to promote the end of Native resistance, among other things. Removal had been made palpable to Americans because of the supposed protection offered to Natives in Indian Country. Settlers now destroyed that construct by defining what had been considered hostile as safe and then ensuring that what had been declared safe became theirs. In this way, Indian Country became the chief casualty of Manifest Destiny.

Ideology is only as strong as its practitioners. Those heading west held economic convictions that propped up a creed that had ill effects that they refused to acknowledge. Settlers desiring land were the worst offenders. They left the East looking for new opportunities, but scholars do not define these motives as one of escaping poverty. Too much capital was needed to move west, so the abject poor did not make the trip.[8] This is accurate enough. In addition, a settler's life's treasure was frequently invested in the trip, which underscored its economic imperative and the desperation to succeed. What future did these men and women have if a move west floundered? Few people attempting the trip returned East.[9] It happened at times, but going west was a key and powerful motive, meaning settlers were a formidable group at the apex of the American assault on Natives inhabiting the Western Plains, the Pacific Coast, and the Southwest.

A large number of settlers who were consumed with a strong financial motive sustained a drive offering many advantages to the disenfranchised. These desperate souls in some ways polished the image of the most economically driven of those streaming west: gold prospectors, hunters, and railroad speculators. More disreputable ends defined these additional travelers. Those seeking gold looked for quick riches, plain and simple. Some of these individuals may have enjoyed a more pastoral contribution as farmers but only after getting (or failing to get) rich. Prospectors also tarnished the lore of families moving west, since men too often left their loved ones in pursuit of gold. Hunters helped accomplish a stunning feat, since entire species faced elimination at their hands, the buffalo being the most famous and important example. Railroads impacted the environment as well, as whole forests vanished before them because the wood was needed for the tracks. Any such damage made life more precarious for Natives, as did overgrazing from the settlers' cattle, or the despoiling of water holes and rivers due to the increasing human traffic frequenting these key resources. The combination meant the Natives faced an onslaught from ideologically devout Americans all subscribing to an economic creed of exploitation, even if not overtly declaring themselves a cog in the wheel of Manifest Destiny for this reason.

One cannot overstate the rapacious nature of settlement. Miners devastated miles of landscape that remained permanently blighted. Hunters made a sport of slaughter extolling waste in a land necessitating frugality. Railroads implemented inhumane labor practices on a large scale. Farmers and ranchers laid claim to homesteads and estates that carved up open spaces, leaving Natives homeless. Because of this carnage and that of other examples extinguishing Native existence and therefore resistance, there was little separation among these Americans collecting in the West. Dominating tribes much like the effort to dominate the land, became expected and all involved certainly accepted that end. Eclipsing Native civilization was merely one more hurdle to overcome in winning the West.

The economic lure enticing settlers west forced the U.S. military to devise a method of protection and consolidation of land not always settled and too often possessing dangers to Americans. This recourse did not automatically make settlement a completely rational outcome, particularly in terms of soldiers fending off Native attacks on civilians. Contacts between the newcomers and Natives were intermittent for the most part. A settler could very well travel west and not encounter a single Native.[10] No matter, the U.S. Army strove to placate the pioneer's cry of needed defense. Forts stretching north and south, from Fort Snelling, Minnesota, to Fort Jesup, Louisiana, might be expected to safeguard the permanent Indian frontier, but they hardly protected the people moving west.[11] Instead, in the most dangerous areas, a cluster of forts arose all within a day's march of each other. Texas, Kansas, and the Powder River region of the Dakotas contained enough forts that, when taken together, appeared to be a shield that extended north to south. This was the intent, at least. The move west repeatedly eviscerated any permanent frontier and added to a confused government policy. Were forts intended to restrain settlers and protect Indian Country, or were these outposts intended to end

Indian Country altogether as a means to a more peaceful outcome of moving west? As always, the grey areas worked against the Native population that was losing a demographic struggle that redefined the issues in favor of Americans.

This problem presented itself early on. When General Stephen Watts Kearny arrived in Santa Fe in August 1846, he announced American rule in the wake of the outbreak of the Mexican American War and a new reality that in his estimation promised a great boon to those present. He declared that all inhabitants would share the bounty of the promise of the United States. However, Kearny's guarantee failed to set an amiable tone for the treatment of Natives in the West at the hands of Americans. Instead, his mere arrival meant a bulge driven far beyond the permanent Indian frontier. For this reason, his boast shattered Jefferson and Jackson's hope for tribes already moved west to live a sheltered existence. Somehow Natives were to co-exist in a world shaped by peaceful settlers guarded by a virtually unneeded military. This benign view proved the opposite of reality in the years to come, as Americans demanding more land also demanded more military action from the U.S. Army.

As settlers advanced across the plains, relations between them and Natives may have remained tense but not explosive, except for the problem of settlement. It was conceivable that expansion meant a heavy American presence in pockets along the Pacific Coast, notably less so in the interior. Indian Country, particularly considering the malevolence associated with it in the minds of settlers, might still be avoided and left largely intact, if settlers could be moved west in an orderly fashion. This appeared the norm before the Civil War, as trade and a mutual curiosity defined the majority of American-Native interactions. Any coexistence was shattered after the war because of territorial aggrandizement by settlers.[12] Sherman had long recognized the inevitability of expansion and hoped to control it by establishing a corridor between the Platte and the Arkansas Rivers that could be made free of Native molestation of settlers and railroads.[13] Conceivably, this divide could be defended as something concrete and manageable, leaving the Army free of having to defend the entire West, and, therefore, American inroads could be something less intrusive and less provocative to Natives. At the very least, this channel was a temporary solution to a larger problem, settlement, that did not have to be solved all at once. The Army simply could not do so given the limited men at hand. In a sensible manner, Sherman strove to bring order to the West.

Whatever path Sherman envisioned guiding settlers, the West fell before a less tidy onslaught. Four great highways emerged, and these routes served as a means of a projection of power with settlers very much in the lead of carving out an expanded America. The Oregon Trail was the early favorite.

It started in Independence, Missouri, and advanced along the North Platte River to the Rocky Mountains. This path marked travel long facilitated by mountain men, so the real difficulties started after reaching Fort Bridger. Once past this landmark, the trail split in two directions, one going north into Oregon and the other southwest into California. This duality explained its popularity. Either route required travelers to move hundreds of miles and test their endurance crossing endless, dusty prairies, and at times, rivers and streams. Then the pioneers faced the final obstacles: the Sierra Nevada Mountains if pushing onto California, or the Columbia Mountains if headed to the Oregon Territory. A good trail guide, some luck, and a large amount of determination were needed to ensure success. Those making the trip also had to overcome their fear of surviving in Indian Country.

The Army looked to help by defending the path to Oregon first, the fort system in Kansas giving birth to posts along that trail that ran deep into land dominated by the "hostiles." A key east-west artery had been established, with foreboding import for Natives. It accompanied other trails that signaled how widespread American settlement would be and that over time, no trace of Indian Country would remain. The old Santa Fe Trail allowed settlers to move from Kansas near Fort Leavenworth and from the town of Independence to the south, ending at Santa Fe. In following the early traders along this path, Americans helped consolidate their grip on the territory newly won from Mexico. The Mormons added their own trail which started in Illinois with a terminus at the Great Salt Lake. This was more of a northern path and served primarily to help populate the region just south of Fort Bridger. Yet it also helped consolidate a key pivot of overland travel after soldiers utilized this path in 1857–1858 to help the federal government stymie a Mormon threat to establish their own state within U.S. territory.

More forts appeared along the key roads, channeling settlers moving west. These strong points represented the American success in taming the West since these "forts" often lacked a defensive wall. Rather, the outpost was enough, a cluster of buildings housing U.S. soldiers standing virtually immune to attack, forts in name only.[14] The formidable nature of the American threat was all too evident in these way-stations. Moreover, the unique American adaptation of forts rang through as well, since the fortress appearance lapsed so completely as to make them completely unlike the defensive forts found in Europe, a reality of those early forts protecting the enclaves of civilization in colonial America. The outpost with no stockade tied American sensibilities to the openness of the frontier and the pending American victory in the battle for control of the West.

All told, these pathways brought thousands of settlers west, some

250,000 people during the twenty-year period of 1840–1860.[15] More were to come after the Civil War. The Great Basin stood as a lodgment of Native resistance to this emigration, a sanctuary, but one ultimately vulnerable to the final lunge of American expansion. For a time, Natives living in this huge interior between the Wasatch Mountains in the Utah territory and the Sierra Nevada in California enjoyed something of reprieve. A few settlers passed through that expanse, but only a handful stayed there.[16] Like so often before, subjugation came in stages, and the result was that from north, south, west, and east, the Great Basin was constricted by a growing tide of settlement. To the north, Americans enjoyed the benefit of circumstance when Mormons joined the struggle in 1854. This group soon sent the Paiutes reeling southward. This Native setback was compounded by defeat to the east since Americans had forced the Utes onto reservations by 1855. With the collapse of Apache and Navajo resistance to the south, and with no significant Native resistance to the west, Natives confined in the Great Basin found themselves isolated, with no place to go, and therefore incapable of effective resistance.

Only fortuitous circumstances shielded the Natives there from the worst. The Great Basin was not desired by Americans. A Mormon path from Salt Lake City to California that bisected the basin, or the Old Spanish Trail from Santa Fe to Los Angeles that straddled it in the south, could have proved to be a means of its undoing, but the former route was infrequently traveled, and the latter path received only moderate trading traffic. Of course, the Oregon and California trails defined a northern border. At long last, something of an equilibrium had been found between American expansion and Native existence, a geographical refuge foretelling the solution to this American-Native clash short of Native obliteration. Native ability to survive in the Great Basin continued until after the Civil War when it too would succumb to American control of what amounted to all of the West. It was a shocking outcome since the terminus mattered most in this progression of travel from east to west. However, an emerging federal control via military outposts housing soldiers capable of responding to emergencies, coupled with human enterprise in terms of way stations for resupply or transport across rivers or guidance over treacherous mountains, combined to make the travel more feasible, if never comfortable. Consequently, the land between the start and end of the journey changed as much as the destination. The "West" never meant just reaching an objective. It also meant reshaping a region, and the whole endured as much as the parts comprising the end product.[17]

Natives slowly came to understand the long-range implications of contact with Americans and when able, tribes exerted their power, exacted concessions, and grudgingly gave ground. It was a hopeless struggle. When settlers teamed with the advanced technology of railroads promising to disperse thousands more Americans throughout the West, the Natives faced a flood they could not stop and one that did in fact fill up the open spaces, thereby ruining the Native lifestyle and existence. Indian Country no longer existed. Settlement, in this sense, had won the West as settlers streamed unimpeded throughout the region. They certainly did more than the feeble garrisons of soldiers strung out along these paths. For example, Fort Leavenworth sat alone on the Missouri River in 1827. After 1849, Forts Kearny and Laramie extended the Army's reach along this river further west. It was measured protection for one path of travel, and pitiful for this reason, but not so in the larger picture. Although a tentative start, forts combined one key purpose present early on in the settlement of the West with another proceed that came from the prolonged sustainment of these structures. Forts protected the small numbers of soldiers, of course. However, more significantly, the fort system cast doom on Indian Country. A military presence moved west as the expanse of the United States increased as well, and the result was the defensive posture of forts became an offensive tool by projecting military power deep into Indian Country on behalf of the settlers' quest of going west. This was the case even though forts represented less military occupation and more a skeleton force looking to offer moral support in terms of extending occasional military protection to civilians. In a real sense, settlers had swamped the U.S. military presence on the prairie.

Renewed Military Campaigns

This state of affairs brought George A. Custer to fame along the Washita River. Here on the Southern Plains in late November 1868, Custer emerged as a famous Indian fighter for the first time, claiming to lead 800 men to victory by decimating a concentration of mostly Cheyenne situated along this river. The parallels with Sand Creek were ominous, including targeting a village home to a chief favoring peace with Americans. Among the dead were Black Kettle and his wife, who together had survived nine wounds at Sand Creek; both were killed in action at this "battle." Custer, like Colonel John Chivington, the architect of the attack at Sand Creek, descended upon this unsuspecting target at dawn. The surprise was complete; the 250 or so Natives were dormant as winter descended over the land. An initial rush both surrounded the village and collapsed any last second defense. In a matter of ten minutes the Army controlled the village, but then the fighting intensified since a few warriors fired from cover and forced Custer's men to concentrate on clearing the area.

Soldiers overcame the remaining resistance and rounded up captives. Still, hours later, sporadic firing continued, and more significantly, a large number of Cheyenne, Arapaho, and Kiowa warriors massed above river, having come from neighboring villages to threaten Custer's position. With wounded personnel and a large herd of ponies in his charge, Custer suddenly realized that he occupied a precarious location. Having killed over 100 braves and taken some 50 women and children prisoner, he slew all ponies within reach and withdrew. The engagement cost the Americans only four dead. Later on, Custer realized a detachment of 18 soldiers had struck out from the village on its own and been destroyed by warriors, adding those soldiers to the total killed.

The Army heralded Custer's attack as a great success for having sternly rebuked an element of the Cheyenne that was refusing to abide by the peace; defeat at the Washita sent a message throughout the plains. A message of terror may well have been sent with this assault, and it underscored the Army's purpose of now adapting the "first way of war" mentality that civilians had hitherto championed. Striking villages and sustenance were not enough; the Army now targeted people. Such depredations received countenance because of the lack of success to this point. Custer's strike force was but one of three debarking on the plains in search of Natives that winter. Senior generals intended all three commands to work in unison and drive at least some tribes into a large-scale engagement. Instead, no real unity of action had been achieved, and Custer's winter attack was a poor substitute for the failure of this grandiose scheme. Still, Custer arrived back at Camp Supply to much acclaim heaped on him by Sheridan. The hero then faced some recrimination from members of his own command for having failed to show more concern about the missing eighteen men. Additionally, a controversy soon arose over the merits of the attack, a surprise attack on a village led by a chief favoring peace, which meant the value of the battle gained prominence at the expense of any analysis of the winter campaign. In fact, Custer had beaten a hasty retreat. Here was another parallel to Sand Creek, a strike that left intact a number of adjacent Native villages. Why not continue to attack? In truth, Custer had fled the battlefield or had been chased from it. If this shortcoming lessened the benefit of the victory at the Washita, another element of the winter operations redeemed that attack to a great extent. The battle spoke to the Army's willingness to engage the Natives on a year-round basis. The war on the Southern Plains would all but end in this way, one marked less by combat than by want. The Natives simply could not sustain their livelihoods, let alone a military stance. Custer's attack on the Washita made this clear. The first way of war paid this great dividend: less blood and more deprivation.

This result took some time to register. Unrelenting Army pressure continued into the following year. Custer again exemplified the effort, and the near miss element of success. He caught up to a party of Cheyenne after weeks of hard riding in March 1869. Once again determination almost yielded to folly. Custer's 800 troopers were exhausted and nearly out of supplies when finding and having to confront a large concentration of warriors. He negotiated, partly out of the necessity of masking his weakness, and apparently in a desire to avoid another incident such as that of the Washita. Custer's negotiations earned mixed results. The Natives did not accompany him back to Camp Supply, as he demanded. They did release some American captives, a step that appeased the volunteers among Custer's command, the 19 Kansas Cavalry, a unit clamoring for military action. Regular officers restrained them and avoided a likely blood bath.[18] Custer withdrew and, by the end of March 1869, declared his operations over and successful.

That success was in question as much as the means of achieving it. The Army again had made a maximum effort, and while no major engagement was the result, in the south the plains tribes were left in dire straits. Continued Army attacks meant Native surrender *enmasse* by the summer of 1869. Cheyenne, Arapaho, Kiowa, and Comanche all sought reservations to escape the Army columns. Regular forces had paid at least some dividends, and if Custer had played a leading role in this result, he was not alone, far from it. In the summer of 1869, Colonel Eugene Carr with the 5th Cavalry, managed to surprise a Cheyenne encampment near the Platte River at Summit Springs. Once discovering their path, Carr had taken the extreme but now accepted step of abandoning his heavy wagons and moving forward rapidly to overtake his foe. That soldier's temerity earned him a strike on a village and a battlefield victory. For the cost of only one wounded man, Carr killed at least 52 Natives and scattered a tribe under Tall Bull's leadership.

The Army's dispersal of several hundred braves heading north to join forces with the Sioux shook the resolve of the Cheyenne, including the heretofore recalcitrant Dog Soldiers, who now sought accommodation and agreed to life on reservations. For this reason, the Battle of Summit Springs appeared a greater victory than Custer's attack on the Washita, to say nothing of the recent winter offensive. Carr had played a role in this operation as well, seeking battle along the Canadian River but achieving little. Yet the combination of the winter campaign and Carr's attack the following summer represented a season-round offensive that was determined to find Natives in their villages. This approach spoke to Native defeat, and it clearly rested on something more than a triumph of military arms. Senior commanders, and their energetic seconds, offered the enemy no reprieve, leaving the target only two choices: reservations or eventual extermination.

This ultimatum was beyond the Army's power to enforce. Bottled up on reservations, the Natives on the Central Plains appeared pacified. However, peace was not the outcome, far from it. The Army's efforts merely pushed those Cheyenne not on the reservation northward and into the hands of the Sioux. The result was a militant concentration threatening the equilibrium just now coming into place. In the end, military success on the prairie led to more fighting. However, one way or another, Sherman had managed to open his coveted route westward, that great artery between the Platte and Arkansas Rivers. It took the far-ranging infiltration of civilians throughout the West to undo this success and force the military back into action on the plains.

When the east-west boundary endorsed by the general proved too restrictive to be effective, Sherman looked to ease his situation by deliberately facilitating settlement via indirect means. In 1862, after the Sioux had successfully repelled the Americans, Sherman's exasperation boiled over because of civilian mandates asking the Army to end Native disturbances but not act ruthlessly. He asked out loud, why not allow hunters to target the Native's means of existence? The general wrote: "I think it would be wise to invite all the sportsmen of England & America there this fall for a Grand Buffalo hunt, and make one grand sweep of them all."[19] He referred to the buffalo, but he just as well could have meant the Natives. Devastating Native settlements was one thing, destroying the very sustenance of the Natives another.

This statement in passing soon became made official policy. The ruthlessness of this war came mainly from results garnished by environmental engineering. The plains tribes relied on the buffalo to such an extent that exterminating the one became the key to vanquishing the other. The destruction of these herds by hunters advancing westward with the spread of the railroads went a long way to explain why the Sioux rapidly faced a bleak plight. Sherman could be complimented for this perceptive look into the future. When it came to buffalo, circumstance had been permanently adjusted to favor American expansion. Before 1870, Natives themselves had overhunted herds, horses competed for grazing land, and a severe drought radically altered the environment. Sherman inherited this arch, a fortuitous if now clearly sought-after end and one in the works for a number of years, at least since 1850, let alone after 1876. If settlement eliminated these beasts, Natives could not continue to exist. Correctly understanding the buffalo's vital role in sustaining the Plains cultures, the military made eroding these herds a top priority.[20]

To achieve this end, the U.S. Army took the first way of war to unprecedented levels when it opted for a clever escalation of the war on the plains by singling out the buffalo for destruction. That end already had overtaken

Natives to the south. There, as in the north, hunters targeted buffalo herds, and those Natives engaged in a last gasp effort to end that practice paid the price in the "Buffalo War" of 1874. With a decreasing source of food because of this slaughter, and an intermittent supply on the reservation, Natives faced starvation if they did not attack. At least, this is how the Natives saw the sit-

A gathering of Civil War generals, January 2, 1865. Left to right: Generals Wesley Merritt, Philip Sheridan, George Crook, James William Forsyth, and George Armstrong Custer (Library of Congress).

uation, and a large number bolted from the reservation. Their target was the hunters decimating the herds, and a number of these men were caught off-guard and killed.

Other hunters mounted a desperate defense against overwhelming odds and survived. The most famous stand was by two hunters and a handful of companions, holed up in a strongpoint consisting of a few wagons on a solitary farm. They withstood a siege lasting a number of days, inflicting at least 70 casualties including a large number of dead, eventually compelling the Natives to break off the attack. From the perspective of battle, the American victory was obvious. However, the telling insight of this engagement was not in the number killed alone, although this scenario repeated itself numerous times and enough of these successes underscored that Natives struggled to eliminate even very small numbers of settlers. The more alarming truism was that the civilian element wreaking the Native way of life could operate with near impunity, and when assisted by the intervention of soldiers, the combination was insurmountable. In this case, the Natives were forced back onto the reservation after five Army columns closed in on the Canadian, Washita, and Red Rivers, underscoring the futility of Native resistance. The Red River War ended in 1875.

The same occurred in the North as the Sioux eventually became the focus of a major military campaign as soldiers clashed with those Natives supporting a last-ditch defense of the Black Hills Mountains. Thus, another Plains war erupted as, once again, the U.S. military could not prevent civilians from entering Indian Country. The soldiers were then charged with protecting the civilians. Executing that duty ran into difficulties, the most famous example being Custer's defeat in June 1876 along the Little Bighorn River. However, Custer's demise underscored the challenge that the Americans faced in the Northern Plains. The expanse there suggested possibilities for resistance denied to tribes east of the Mississippi. Try as it might, the Army could not prevent the Natives from capitalizing on the open plains and merely melting away before its advance. The chance of avoiding conflict and thereby extending the war was genuine. This evasion continued to occur until salient circumstances again came into play and doomed any Native "last stand" in the North or elsewhere for that matter. In this regard, settlement compromised those Natives still at large in the West and prevented them from mounting an effective resistance. Indian Country was no more, and any notion of sovereignty increasingly gained meaning only within American declarations of reservations, a tenuous proposition in its own right.

When further inroads into Sioux territory became a priority, it was clear that settlers were the foremost tool of the U.S. Army's first way of war. As with Removal, a few voices understood this process of expansion west as ending with Native destruction and spoke out. Preachers and some dutiful bureaucrats managed to get President Grant's attention, resulting in his endorsement of a Peace Policy. It had been a startling turn around for a president who, when running for election, engaged in inflammatory rhetoric matching that of Sherman. He had declared himself a proponent of settlement and of the extermination of Natives if necessary in pursuing this end.[21] Now, with a chance to craft this policy, he fell into the familiar American ambiguity of defining relations with Natives by trying to advance ideals without obviously invalidating those ideals through the obliteration of a people. His critics, then and now, lamented the use of military force that continued even with the objective of a peace policy. By blaming soldiers, they too simplified the reality and ignored the civilian onslaught that had dictated the violence that so often defined this confrontation. These dissenters saw only ambiguity in purpose and execution: the constant fighting was an emblem of Army failures. However, Grant's policy had not endorsed a "Janus-faced" approach, as one critic at the time labeled it.[22] Rather, it accepted what had come before and what was to come as settlers pressed the Natives into areas where only conflict could result. In response to this reality, the president looked to safeguard what he could of Indian Country by endorsing reservations. In seeking to bring this war to a close in this manner, Grant authored a clever pronouncement that both ended the frontier and established a middle ground. Here was the triumph of the Peace Policy: a cause and effect no doubt callously embraced, but still advancing an effective policy.

Grant bowed before the inevitability of the unfolding economic process of settlement, something Sherman had accepted long ago. Even when forced to abide by the calls for peace and conciliation of Natives in the north in 1868 and 1869, Sherman contemplated the wave of settlement and the consequences for Natives that it entailed. Sherman wrote Grant, "The Chief use of the Peace Commission is to kill time which will do more to settle the Indians than anything we can do."[23] Ultimately, he expected the U.S. Army's weakness to be remedied by the tide of settlement sweeping the West. Sherman observed the grit of these overland travelers and the potential of railroads to increase the number of people heading westward and taming regions they might not have reached otherwise. Technology had unleashed a deadly foe.[24] Of these, the settlers were the most dangerous. The assumed innocence of their purpose (securing land) and their entitlement to it, that produced a never ending wave their increased size each year. After 1865, as Sherman directed the war in the West, Americans no longer feared for their survival, hoped for coexistence with Natives, or espoused the innocence supposedly undergirding Manifest Destiny. The drive westward amounted to the extermination of Natives, and while this aspect of Manifest Destiny was opposed by those calling for a Peace Policy, the combination underscored American ambivalence to the Native question and to that people's dire plight. In fact, their impending destruction was just as manifest as the near public-wide refusal to see this as a black mark on the American experiment. Americans had built a nation, and this success remained paramount in their minds.

End of the War

The quest to define the United States kept the consequences obscured from Americans in the intent if not in the results. The benevolent rationales of settlers excused the human cost of expansion, but the act now was a war for defining civilization across a continent, and the cost of failure in this war was cultural effacement. As it was, Americans could compliment themselves on including Natives in the new experience, a "compromise" all the more tangible given that Americans were shaping the economic bonanza that defined that emerging entity. Not surprisingly, conflict marred this effort, and the resultant wars begat more wars, so that not all that long after 1876, a secure frontier meant that Natives were shuttled onto reservations as the last refuge from which to assimilate into American society. Civilians were the main cog of an invasion so insidious as to deny this purpose, all the while serving at the tip of the spear to achieve this isolation, and this done in order to secure economic advancement for themselves. Soldiers had to follow the civilians, but the key to this success was a growing population of those identifying with the American cause, changing the complexion of settlement in the West. This onslaught left the Natives with no place to go and no way to survive other than on reservations. The war in the West underscored a long-term reality that aided American expansion and undermined Native resistance as settlers ensured the defeat of Indian Country. It was as impressive and unique an accomplishment as it was heartless, dangerously treading on the American sentiments of seeking Jefferson's Empire Liberty in the open expanse of the West.

8

Security Force Operations

Reservations and the "Last Indian Wars"

The irrational proved deadly. General Edward R.S. Canby did not believe the violence could go on, and he moved forward alone to meet the outlaw "Captain Jack" of the Modoc. Canby knew he had the presence of America at his side; the pointlessness of continued Native resistance was so pronounced that there could only be a negotiated settlement of surrender. Canby's rational world did not last the hour. When they met to discuss peace, Captain Jack drew a revolver and shot Canby in the chest. As Canby staggered away, the Modoc dragged him down and finished him off. It was a senseless death from only the American point of view. For these Natives, violent acts leading to unsure ends had defined their existence for so long that this killing merely blended into the hard-to-fathom depths of their own despair. In this way, the Modocs had in fact met Canby halfway; the Natives were as tired as Canby was of violent acts but accepted them as a routine part of existence.

Native surrenders proved a coveted commodity to Americans. Peace was to enshrine the final acts of military brawn, a recompense for a tortuous path leading to the extinction of Native martial resistance. Americans got what they wanted in these final clashes. Chief Joseph of the Nez Perce surrendered a portion of his tiny band just short of the Canadian border, an admission of the Native futility of trying to escape American clutches. However, the military exploit of Chief Joseph's surrender grated against the passing of an era already at hand, stopping this last spasm of defiance a reminder of what had come before. Even harder to see was the measure of the triumph in the surrender of Geronimo, the famed Apache who had waged a seemingly solo fight in the Southwestern desert. This desperate soul achieved recognition for a resistance so out of place that Geronimo appeared to be a criminal bent on a violent path.

Taken together, these final figures impressed a violent resistance so indelibly on the American consciousness that this memory deprived them of a sense of victory. However, the vanquished remained defiant only in the nostalgia of Americans for on the ground, Natives had capitulated. These last Plains Wars came about as nothing more than fate and tragedy, depending on where one stood. All those involved assessed the results and turned away from the story it told, that of a war rhyming in purpose if not always in the means. To understand what had happened, new truths were needed and would be found by facing the totality of American-Native interaction as resting on military successes rooted in a civilian acceptance of peace. Yet, with Natives still present on the U.S. landscape, the long war of contact had produced a middle ground after all, even if Americans refused to recognize this outcome as success.

Reservations

From 1876 to 1890, the Americans overcame the last vestiges of Native military resistance in a series of clashes they labeled "wars." When finished, Natives accepted reservations at last. They had no choice. Facing defeat, only desperate flight or submission remained: most chose submission. In this final period of time, military force became imperative in achieving this result. However, it was the way that force was dispensed that marked the difference from earlier times. Gone was any spirit of adventure and exploration. Rather, the federal government had to solve a problem after being pushed to do so by its citizens, who favored both the extermination and protection of Natives. The U.S. military struggled to find its role in this stage of the conflict and it did so as the need to end the violence became paramount. It also succeeded, and the Army completed its victory with the attack at Wounded Knee in 1890. However, the hollow nature of this battlefield success and its tragedy laid bare the truth that the consolidation of the entire land mass had become the aim, and Natives had no place in this completed nation other than on reservations. This permanent frontier was not genocide more than it was the fruition of the Peace Policy, though the method of enforcement was no less ferocious as what might be termed "security force operations" ended the last spasms of resistance.

The plains tribes remained the final obstacle to American expansion. By 1868, the last formidable Native people, the Sioux, signed the Treaty of Fort Laramie, committing themselves, as other tribes had done, to a reservation, which in effect sectioned off portions of their former expanse of land.

Proponents of the Peace Policy initiated within the Grant Administration used this treaty to advance a program that would ensure federal protection of the Natives in order to then facilitate their successful assimilation into American culture. In this view, the Natives in the Northern Plains would take their place as farmers and eliminate any need for independent sovereignty. The treaty and program going forward after 1869 were not advocating a Native nationhood but were advancing a holding action designed to make Americans feel better about the fate of the "original occupants" of the country, as Grant referred to Natives in his first inaugural address. "Proper treatment" would result in their "civilization" and eventual "citizenship," Grant declared.[1] In effect, the U.S. government was to bestowe to the northern tribes the same gift of sanctuary as had come to the five great civilized tribes of the south, now supposedly living a blissful existence in the Indian Territory.

U.S. authorities viewed the Treaty of Fort Laramie as a palpable timetable for assimilation that would disintegrate the guarantee of reservations. Although exaggerating the benevolence extended to those tribes now confined to the Indian Territory, members of the Peace Commission presiding over this outcome could tell themselves they had indeed offered a solution to the latest round of trouble with Natives. The Sioux could count themselves lucky that removal was not in the treaty. They remained in place as long as they ceased attacking settlers. Here was a moment of triumph, thwarting American expansion west. It stemmed from championing resistance to outside threats by men such as Red Cloud, Sitting Bull, and Crazy Horse, and from the Sioux's ability to maintain internal cohesion despite the always present tribal factionalism. The Sioux had earned their place on the prairie due to more than their war-like disposition. A Sioux identity was such that no unity movement preceded the call to arms. Militant action was the norm.[2]

For this reason, in the Treaty of Fort Laramie, the Sioux did not admit defeat, as had been the case when American authorities had dictated terms to those tribes east of the Mississippi. Rebuffed by Red Cloud's diplomacy, checked militarily by Sioux warriors successfully isolating the forts along the passageways west, and to the north, the United States made peace as a result of Red Cloud's "guerrilla war." The U.S. government destroyed its forts along the Bozeman Trail in 1868, accentuating an apparent Sioux victory.[3] In other words, the Sioux believed they had rebuffed an invasion and that the treaty suggested an equitable exchange leading to American acceptance of Sioux territorial boundaries. Subsequent American actions made their agreement with the Sioux mean otherwise.[4]

Reservations demonstrated to what extent Americans had grown impatient with treaties as an instrument of governing Native affairs. Those charged with increasingly military actions found themselves too circumscribed by the legalism inherent in these previous agreements. With the demise of Indian Country, the treaties no longer matched the realties on the ground. Since Native land could not be made solvent, there would be no more guarantees defining their land. Instead, enforcement of the reservation system became the objective. As a result, the final Army operations against Native Americans sought to confine them to reservations. However, dictating this new objective nevertheless raised the old ambiguity of understanding Natives as either representing a sovereign state or a dependent nation. Natives still found themselves a hunted minority, denied protections inherent in citizenship, all the while being asked to accept the suzerainty of their new nation, the United States. In sum, tribes found themselves waging a desperate, largely futile struggle against a determined foe claiming them as part of the nation but seeking their removal.

With reservations, a strong dependency also evolved. Natives now were completely at the mercy of the Americans, needing food, shelter, and protection, but getting little of any of these things. Here would be the U.S. military's most ignominious contribution to the fate of Natives. Contractors failed to deliver supplies or food, and exploitation when possible occurred, too often with Army complicity. This lapse meant little protection was provided as well. When aid failed to arrive, or arrived in insufficient quantities, the plight of those on reservations became bleak. A few individuals sounded warnings of this dangerous dependency and the discrediting of U.S. honor. It was "the legalized murder of a whole nation ... expensive, vicious, inhumane," a description coming from mountain man Tom Fitzpatrick, one charged with helping to implement the policy in the early 1850s.[5] No one listened, and the results thereafter hardly refuted this dire forecast. The San Carlos reservation in southeastern Arizona suffered from shortages, but also from malaria outbreaks that killed many Apache. The Navajo faced a similar fate. Removed to Bosque Redondo, a barren valley in eastern New Mexico, their condition became so bleak that U.S. government officials relented and allowed these people to return to their mountain homelands and to a reservation there.

These failures were a sad cap to a more noble effort of a military guarantee protecting the reservations. The Sioux were the latest test case. Many crafting the reservation policy hoped that the ability of these people to become American would set a new measure of success. Also, many in the U.S. military tried to make the reservation system work in order to save something of this race before the onslaught of settlement eliminated it. Native obliteration was a real possibility after Custer's defeat. The human tide heading west easily overcame this setback, making clear the doom facing the Sioux after 1876. Americans did maintain the reservations in the North, but the Sioux could no longer claim victory, as they had in 1868. Now, they endured a colonial overseer. Rather than their transformation and a symbol of something new, the Sioux became a people representing a constant, an abusive middle ground as it always had been, something eventually taken from them leaving Natives bereft of their vitality while paving the way for a new entity— the United States.[6]

The trouble with the contrived fiction of assimilation, no matter how defined, was that it fell short in its intellectual construct and also its practical reality. The reservation system made this failure plain. That solution was to be a compromise, although its promise of providing a space for Natives to change and then enter the newly constructed American nation was simply an updated version of Removal. The areas selected were poor in soil quality, refuting the aim of allowing Natives to learn farming and become like Americans. Additionally, the restricted size of reservations meant the plains tribes had to give up roaming and hunting across the prairie, a profound cultural shift to say the least and one underscoring the psychological toll of confinement. Hence, leaving the reservation frequently became a highly desired and, in some respects, a necessary course of action to alleviate mental and physical destitution. However, Americans considered all Natives "off the reservation" to be hostile and therefore dangerous. Soon, Americans identified only "good" and "bad" Indians, those who chose reservation life being the "good." Whatever the mindset, the reservation policy was intended to be one of "out of sight, out of mind." Removal had come to pass after all, even in the far west as government officials looked to use reservations to civilize the Natives.

The U.S. Army could be excused from indulging in the simple motive of merely facilitating conquest by ensuring that Natives remained on reservations. Some benevolence accompanied their efforts. Forts in the West, as before, attracted Natives interested in trade and resupply. A number of Natives remained voluntarily near forts. In this way, the Army could protect Natives from aggressive settlers as much as it protected settlers from violence inflicted by Natives. However, the haphazard nature of this relationship ensured periodic outbreaks of violence producing government efforts to formalize the reservation system. The look toward a permanent Indian frontier had given way to allowing only pockets of Natives throughout the West, meaning no frontier was to exist at all. The final confrontations with Natives in the Plains Region underscored how the Army reaped the benefit of the isolation of the Natives and demonstrated the futility of further fighting. That came nonetheless as the Army overcame the last Native resistance mounted in the rugged expanse of the northern Pacific Coast, on the Northern Plains, and to the south in the Arizona Territory. The outcome was hardly in doubt given the demographic advantage the United States enjoyed over its rivals.

The Modoc War

The Modoc tribe of California was fortunate to have survived that states extremely punitive response to its Native problem. By the 1870s, some 20 years after the gold rush, Natives had either been destroyed or seemingly acquiesced to American rule due to a combination of disease and conflict with settlers. More adept tribes attempted assimilation. This effort floundered for usually similar reasons: a flood of alcohol, subservient working conditions, and a general acceptance of a loss of Native ways, best symbolized by a corruption of Native languages, now including English, and by the adoption of American style clothing. All told, the changes represented a badge of submission to American culture. However, no such concessions impeded both local and federal government efforts to relegate Natives to remote areas, the much-hailed reservations. This confinement was all the easier to achieve given the reduced numbers of Natives. The Modoc tribe, located in what is now northern California, had suffered accordingly, a depopulation all the more devastating because the tribe had never been large, a high estimate totaling maybe some 1,000 members. The remainder of the tribe appeared content to live on the margins of American society, but this compliance changed drastically in 1871, when one Modoc named Captain Jack killed a shaman from a rival tribe after that man failed to heal his daughter. American officials responded to Native protests and ordered his arrest. Enforcement proved impossible, and a year later Jack was not only still at large, but also demanded a new reservation for his people in his homelands near the California-Oregon border. Reservation existence had driven more than a few Natives to desperate acts, so as Jack prepared to leave and claim the rights to the tribe's old hunting lands, over 300 Modocs joined him. The Army set off in pursuit, worried about civilian reactions and the violence that those responses might entail; the Army could do better. However, the very act of 38 soldiers led by a captain attempting to apprehend the now renegade Modocs ushered in a war at the end of November 1872. It was to be the most expensive Indian war in lives and money.[7]

The Modocs rebuffed Captain Jackson's patrol, killing or wounding eight of his small command. After this engagement, the Natives fled and killed fourteen settlers that they happened to encounter. However, the pursuit and the clashes with settlers underscored the hopelessness of the band's situation.

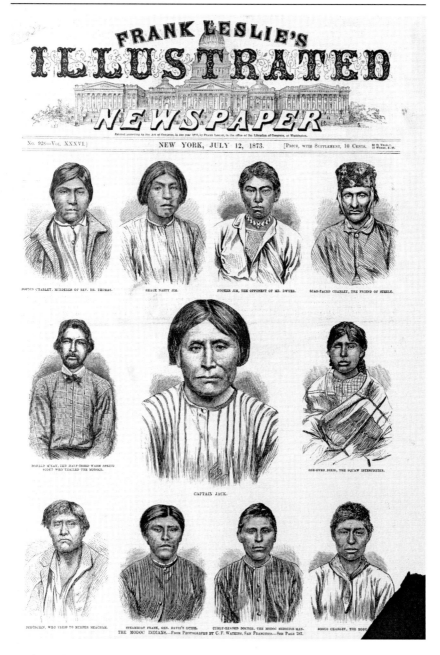

Modoc Indians, as seen on the cover of *Frank Leslie's Illustrated Newspaper*, July 12, 1873. Left to right, top row to bottom row: Boston Charley, Shack Nasty Jim, Hooker Jim, Scar-Faced Charley, Donald M'Kay, Captain Jack, One-Eyed Dixie, Schonchin, Steamboat Frank, Curly-Headed Doctor, Bogus Charley (Library of Congress).

Its resistance was doomed. The Modocs with Captain Jack understood this as well and quickly retreated to a mountainous stronghold located on the south shore of Tule Lake in the northern mountains of California, an area off the reservation but in the former home territory of this tribe. Dominated by an extensive lava bed, the sharp rocks and rugged terrain made defense easy. Here the Army found Captain Jack and some 165 men, women, and children in mid–January 1873. A few probing attacks that month accomplished nothing, and the Army in effect laid siege to the position given the difficulty of assaulting the caves and hideouts.

Modoc attacks on civilians had helped propel this outbreak of violence to a military clash, and so too did the death of the highest-ranking American officer felled during the entire period of time of the wars against the Natives. General Canby arrived to take command of the increasing military force attempting to stop the Modoc. Canby walked to his death when he rendezvoused with Captain Jack and a few of his companions on April 11, 1873. During this parley, Captain Jack shot Canby at point blank range. Mortally wounded, that officer struggled to his feet and staggered away. Another Modoc shot him again, and Captain Jack then pounced on Canby and stabbed him in the throat. Canby, brave to the last, had said goodbye to his wife in a letter he penned that morning, just in case things went wrong later in the day. His previous experience with Native resistance, the Seminole wars and Removal, had not induced him to lower his guard more than it had inured him to the conflict: he had seen much war during his service, and he wanted to end Modoc resistance as bloodlessly as possible. Canby jumped at the chance to negotiate a cease fire even if to do so meant he had to meet with the Natives while out of reach of his men, as the Modocs demanded. In his estimation, it was worth the risk. By doing so, Canby may well be remembered as the officer presiding over the final resistance of this long conflict. When Captain Jack and his companions drew their guns and fired, Canby fell and could not be reached by his soldiers until his clothes were stripped off and his killers had vanished. Instead of immortality for ending the violence, Canby drew attention to a small war serving as a back drop to the larger war. Armed Native American resistance was coming to an end, as Canby sensed, but not before the Modocs and some other tribes attempted a final stand that could accomplish nothing but underscore the doomed status of Natives in a land now controlled by Americans.

The Modocs killed another man and grievously wounded a third belonging to the negotiating party, and then the Natives fled back into their stronghold. Almost simultaneously, a few Modocs under the shaman Curley Headed Doctor, fired on another party they had coaxed from cover. Another soldier died. Stunned by these acts of treachery and the sheer audacity of the attacks, and given the temporary confusion over who was in charge, the Army pressed forward but stopped after confirming the Natives were back in their stronghold. As the Army had learned in January, the rough terrain made any approach difficult in terms of simply traversing the ground, but also tended to funnel advancing soldiers onto natural strong points. Having been reinforced with artillery in the succeeding months, the guns were to provide covering fire and make an advance feasible with few casualties. An attack unfolded on April 14, three days after Canby's death. Calls to "exterminate" the Modocs came from Sherman, managing the war from afar, and in the bravado of the commander in place at the lava beds, Colonel Alvan Gillem.[8] Over the next few days, the Army pressed the action at a very slow pace, methodically enough to come close to the Native positions. However, the cordon was not complete and when short of water, the Modocs abandoned the stronghold and easily slipped away.

This escape pointed to the resourcefulness of these Natives to prolong this struggle by taking refuge in the lava beds endemic to the area. This advantage on the defense did not explain why just a few shots coming from a cave or bluff scattered the Army units now assembled to overcome the enemy. The most recent American advance suffered this fate. When it was determined that the fugitives had fled the stronghold, a cautious pursuit ensued. A conglomeration of Regulars and militia again moved slowly into the lava beds looking for Natives. Captain Jack stymied this attack as well with a scattered volley that first held the attackers in place and then chased them from the scene. In the confusion, the Modoc isolated a contingent of 24 soldiers under Captain Evan Thomas, all but wiping them out. The Natives escaped without loss from this debacle, so the campaign wore on.

The repulse of this Army detachment was not enough to bring Captain Jack and the Modoc victory; nothing could do so. The Americans remained in place, and when the defenders tried a similar ambush, they were discovered by soldiers who at last held their ground. In fact, a Native was finally killed, provoking a crisis for the Modoc. Medicine man Curley Headed Doctor had assured his comrades that they could not be harmed. American tepidness almost fulfilled the prophecy—the soldier's early advances the Modoc repelled without losing a man. In fact, the Modocs did not suffer any men wounded or killed until months into the conflict. The low tally of Natives killed was fortunate, since even one man killed shattered the resistance given that death dispelled the aura of the shaman's power. The irony was that, even in disgrace, if not defeat, Americans could not lose this war nor could the Natives win it. The failed "medicine" mattered less than did the absurdity of the resistance to begin with. The end was inevitable.

That came with one last standoff as Natives clung to yet another rugged position where they were trapped. Captain Jack finally surrendered on June 1, 1873, the Modocs exhausted by their six months of futile resistance. His demise underscored the full meaning of the war, more than did the thirty or so Americans he had killed and the two Natives who had died in the campaign. When added to the handful of civilians unfortunate enough to be killed, this constituted the casualties of this war. The duration of the resistance cast a certain heroic light on the defenders and, in turn, led to a better understanding of this clash as one precipitated by the Americans enforcing life on the reservation. Captain Jack echoed this sentiment when he stood trial and explained why he had killed General Canby: "I see no crime in my heart although I killed Canby.... You White people have driven me from mountain to mountain, from valley to valley."[9] In this context, the just cause of the Natives could be seen, but not when those prosecuting the Modocs decried their resistance as a war. Their act of defiance, and its criminality, was an attack on the United States as a whole, not individual citizens of the nation. As such, no pardon could be issued, only a surrender accepted. Execution followed on October 3, 1873. Four Natives were hanged for having started this struggle, among them Captain Jack. The others the Army declared prisoners of war, rebuffing an attempt by civilian authorities to gain custody and hold more trials. The Army then removed 150 Modocs to the Indian Territory. The transplantation of this group became another example of victory in the Plains war. It was more than this. Isolation had again rendered resistance pointless, yet violence came nonetheless. In a way, these criminals got what they deserved. At the same time, this beleaguered rabble symbolized what the Natives had become, hunted men in their home land and ones no longer able to live by their own rules.

Chief Joseph

The Modoc War remained an epitaph to the American resolve to finish the Indian Wars, producing these final, tragic campaigns. However, the height of this determination rose clearly to the surface on the Northwestern Plains. Here, a peaceful tribe, the Nez Perce, waged an epic struggle to survive in the summer of 1877, as approximately 800 Natives refused to relocate to a reservation and instead headed for Canada. Soon, several thousand U.S. troops were on their trail looking to prevent this escape. The pursuit climaxed in some four months with a multitude of compliments by these giving chase. The Natives had conducted themselves with hitherto unseen restraint along the hundreds of miles they traversed so that few civilians were harmed even as the Nez Perce situation became desperate. These Natives also had executed a fighting retreat of admirable proportion in military terms. Sherman, not one sympathetic to Natives, praised their courage and martial skill stating, "The Indians throughout displayed a courage and skill that elicited universal praise" in terms of military performance. Local observers complimented the Natives for waging war and observing a high standard of morality. A "frontier newspaper" proclaimed that the Natives involved in this struggle fought according to "the highest characteristics recognized by civilized nations."[10] It was recognition as a badge of honor bestowed on a foe hunted to near extinction. The Nez Perce now represented the entire fate of Native Americans. However, the compliments hid the hopelessness of the quest of flight, albeit because of a surprising determination by Americans to prevent these Natives from leaving U.S. territory.

What underscored the tragedy of this confrontation was that the Nez Perce had enjoyed friendly relations with Americans reaching back to the Lewis and Clark expedition.[11] Some Christianity surfaced in the tribe in the mid–1830s, but it primarily reinforced divisions among these people. When Americans laid territorial demands at their feet in the 1850s, the Native response was confused and provoked crisis leading to a stringent treaty imposed upon them. By 1876, the Nez Perce were slated for removal entirely, the already punitive Treaty of 1855 and then that of 1863 swept aside and the U.S. government preparing to send them to a reservation far away from their homeland. A rush to violence and therefore war was typical in American-Native encounters, and this was no exception. Increasing numbers of settlers in the area at times clashed with and killed Natives. These acts went unpunished by local authorities. Subsequent Native retaliations were deemed criminal by government authorities and more evidence of the need to remove these people. This standoff climaxed in June 1877, when intoxicated warriors lashed out at those around them and killed 15 settlers in two days. Thus, a handful of incidents produced a war in the summer of 1877, as a small number of Nez Perce refused sanctuary on a reservation and tried to flee American control altogether by reaching Canada.

As a result, a year after Custer's demise, another great struggle unfolded on the plains. Led by Chief Joseph, the small number of Nez Perce possessed excellent mobility, and this asset prevented easy detection and capture. Moreover, that community showed in flight the ability to maintain skirmish lines, protect its women and children, and feed and resupply itself. Yet, Joseph was only in nominal control, and he was the last surviving chief when the end came. American adulation of their ability to capture these intrepid Natives concentrated on Joseph, but most resistance was spontaneously effective. In fact, the Natives were surprised by their pursuers too often, revealing a lack of command. When something more was needed, another Nez Perce, Looking Glass, not Joseph, led the defense. The result was an epic retreat impeded by a relentless Army in pursuit. The larger referendum was asking why Americans would go to such lengths simply to prevent this Native exodus.

The natural discipline of this small group meant the first efforts at capture by the military failed. General Oliver Otis Howard, the same officer who had negotiated with Cochise, sent a few soldiers to capture the Nez Perce, but these efforts met defeat. So the Army went into action. Initially, Captain David Perry, with 75 soldiers of the First Cavalry, attacked the tribe. He surprised the Nez Perce in White Bird Canyon, where an equal number of warriors demonstrated excellent marksmanship and an above-average sense of tactics. They used enfilade fire to bloody Perry's ranks and he was repulsed with the loss of 25 men. The Army, conversely, showed none of these skills and, in fact, demonstrated such poor discipline as to bring that unit ill repute. This was a bad defeat, and one Howard made worse by sending another detachment to apprehend a small group of Natives under Looking Glass. This chief was seeking neutrality, but he joined Joseph in flight after troopers opened fire on his village. By the end of June, Howard had not only failed to stymie the violence, but he had actually fanned its flames. Howard asked for and received more troops, bringing his total to 400, but he soon faced a larger number of hostiles, some 300 fighting men and 500 women and children.

The Natives now had a chance to withdraw, and Howard had to pursue an emboldened foe. Another engagement unfolded much as had the previous encounter with Perry. Howard sent his men forward into a small

Chief Joseph of the Nez Perce (Library of Congress).

canyon near the Clearwater River. The warriors dispersed, ringed the advancing troopers with fire, and mounted another spirited defense even withstanding Howard's artillery. A timely reinforcement allowed Howard to flank the Natives and expel them from their defensive positions. However, Howard had suffered another 13 dead, and this loss checked his advance. With this reprieve, the Nez Perce fled north probably after suffering no more than four killed. The Battle of the Clearwater had been another Native success.

Howard had fumbled badly, and the apparent near capture of the fugitives only added to the Army's determination not to allow the Nez Perce to escape. However, Howard tarried for two weeks along the Clearwater, causing senior leadership to question if he was the right man to complete the job. Fortunately for the Army, these Natives did not always travel at full speed, being content to make the journey at a rate that conserved the strength of women and children and also that of the pony herds with them. They also believed the military would not follow a retreating, insignificant number of Natives. Their calculation was erroneous. The Army redoubled its efforts. As the Nez Perce headed northward, another Army detachment of 100 men under Colonel John Gibbon surprised their camp. As before, the results were the same. Mounting a haphazard but spirited defense, they quickly blunted the attack, killing 30 men and wounding another 30. It was a pitched battle, and one that cost the Natives as many casualties including a number of women and children. The parity of losses left the Nez Perce in the untenable situation of facing threats from multiple directions and of not being able to prevent the attacks. The Army had its own troubles. Marching with raw recruits in its ranks, it displayed a mediocrity in not being able to capitalize on a surprised, vulnerable foe. This round of American-Native confrontation was clearly taking on a tone of folly due to the ferocity of both combatants and the casualties sustained as a result.

The greatest travesty came when the Natives entered the Montana territory. The Nez Perce followed a predictable trail, and Howard acted to cut them off. He failed to do so, and the Nez Perce raided his camp in a surprise attack and made good their escape into the vicinity of present day Yellowstone National Park. After this clash at Camas Meadows costing Howard one dead and seven wounded, he stopped again, pleading his case to his superiors that his command was worn out and could only hold their positions. Sherman ordered Howard forward, and Sherman ordered more soldiers to the region. The Nez Perce were not to make it to Canada. The pursuit continued.

As it turned out, the Army succeeded in stopping the Nez Perce just short of the international border. Colonel Nelson A. Miles, a soldier eager to make a name as an Indian fighter, blocked the escape route with 400 men.

With Howard still in pursuit, the Nez Perce were trapped at Bear Paw pass only 40 miles from their destination. Miles' initial rush cost him 22 dead and 38 wounded, but he had sprung the trap. Thus, the long chase was nearing an end. After a five day standoff, Joseph surrendered 400 Nez Perce in the first days of October, famously declaring, "Hear me, my chiefs.... I will fight no more forever."[12] The remainder, maybe 100 warriors and two hundred women and children, did make it to Canada.

Here was another U.S. triumph and Miles joined those paying tribute to his enemy and to Chief Joseph. Miles said, "The Nez Perce are the boldest men I have ever encountered, and Chief Joseph is a man of more sagacity and intelligence than any Indian I have ever met."[13] However, the flattery was again off the mark. For one thing, Miles sought recognition for his role in the chase, and extolling the virtues of his enemy served this end. For another, if epic in scope, the retreat appeared less flattering to those involved when the final costs were measured. Since a number of Nez Perce did make it to Canada, the American victory was less than complete. The focus on Joseph was all the more telling in this respect. He was a convenient symbol of the resistance.[14] Yet Looking Glass, given his military abilities, was in many ways the key leader. Even the continued adulation of Joseph by his pursuers, a chorus that grew in retrospect as that man argued for his people to return to Idaho, and eventually succeeded in achieving this end, could not hide the more sobering dimensions of this campaign.[15] The U.S. Army lost just over 100 dead, the Nez Perce something close to that number. The estimated 1,170 miles Howard's command traversed underscored how frequently his men fumbled repeated chances to capture the Nez Perce. Neither could these Natives claim even a moral victory for having put up a good fight: those who made it to Canada soon grew dissatisfied with life there, and they returned to the United States and to a reservation. Heroic in the act, the Nez Perce fate was less so since it primarily underscored the lengths to which the U.S. military was charged to go, and was willing to go, to end the last vestiges of Native resistance.[16]

Geronimo

This resolve meant was that there would be no Indian Country. Only confinement on a reservation would do. Therefore, this supposedly humane gesture became a punitive response, with the Army in the lead during the closing years of the American war against Natives. The soldiers proved up to the task, and these final wars became a grim story of pursuit and engagement.

In this reality, any Native off the reservation was considered hostile and merited killing.

Geronimo tested the American resolve in this respect. His small band of Apaches evaded capture on several occasions; his just as frequent surrenders appeared to be mere pauses until his next challenge to life on the reservation. His motives for extending a war that was all but over underscored the desperate acts of Natives at this time, and the just as desperate U.S. doggedness to end this conflict once and for all. Geronimo was the key figure in the final stages of this long war as he led a mere handful of men, women, and children who drew several thousand U.S. soldiers in pursuit to try and seal the border with Mexico and end his forays. The U.S. Army accomplished this task only after much trial and error.

Geronimo was not a chief; he was only a skilled warrior who had survived a great number of perilous events in his life. In the 1880s, Geronimo was old enough to have been raised at the tail end of Apache dominance in the region, and therefore he remembered Apache existence as blissful. Roaming the southwest desert, life was hard but rewarding in terms of distinguishing one's character; only the strong survived there, and the Apache were the strongest. Mexicans and Americans challenged this outlook, naturally, and Geronimo appeared content to vent his fury on Mexicans. This was all the more so when a Mexican detachment of soldiers struck his camp and killed his wife and child. His Apache name was Goyahkla, or "One Who Yawns." The Mexicans called out Geronimo when confronting him in battle and did so often enough that the Apache adopted this as their war cry. These confrontations were so frequent that the name soon stuck to one man.[17]

Geronimo's lifelong vendetta directed southward soon included the Americans once it became clear after 1865 that here was a new and more far reaching challenge to Apache existence. However, the violence he participated in during the five years from 1881–1886 appeared a desperate lashing out at both enemies, and in no measured way. It may have been the last Indian War, and chronologically it was, but it was anti-climactic in the extreme in terms of deciding who was winning this war. The Americans, and to a lesser extent the Mexicans, had triumphed, and Geronimo's struggle could do no more than remind his followers (and himself no doubt) of what had been lost. This motive to resist spoke to inevitable defeat, a poor reason to go to war.

The violence that ensued at this time only punctuated Geronimo's now discredited existence. Passing time on the reservation was a daily humiliation in terms of abandoning the roaming Apache way of life. The indolence his detractors accused him of when he lived on the reservation, if true, also transgressed on Apache values of stolid hardship and endurance. Geronimo had

Geronimo, Apache warrior, before the surrender to Gen. Crook in March 1886
(Library of Congress).

excelled in these characteristics. As a younger warrior, he consistently exhibited bravery in battle and could claim a number of kills. When training youthful warriors, he inured them to hardship by forcing them into cold water and then to exit and remain motionless for a long period of time, a treatment he had no doubt endured himself. But, at the same time, he appeared inconsistently cruel, such as when he allowed his men to torture settlers taken in his 1881 flight from the reservation. Such harsh acts lent credence to the efforts of the American authorities to capture him and execute him, but he cared little. His own resolve may have been a fatalism dictating his actions, but if so, his behavior was too erratic even for his own people. He led these final acts of desperation primarily because no other leaders were left, not because those sharing his grievances trusted his judgment.[18] This shortcoming was all the more apparent because of his successes as a warrior. Geronimo was, after all, the ultimate symbol of Apache resistance: futility, desperation, violence, and oblivion.[19] Now, Geronimo emerged as a leader of a time passed, and he appeared unwilling to face this truth. However, this man survived these final wars and, in so doing, faced exile from his beloved country and did so as a lackey of the Americans. Geronimo became an exhibition as a war trophy and novelty of a bygone era, one more example of tamed Native ferociousness and a symbol of their defeat. This great humiliation he apparently accepted and carried to his death in 1909.

The Apache found reservation life at San Carlos in Arizona objectionable, spurring their discontent, but it is hard to say this was the main reason why some 200 Chiricahuas left the enclave in September 1881. Geronimo at this time was part of a band that reunited the last great Apache leaders. These included Juh (perhaps the best tactician among them), Natchez, and Chato. Holding off pursuing soldiers, they fled south into Mexican territory and to the familiar ground of the Sierra Madre Mountains. There they met Nana and the survivors of Victorio's band, who had also fled the reservation. However, the objective, again, was not to win a war but merely not to surrender or to accept life on the reservation: better to die a great death in battle than to accept their blighted existence. The scope of those so determined was limited. In fact, Geronimo's band could not fathom its own small numbers, and after bolting from the reservation, it returned to that place and forced a great many Apache under another leader of distinction, Loco, to leave the reservation and join them in April 1882. This act revealed that not all Apache longed to return to life as it once was: that even the daily hardships on the reservation were preferable to living the nostalgic life of what had been. This was all the more so given how the U.S. Army acted to end the Apache violence in the area. When a large number of Apache joined the soldiers in pursuing their people, this betrayal or acceptance further eroded legends of Apache warriors at home in the desert determined to live as a free people.

Native scouts and a large number of soldiers were just two ingredients needed to capture Geronimo and the others and end this latest round of Apache violence. The third was the return of the renowned Indian fighter George Crook in July 1882. Crook had achieved some results after almost four years of campaigning in the southwest by forcing the Tonto Apache to the reservation. While he considered his success incomplete because he never had the chance to pursue Cochise, and because that man remained defiant, Crook had ended his time in the southwest with distinction. This praise received a check in 1876, since Crook participated in the campaign that led to Custer's death, and Crook had in fact failed to win any significant acclaim against the Sioux. In many ways he carried his own desperation to succeed with him to San Carlos. This drive explained his more than liberal interpretation of the agreement between Mexico and the United States to wage this war against the Apache. As Apache violence increased, resulting in at least thirty dead Americans, General Crook went south and pursued Geronimo far into Mexican territory.

Crook captured Geronimo, and he bragged he did so by mimicking Native tactics. The general again deviated from conventional Army practices by discarding baggage trains and using pack mules, forcing his men to match the arduous pace of the Apache, and, when this proved nearly impossible given that few soldiers could physically endure the strain, employing armed parties consisting almost entirely of Apache. These acts mattered most in wearing down Geronimo's will to resist, and the constant pursuit forced him to discuss terms of surrender. However, first Geronimo opted for one more offensive, launching raids against Mexicans and Americans before agreeing to return to the United States and life on a reservation. Chato raided north back into American territory, and in just a two-week period of time, he managed to kill 26 more citizens. Neither the militia nor soldiers sent to stop him saw a single Apache, let alone eliminated one. Geronimo led another war party south and exacted his usual vengeance against Mexicans. Panic ensued on both sides of the border due to the temerity of the attacks and the clear inability of the military of either nation to end the Apache threat. The termination of the violence again appeared to rest entirely on the Apache tiring of the fighting.

Crook acted decisively. In May 1883, after consulting with Mexican officials, he moved his strike force of almost 200 Native scouts and only 45 troopers back into Mexican territory. Crook allowed the scouts to race ahead of the soldiers who were slowing the pace. A scout who the troopers called Peaches because of his fair complexion and who recently had defected from

Chato's raiding party led the way. In a few weeks, Crook's force surprised Geronimo's party in its mountain stronghold. Shocked by their discovery and that it came at the hands of other Apache, 121 of his company surrendered immediately. Soon, the number swelled to over 200. Crook had delivered a telling blow, certainly, but perhaps more significant in its larger parameters. Crook demonstrated he was willing to disregard the border and chase Geronimo into the Apache sanctuary of the Sierra Madre that had sheltered them for hundreds of years. This reality defeated Geronimo, the elimination of the division between Mexico and the United States, at least in terms of military exigency, registering a loss of freedom of movement that inflicted a psychological wound on this hunted man from which he did not recover. Leaving Natives with no place to go was the same ill impacting Chief Joseph, a realization that the Americans had curtailed a way of life of a people, not just the few individuals now paying that price. The U.S. military may have executed the blow, but the result came from settlers that now reached across all of Apache land. Geronimo could never kill enough of either Mexicans or Americans to alter this clear reality.

Once seeing Crook in the Sierra Madre stronghold, Geronimo and other Apache sought terms. After a weeklong parley with Crook, Geronimo and most of the band agreed to surrender. Geronimo, however, insisted he had to remain to collect the rest of his party. Crook headed north with some 275 women and children and 50 warriors, leaving perhaps another 200 Apache— mostly warriors—at large. The majority of these bands trickled back to the reservation in succeeding months. Only in March 1884, over nine months later, did Geronimo make good on his promise to cease fighting and arrive at the San Carlos reservation with 15 men and 70 women and children. When he did so, he brought a souvenir from Mexico, a herd of cattle totaling over 300. It was an act of defiance all while submitting to American authority. Still, Crook accepted accolades for having captured the now most infamous Apache in the southwest and having done so by having that warrior surrender himself. It was a tremendous accomplishment.

Geronimo returned to the reservation only to leave once again in May 1885. This time he argued that his life had been threatened, whether by other Apaches or Americans is not clear. It was not clear if his life had been threatened.[20] No matter, Geronimo and 42 men and 92 women and children headed south to Mexico. One warrior, Chihuahua, soon clashed with Geronimo for manipulating him into leaving the reservation. Chihuahua tarried along the border, perhaps looking to return peacefully to the reservation. An Army detachment assaulted his position ending this hope.[21] The familiar pattern of raiding north and south soon reappeared. Twelve warriors embarked on a rampage that in New Mexico and Arizona left 38 dead in four weeks; Army units failed to engage them. Crook sent a trusted man, Captain Emmet Crawford, at the head of a number of scouts, and these men chased Geronimo in Mexico. Once again, Apache strongholds fell before Apache scouts and a few Regulars. Only Crawford's death allowed Geronimo to remain at large. That soldier was killed when a Mexican detachment fired on his position, and he exposed himself to call off their fire. The hunt collapsed in the wake of the captain's death, but even Geronimo grew tired of the struggle. He requested a meeting with Crook who traveled 12 miles south of the border to negotiate another surrender. Geronimo agreed to return to the reservation and to serve a brief prison sentence. After talking with Crook, Geronimo and a handful of others repudiated their surrender terms and fled into the mountains. This blow discredited Crook in the eyes of his superiors who thought the terms too lenient. When they learned of Geronimo's continued resistance, they sought more of an "Army" response, one defending key points along the border in order to protect Americans. Crook disputed the strategy that yielded the initiative to the Apache and that rebuked his approach of relying on scouts. In his view, it was futile to try and stop raids by defending the border. Senior leadership granted Crook's request to be relieved. In this way, Geronimo beat Crook, who was dismissed for failing to bring that notorious man to justice.

His replacement was none other than now Brigadier General Nelson A. Miles. He arrived in April 1886, and he intended to end the Apache resistance once and for all. Instead of relying heavily on scouts, Miles asked the Regulars at his disposal to finish this war. He attempted to better defend the border with an observation system allowing the dispatch of punitive columns to chase down Apaches. Some scouts accompanied the troopers and often led the way, but the border remained as porous as before. The war dragged on and became increasingly criminal in nature. Geronimo, now nothing more than a renegade, rapidly lost any meaning to his actions. He led only ten followers, six men and four women, as he came north, evading border security, killing a number of civilians in his path, and taking a few captives as well. He then retraced his steps and entered Mexico and continued killing any person he encountered. It was not a great swath of destruction given his pitifully small numbers, but it was an act of terror, and his name and the fear associated with it reached new heights. Miles sent 5,000 men after him, a far cry from Crooks' strategy to rely on a few hundred Native scouts. Geronimo and maybe some eighteen Apache remained free.

Ultimately, Miles changed tactics. Henry W. Lawton, a captain leading 100 men, set off into Mexico in pursuit of Geronimo. After five months and over 3,000 miles of pursuit, Lawton had not killed or captured a single Apache. Conversely, twelve Americans and perhaps over a hundred Mexicans lost their lives to Geronimo at this time. Eventually, Lawton and another soldier, Lieutenant Charles B. Gatewood, with the help of two scouts, located Geronimo and opened discussions. Miles concluded the surrender on September 4, 1886, at Skeleton Canyon, 65 miles southeast of Fort Bowie, but on duplicitous terms. Geronimo was to join his people already sent to Florida. He succumbed to despair after hearing of the removal of 434 Chiriahuas to that state, and his surrender came at least in part because of this loss. Exhaustion was another reason, so much so that Geronimo agreed to deportation to Florida as well. These were hard terms, but he was to return in two years according to the conditions of his surrender. He never did return, however. The government repudiated this condition because of his resistance, the repeated offensives forfeiting a life on a reservation in Arizona, one that had appeared so odious to him before this point. Therefore, this war ended close to where it had started at Fort Bowie, with guile and duplicity among all participating as its trademark.

Only Geronimo's exile from his homeland, and that of his people, concluded his war against internment. It had been glorious only in retrospect, the immediacy of his resistance producing a great sense of loss spelling disaster for his clan of Apache and others, now removed to Florida. However, the Army did him a final favor even with this result. He was a prisoner of war, and for this reason avoided a civilian trial that would have ended with his execution at the hands of Arizonians determined to be rid of him once and for all.[22] Apache resistance in the Southwest ended this way, a handful of Natives finally admitting defeat, sheltered by their nemesis, soldiers, who blunted the civilian predilection for vengeance a final time. For this reason, Geronimo represented the entire conflict of 300 years duration, even if he was localized to a region expansive in territory and in symbolic meaning, but his actions so reduced in scale as to be hardly a war. It was, instead, the epitome of Americans versus Natives and a guerrilla war. In this way, he represented the end of Native resistance more than did the violence at Wounded Knee.

Wounded Knee

Wounded Knee meant one more tragedy, one more massacre, punctuated American-Native interactions. This incident involved the Sioux, formerly the strongest of the plains tribes and, with this action, the last to capitulate. However, Wounded Knee arose from confusion; Natives did not intend to engage the U.S. military. That clash and the sad fate of a proud people came nonetheless as a ceremonial dance rekindled old feelings of a nostalgic existence on the plains. The Ghost Dance was a challenge to the loss of freedom so clearly evident in Geronimo and Chief Joseph's fate. However, feelings only briefly moved past this when in December 1890, a number of Sioux, perhaps as many as 300, moved off the reservation, they soon recalled the ease of dependency rather than the joy inherent in the exertion needed to regain the freedom of the plains.

Exemplifying this reality, their leader, Chief Big Foot, fell ill almost immediately and longed for the comfort of the reservation and a chance to recover. Whatever nostalgia there was for a past way of life, it cooled rapidly so that the Sioux looked to return to safety. It was a humiliating epiphany that bred deadly consequences. When confronted by pursuing soldiers, these Sioux surrendered willingly and accompanied the escort to Wounded Knee. There a weapons search commenced, and tempers flared, leading to shots and a massacre. Like many of the massacres before, the tally pointed to American brutality—214 dead Sioux. Worse, soldiers hunted down those fleeing, often defenseless women and children, and killed them. After Wounded Knee, the Sioux found themselves cut off from a way of life, from their culture. Any nostalgia about resuscitating a Native past died in that field with the 300 Sioux. The Ghost Dance had animated the movement, a call to believe in an afterlife that was entirely free of American influence. Now, even this spiritual escape was stopped. Wounded Knee became an abrupt reminder of a complete isolation, one more profound than could be believed. The Sioux faced American dominance reaching into their most cherished dreams.

The incident highlighted the worst of American motives and sentiment, and spoke to a Native hopelessness. This was the sum total of the Peace Policy, Natives decimated by the circumstance of isolation brought home as a final measure of American victory. There was no glory here and few Americans claimed it as such. The Republican call to put down an "uprising" was a clearly overstated declaration smacking more of seeking political gain with voters than as identifying a credible threat.[23] Instead, the incident at Wounded Knee was the final battle of a long war that had robbed all combatants of a sense of rightful purpose. Americans were no freer than Natives, since the haunting memory of this massacre ensured Americans inherited a negative recollection of the Plains war and the wars that preceded them. What Americans had done right over that long period of conflict was now lost as a casualty of this tragedy. Military virtue had never suffered so greatly as at Wounded Knee because Americans had exercised their own demons over the long haul of completing the enforcement of reservations as the hallmark of the Peace Policy. Whatever legacy could be found on the plains was negative and alarming. Posterity would have to sort out the implications of the long war of contact.

End

As Americans created one nation, they were completing their dismantling of another culture. The extreme imbalance of the combatants and the rationale of the struggle, to confine tribes to reservations, underscored the doomed fate of the Natives. That end may have been accomplished by acts of war, but again, it was more than this. Settlement had made it possible. Cut off with no place to go,the Natives forced defeat as senior commanders plotted Native destruction leaving only two choices: reservations or extermination. Assimilation had to be found between these two extremes. Natives were asked to redefine themselves as Americans, to contribute to a new nation by staying aloof from that nation until they had profoundly changed. While Americans held out the hope of Natives converting to American norms and customs— whether in terms of religion, a sedentary lifestyle, or trade—this expectation was as false as the reservation solution itself, which, of course, meant the end of the Native way of life, not its perpetuation. The Peace Policy that came to fruition after 1868 suggested a desire to see Natives survive, but only on American terms. The lack of symmetry in cause and effect did not expose an incongruity between settlement and the military actions after 1876, far from it. Rather, these security force operations meant the Peace Policy brought these two efforts into harmony and in so doing, exposed the lie that had been coexistence as a justification for a conflict that had remained in place for 300 years. The last attempt by Americans to include Natives in the United States in fact left Natives as outsiders, all the while enjoying a middle ground, making clear that any concept of nation building had only one group in mind, Americans.

9

The Ultimate Counterinsurgency Success

The tale is fearsome to contemplate. At the end of a 300-year sweep of history, Europeans and then Americans had reduced Native peoples in North America, once numbering in the millions, to a few thousand souls marooned on a handful of parcels of land. Europeans had escaped that fate themselves as their tenuous grip on settlement sparked desperate resolve on the part of the colonials. From the first moments of contact, these settlers looked to strike a major blow and stabilize their foothold on new land. This they did during a series of wars in Jamestown and New England, and by 1680, their lodgment was secure. Certainly by that date, they were here to stay, and only the extent of European expansion remained to be determined. That this tide reached the Pacific Ocean and a new people formed an entirely new nation, one defeating all rivals inside and out, spoke of success that emphasized the proceeds of the ultimate counterinsurgency.

The long war of contact as a counterinsurgency requires insurgents. This the Native tribes provided, even without a compelling, unified identity. They earned this label of insurgent to a large degree by waging an "Indian way of war" that spoke to more than tactics; its most complete understanding also spoke to co-existence with the new arrivals. A shared sovereignty with settlers, a middle ground, was a goal that framed the Native outlook of their changing world after contact with Europeans.[1] This view also suited Europeans, for a time, but at each stage of expansion, they rewrote the norms, from a middle ground to seeking exclusion. The new arrivals mostly succeeded but Americans eventually settled for something short of Native obliteration and sought out some sort of accord. As Wayne Lee characterizes European expansion in the Americas, the Native response had much to do with that outcome:

It therefore was not always, or even mostly, a story of direct "conquest" but, rather, a story of convincing, cajoling, and coercing indigenous agents to harness their own resources and to project power, either at the imperial behest or at least in the imperial interest.[2]

All told, these Native "agents" defied conquest. To put this another way, any absorption of one society by another represents only the first step by which a society imposes itself on another. The most crucial development after domination is the "rationale" that explains why one group has conquered.[3] To lend credence to this outcome, the story is simplified in that one party triumphs, and that story ends as the victor begins anew, free of any consequence.

The naiveté of this understanding lies in believing actions can be free of consequences. This is never true. In the case of this 300-year war, to accept a rationale of discovery or exploration purposely lauds only one group of participants. To look to disease as producing a demographic impact that explains success lacks intent. However, to assess a process across any number of regions eventually totaling a complete landmass, where multiple parties made decisions producing conflict and accommodation, this more holistic rationale means the war of contact went beyond conquest and also served as a measure of accord among survivors of trauma and among the beneficiaries of mutual growth. Winning a counterinsurgency means all those involved undergo shared changes among dynamically changing peoples; it does not mean that one side emerges unchanged after imposing an outcome on another.

The method of that COIN success is as imprecise now as it was then. A referendum on Native American warfare as undertaken after European contact lacks consensus.[4] How can there be? A "first way of war" grew out of Europeans copying Native methods of warfare, the so-called "skulking war." Natives struck noncombatants and struggled to minimize the impact of war on those engaged. Not surprisingly, so too did the new arrivals. This is not to say that this dynamic surfaced as a result of contact. Rather, the frequently confused terminology in application and purpose highlights a process and, therefore, reveals the changing forms of warfare impacting all combatants in North America as a middle ground. One should listen to those warning against the folly of overusing this metaphor, of finding a middle ground everywhere.[5] However, it matters how one gets to the end result of the Natives facing a loss of sovereignty. Understanding, let alone controlling, a mutual outcome left all combatants measuring ways of accommodation as well as annihilation: a hallmark of a counterinsurgency. To liken the long war of contact with the COIN practices of today may appear ahistorical until one realizes that the aim of the counterinsurgents is to gain favor among those contacted via pacification, winning hearts and minds, and conducting security force operations but, when necessary, dispensing violence upon that process, upon that middle ground.

COIN theory expressing this military reality purports its own frontier thesis, a tale of expansion seeking accommodation even as outliers are expunged and seldom converted. In North America, this process repeatedly met destination as the settlers rediscovered a "west" any number of times. Tensions arose due to contact, and military practices fluctuated, but the violence inherent in the confused middle ground reverberated in favor of Americans, often in unpredictable fashion. The challenge of winning hearts and minds via military means was a contradiction then as now since an Empire of Liberty framed an inclusive boundary that never did pull in Native Americans. Instead, mountain men, explorers, and those celebrated today as frontiersmen, all who could be Native-like in many ways, accelerated the destruction of tribes by opening the West. In their wake came frontiersmen of a different sort who emerged in reference to a rampaging militia and volunteers who sought to kill Natives wherever they could be found. Altogether, these paramilitary agents helped conventional forces first isolate enemies and then "remove" them altogether.

The U.S. Army's "counter-guerrilla" military operations forced it into launching attacks across the prairie against recalcitrant Natives, manning forts to extend an umbrella of governmental authority across the West, and confining the defeated peoples to reservations.[6] Functioning as an attack force, a constabulary presence, and an executor of government policy left military personnel engaged in search and destroy operations and pacification efforts. The Army preferred the label of "total war," an effort to finish a campaign that never had an end via military means alone, a dimension that spoke to Army ambiguity toward a first way of war. A larger framework was needed to get beyond the incongruity of using punitive military force to save peoples from obliteration and was present as Americans forced Natives onto reservations. As the Army strove to stamp out the last elements of Native resistance, these final defeats registered the means to this end: a civilian push that made possible a strictly military effort in the 1870s. This groundswell of support rendered Army actions no more than security force operations, a popular mandate having relegated any lingering opposition to the fringes of society and to an anticlimactic role in a war all but won.

This reality at that time appears a lure today when the counterinsurgents declare the war to be in this final stage but, in truth, operate far from this desired end-state. Still, that goal is a needed pursuit, but it is more systemic than it is climactic. From this perspective, the United States has witnessed a long struggle in the post–World War II era, just as settlers did over the course of the establishment of colonies leading to a nation, and then the full expression of that nation from one coast to another. Today, the systemic nature of success has become lost in a push for victory that identifies friends and foes. The more complex world that that dichotomy suspends does not go away, but remains in place as new relationships are formed among differing peoples. The American push to maintain its global standing requires this understanding as much as did the founding of the nation. The U.S. home front never wavered at either time; rather, it best sustains itself by accepting success in process rather than seeking finality in victory. The difference is that today, a focus on process must be conscious, guided by past actions that benefited from that view now imposed on these events. That the previous era found virtue in progression only in retrospect, does not excuse the current age for failing to accept this focus as a best practice. In both of these instances, conflict as an ongoing reality germinates confusion other than as a COIN reality.

One must go further and stress that the greatest imprecision in measuring this past COIN success lay in assessing who won the war. By conflict's end, Americans had confined Natives to reservations, and this blighted existence served as a horrific measure of how far these people had fallen after contact with Europeans. Yet, they were still there. If the Natives had survived, their culture had been radically impacted and transformed, so any accommodation leading to survival on reservations spoke to something acceptable on American terms, and not much more than this. However, Natives do benefit from an Indian identity today, enjoying a unity they had never subscribed to before. This success, beyond mere legal standing or life on a reservation, has produced a shared existence with Americans.[7] Natives did not win the war of contact, nor have they enjoyed a greater reward from having more faithfully favored a middle ground than have Americans, as perhaps they should have, but they have endured. This ability remains a reminder today that victory in war is less military and more cultural, and this kind of result defies a totality of success.

Natives survived, and when necessary, their resistance and coexistence continues. This purpose belies a break at 1890, as if the history of American-Native interaction came to an end at this point in time. Yet, the tone of the conflict has shifted markedly since then because the struggle is no longer frequently violent. Moreover, after this date, the battle between Americans and Natives was one of wrestling with the totality of the experience: Americans saw western settlement as leading to an end of the frontier, and Natives viewed that same result as a reprieve to reconstitute themselves.[8] Such decrees were as false then as they are today. Like victory, frontiers never mean an end of a process, only its continuation. The struggle of early America exemplifies this larger perspective, leaving victory in this war as unclear then as it is on today's COIN battlefields. At that time, the end product was accord among differing peoples seeing virtue in interaction, something still ongoing today. Frontiers yield to borderlands.[9] Today, that same mantra comes as close to a universally accepted COIN theory as might exist when speaking of "population centric" counterinsurgency.[10] The harmful dictates via military force, such as search and destroy that targets the insurgents and eliminates them, and the isolation of the insurgents from outside reinforcement, are to yield to approaches looking to gain favor with an assumed disinterested public. For this reason, the counterinsurgents look to pacify the population, preferably with paramilitary forces, or elements of that population now working alongside the counterinsurgents. These terms are as mercurial as one can imagine, suggesting the mitigation of the use of force, but allowing for more punitive measures in the name of achieving success.

The hoped-for restraint in population-centric COIN implies an abandonment of victory as a measure of success. If so, this limitation stands in marked contrast to the push west that defined the settlement of North America. The shift in fortunes of Americans and Natives was so pronounced by 1890 that some verdict on victory is needed. To "win" this war, Americans did three things well. First, they prevented the Natives from forging a lasting alliance with other European powers or among themselves for that matter. Had a number of tribes done either one of these things, colonial expansion may well have stopped at the coast, or American expansion at the Appalachian Mountains, at the Mississippi River, or well short of the Pacific Ocean. That this did not occur spelled the doom of those Natives living "west" or wherever settlers transplanted themselves. Second, Americans sustained the struggle for 300 years. Of course, this imposing figure in the aggregate is less imposing in the incremental parts of expansion. These took considerably less time. Still, the ability to advance in parts, to continue to do so, and to do so to the point of settling a continent, was an impressive accomplishment. Third, Americans teamed military power with the tide of settlement. This dual effort often produced the startling outcome of military forces reigning in civilian volunteers, but no matter this attempt, Natives faced obliteration on the North American continent. Civilians did not always deliberately or even consciously pursue this outcome, but this was the result.

A focus this counterinsurgency reveals that this success hardly stemmed from military prowess alone. While the lack of major battles has been noted, the label persisted. Yet, the fighting was small in scale. Either the numbers engaged were few, or the losses incurred were slight, and sometimes both cases applied suggesting that the title of "battle" be replaced with "skirmish."

Skirmishes, of course, typify guerrilla fighting, often best describing the means of the resistance of insurgents, who employ hit-and-run attacks. That is the case here, as very small bands of warriors engaged settlers and soldiers. In other words, Natives by and large imposed the kind of war they wished to fight on the battlefield. Tales of epic battles perpetually reached an interested public, a dubious salute in so many ways other than that these "battles" totaled a decisive victory as seen in the prism of counterinsurgency.

Americans often overcame Native resistance in violent engagements, and these skirmishes, massacres, and occasionally larger fights were the key battles in a long war. The ongoing clashes made it clear that the many wars all taken together totaled a counterinsurgency effort that allowed Americans to win this struggle. The progression of the fighting reveals this, from that characterized by colonials merely surviving to that indicative of Americans enjoying a shift from co-existence, to Removal, to westward expansion, and finally to enforcing the reservation system. However, even this progression did not fully spell out the full measure of success, a continent-wide effort by European and then American settlers employing a mix of military force and civilian activity to overcome resisting Natives. Manifest Destiny, one of the few formal pronouncements of American intentions in this regard, meant only a western fulfillment of this reality, but it also clearly referenced the path taken to attain the now formally recognized parameters of the nation. When the counterinsurgency is seen in its entirety, the war for the West was merely the last stage of the halting nature of expansion.

Americans could not face this big picture because of the overall consequence of that war: conquest. The denial of this act, abhorrent to a nation founded on proclaiming liberty for all peoples, was underscored by how the conflict was won. With no recognition of the war to claim a continent, no victory over a "nation" was possible. Instead, the ambiguity inherent in American and Native interaction surfaces again. Since Natives had been denied independent state status, Chief Justice John Marshall phrased this relationship as one of dependent states within a state. Thus, Americans were not aggressors marching into lands populated by others. It was a confused situation to say the least. Americans managed the confusion to their advantage and achieved a singular purpose—expansion—more so than Natives achieved their defensive aim—retaining their homeland not so much with the expulsion of Whites but by becoming part of this new world. The starts and stops of the conflict, the intermittent gains of settlers and the at times successful defense mounted by Natives, underscored that the Americans could not sustain the resultant "war" in the name of self-defense except when characterized as a failed effort to include Natives in the new creation. Somehow, this justification meant

developing empty land and civilizing the Natives, and these actions stopped
short of war. Consequently, settlers both welcomed and renounced Natives
producing a successful counterinsurgency.

Coming to terms with a changing cast of characters over 300 years makes
continuity difficult to gauge other than by this focus. No matter who is
selected, important names share little other than the purpose that clearly fell
to them: either insurgents or counterinsurgents. From the Native point of
view, for example, a look at famous chiefs makes for entertaining reading,
but what do they have in common other than the struggle they waged?[11] Chief
Powhatan, the most powerful leader of the Algonquian people located in the
region where the colonials established Jamestown, had little in common with
Sitting Bull, the Sioux leader waging war against the U.S. Army on the Northwestern plains. The one chief faced an incipient threat from Europeans, and
the other confronted the full maturity of American aggression. Both men
met defeat. King Philip, the Wampanoag chief, tried to maintain himself in
the area of Puritan settlement by arguably remaining a part of colonial culture.
The Shawnee Chief Tecumseh, emerging after the Native defeat at Fallen
Timbers, completely rejected European culture and called for its eradication.
Neither man succeeded. Even a more compelling circumstance does not produce strong commonalities. In Florida, the Seminole leader Osceola fought
a guerrilla war and a number of Apache warriors in the Southwest—Cochise,
Victorio, and Geronimo among them—also fought guerrilla wars. Including
them in the same story means they participated in this clash, but to what
end? To conclude that these famous resistance fighters failed at the collective
purpose of stopping American aggression is false. No Natives did this in concert with other Natives. Instead, the juxtaposition of these famous names and
others speaks to the foremost characteristic they did have in common: leading
a scattered, isolated resistance unable to rally to a common cause due to
Native peoples often seeking supplication, not conflict, with settlers. The
question is, what can be learned from the commonality establishing them as
insurgents, and what can be learned from its opposite, falling victim to a
counterinsurgency?

Those in service to a rising America have no such log of combatants.
There is no study of great Indian fighters or of those leading a common crusade.[12] More than a few efforts profile soldiers of many ranks and eras, and
these are often compelling studies. However, colonial arrivals had no more
in common with a cavalry officer in the West in the 1860s than chiefs acting
at these different times. Settler ideologies had shifted arguably from pursuing
a religious crusade to building a nation, something the new inhabitants never
dreamed of in the 1600s, at least not on the scale that it had become after

1845. Myles Standish, the military captain directing early Puritan efforts, and George Custer, at war with the Sioux in the post–Civil War period, may well have both been soldiers, but that superficial comparison does not survive the above test of ideology; it personifies it. Standish served a religious purpose, even if not gripped by that ferver. Custer acted from multiple motives, but the foremost cause was to sustain the nation he had just defended in civil war by helping it "settle" the West.

This roll of opposites continues. Andrew Jackson may have embodied the pulse of a rising American democracy, even as he famously held a contrasting view of republican government from many Founding Fathers. Yet he shared a similar reputation with that foremost of Founding Fathers, George Washington. Both men had earned fame for making war on Native Americans and the Natives' sometime benefactor, England. This admission is all the more unpalatable because Washington and Jackson, both great Indian fighters and both great counterinsurgents for this reason, must take their place alongside those who more overtly embraced the mantle, Robert Rogers, for example, and Kit Carson for another. When this occurs, the melding of military and civilian figures is complete. Now, a tale of American leaders can be told—only the word "great" is harder to award given the consequences of the act they were all a part of, and that is a counterinsurgency that exacted a fearsome human toll.

As was the case with Native leaders, what unified the different outlooks of Americans was the unfolding struggle in which they all found themselves. The difference was that the chiefs failed to overcome division on any permanent sort of basis, and Americans did. This evolution in the fighting came after an extended period of trial and error, and the resultant lessons were only reluctantly accepted by the U.S. Army. When it finally did so, no matter how imperfectly, the Plains war besetting the West came to a rapid end. However, the late American push to finish this conflict was strikingly different from the colonial impulse that had initiated it. The first arrivals had themselves assumed the mantle of insurgent, competing with Natives in this fashion. A different goal may have been preferred, but early on the colonists numbers were so small as to prevent a decisive blow from being delivered. Even when colonials destroyed entire tribal communities, the point shone through. Other tribes were intact and had to be dealt with and defeated. This was true from Mystic to Fort Mims. By the time of Jackson's triumphs in the wake of the Fort Mims disaster, however, the tide had turned. Americans were clearly past the point where they represented just one more insurgent group. Now, the push to defeat all such insurgents was the American aim. When possible, they lashed out at a vulnerable tribe, and they rebuked European inroads on the continent as well. These efforts gathered momentum, and as a consequence, they assumed the role of counterinsurgent in order to gain an empire.

The trouble with assigning unity among settlers as the foremost cause of Native defeat is that a lack of identity, and for the same reasons as Natives, factionalism and regional divides, characterized first colonial and then American culture too. Jamestown's internal problems are famous, and colonials in New England ostracized many of the faithful, leading to the creation of new colonies. Such rivalries did not end, as seen in the English and American confrontation during the American Revolution. The Civil War serves as another, obvious example. Yet there would be an American culture after all, given its mission of counterinsurgency. This binding goal proved superior to the motive of "survival" by Natives. Americans embraced the means (expansion) and gradually the end (conquest), and enjoyed the initiative throughout the conflict for that reason, a drive to be more than insurgents and become something else—conquerors. This would never be the term used, however. Settlement was the label, but as has been seen, it was no more than a method of counterinsurgency.

Natives mounted an insurgency, but only in the sense of *de facto* resistance to colonial and subsequently to American expansion. Consequently, a Native cause never existed beyond this base measure, so their successes had little relation to each other. Strategy ending a war enjoyed only a limited place in Native combat. A failure to grasp the stakes of the conflict spoke to a disunity plaguing Natives, and even like tribes often could not get free of this infighting. This reality bolsters those who question the establishment of Native empires. There may well have been a Comanchería, or an Apacheria, and even the Sioux may have assembled a great power structure, but in each case these tribes never surmounted the method of leadership by personality designed to overawe dissenters. However much this bond pulled them together, it failed to keep them from emphasizing the parts more than the whole. For this reason, empires did not confront the American advance, individual warriors did, and they seldom represented more than a handful of family members. The clash should have pitted Natives allied with one another against the emerging American nation. Instead, Native peoples sought enmeshment in an increasingly dominated American world and often did so at the expense of one another. The lack of cohesion and the tendency to seek accommodation from Americans were crucial weaknesses and did more than any other factor to undo Native resistance.

Settlers benefited from the opposite of this progression. They were no more aware that they were involved in a struggle requiring them to adopt a counterinsurgency than Natives were aware that they needed to rise above the condition of insurgents. Yet, this is how the clash developed. A unity of purpose, no matter how subconscious or beset by starts and stops, defined the American experience. It was a key advantage, and largely explained the defeat of the insurgency by Americans advancing a sophisticated counterinsurgency since each of their successes contributed to an overall strategy forcing insurgents to capitulate. The goal of controlling the entire expanse of the West ensured this last step, and submission stood in marked contrast to the Native failure to grasp a similar "big picture" reality. Natives lost this war for survival due to this lack of awareness as much as Americans profited from seeking an end to the violence altogether. The final western campaigns symbolized the entire 300-year struggle. This last battlefield revealed the American quest for victory, and it came with an enforcement of the reservation system, but that war had been in place since long ago. While the term counterinsurgency was never uttered, the task of winning the overall war spoke to this end.

That end is an endorsement of the ultimate counterinsurgency success. This consisted of several parts, including the correct use of military force to isolate the battlefield. It was one thing for the United States to commit its military forces to prevent outside powers from decisively influencing the battlefield by backing the Natives opposing Americans. It was another to seal these borders, which amounted to not letting the enemy escape—in addition to not allowing reinforcement. Yet, these two aims were clearly related, and the U.S. Army did a superb job in each regard. It was all the more remarkable given the always small number of troops at American disposal. When accomplished, two advantages favored the United States. One was the hopelessness of resistance prevailing among the Natives due to, among other things, the lack of outside support. The other was the willingness of U.S. Army personnel to finish off the last outbreaks of violence perpetrated by Native Americans. To this end, Americans blamed the Natives for starting these last wars even if the fault was shared. Ultimately, assigning blame meant little in either case. Settlement, a civilian reality enjoying increasing military support, overcame the Natives' last ditch resistance and rapidly so, allowing Americans to speak to a fortuitous evolution to where soldiers could act as effective counterinsurgents.

Additional benefits came about as a result of this gradual transformation. Christianity and even alcohol may have signified more obvious acts of assimilation, but success in winning hearts and minds grew out of the unlikely vehicle of forts. The changing nature of forts from defending the colonial toehold in the New World to dictating a reservation system represented some avant-garde counterinsurgency doctrine. At first, Americans used forts to project power into hostile lands and do so with the very small number of troops available; these troops required forts as protection from attack. Otherwise, their small numbers risked complete annihilation. Even if scattered about the hinterland, these bastions were usually impervious to assault, and could therefore serve as the tool "protecting" settlement, and something more. Very soon, the existence of forts facilitated the exchange of goods that occurred. Some interplay increased as a result, a "middle ground," but in the West, it became clear that the U.S. government hoped to use forts to keep Natives within strict confines and maintain a larger principle—separating the guerrillas from the population.[13] This the Americans did by promising amnesty, a "gift" all too often leading to confinement on reservations that belied the assumed benevolence of this approach. When the need for co-existence had passed, best indicated by the scorched earth efforts that sounded the defeat of the plains tribes, first in the south, then in the north, the guerrillas now were those off the reservation. The U.S. military used this convenient measure to good effect by hunting down the final resisters in a series of clashes hardly deserving the label of wars. The Modocs, Nez Perce, Sioux, and Apache all offered a final challenge, but this sound COIN practice was enough to ensure the defeat of the last Native resistance on the plains.

When the Americans finally decided the last remnants of Indian Country had to succumb to their control, Native resistance was pointless primarily because reservations had inverted the fort mentality. To Americans, forts lent credence to their belief that the land was empty and theirs for the taking, despite having promised Natives a sanctuary west of the Mississippi River, the rationale undergirding Removal. The lonely outposts, dots of civilization in a barren wasteland, meant Americans could contemplate the void that was the West as something that could be mastered. Here was the key difference in the spatial thinking of Natives and Americans. Openness had to be preserved for the Natives but overcome by settlers. Given this mindset, forts gave Americans a key advantage. These way-stations not only helped to shuttle settlers across the continent, but they also impeded Native movement. These bastions ensured that an already atomized resistance was slowly buffeted about the prairie on reduced land, so that Natives faced an early cordon eventually redefined as the reservation system. So again, these defensive tools became a key part of a counterinsurgency effort, excluding Natives from involvement in the new nation rather than serving as tools of assimilation, rendering hearts and minds an empty appeal. Settlement was to fulfill an Empire of Liberty rather than foster a middle ground.

The zealousness with which Americans made war on Native Americans, and the willingness to cover-up the naked economic incentives for that war with rationalizations such as Removal, and slogans like Manifest Destiny conveys the extent to which American "settlers" remained committed to winning this war. This support was a crucial component of successful counterinsurgency because all too often during this conflict the U.S. military proved inadequate to the task. It could not always protect Americans from Native attack. A steady occurrence of settlers taking matters into their own hands characterized the conflict as much as did the military clashes. This extended beyond volunteers and militia engaged in a first way of war and came to embody virtually all citizens of the new nation. The evolution of this conflict makes this conviction clear in those who held it closest, the settlers, who provoked conflict and, when things went badly, asked for protection. In this arc came a shift in motive from mere survival to that of expansion. While ideology clouded the motives of Americans, and at times was shared by military commanders, the true motive remained economic advancement, an end civilians desired at any cost. It would be fortunate for Americans that the Natives bore most of this cost.

This ugly reality underscored the limits of restraint the U.S. military imposed on the home front. Americans remained determined to wage this conflict, a desire of settlement sustaining the effort over a great many years. This success turns on its head conceptions of what is today called "nation building." Far from protecting inhabitants from tyranny and fostering a democratic government, Americans destroyed the indigenous cultures as they built a nation, one suiting only American interests and one excluding Natives. Over the course of this long war, Americans won a nation at the expense of the inhabitants they contacted. It mattered little if the main perpetrators were civilians, military forces only augmenting their efforts after failing to curtail the aggressions of settlers. In totality, Americans established a punitive expression of nation building that won them a nation and a continent.

With this mandate, Americans found ways to justify expansion, rationales that are less convincing today. That shift in thinking rests mostly with the American military. In looking at the war in Iraq, it is clear that "shock and awe" had a strong precursor in the Native American war with Americans. The punitive call behind this phrase was less than one might expect and clearly worked to sooth an American public seeking a swift end to war. In Iraq, the U.S. military went forth and practiced restraint, an effort to win a war by mitigating conflict in the targeted nation, all the while mollifying an American public at home with calls of achieving victory.

The necessity of this balancing act reveals the American public's standard of success in COIN wars to rest on some vague understanding of the conflict of Americans versus Natives. Today, when engaged abroad in counterinsurgency operations, Americans desire a military victory similar to the one they achieved against Native Americans. This appeal to the past is problematic on a number of accounts. First, Americans never achieved a strictly military victory. Both civilians and armed forces prosecuted this war. Second, the combination of factors leading to success, one of isolating the battlefield, of unleashing paramilitary forces, and of teaming kinetic force with soft power as civilians settled the continent, were unique conditions that may not repeat or only partially so. Third, and last, the outcome of this combination, the demographic destruction, is not desired today. Devastating a population is not just immoral by the American standard of serving liberty, but is also at variance with an expeditionary warfare intended to empower a foreign populace, not eliminate it.

For each of these reasons, the success of the past—if one wishes to call it a success—cannot be repeated today. One of the key purposes of this book is to bring greater clarity to this past war as Americans struggle with questions of what is meant by counterinsurgency and how one wins such conflicts. The public would do well to re-visit the long American-Native war to remind itself of the militarism inherent in the democratic bearing of a nation sworn to peace, but favoring the use of violence. This impulse resonates deeply in the American landscape but gains its urgency from an impatient, hypocritical public that belies the values it clings to when demanding unfettered military action to achieve foreign policy objectives. That contradiction raises the question, what is the United States trying to achieve abroad, and how is it going to meet that end? Answers are badly needed, and they center on a better understanding of counterinsurgency. What such a discourse yields is recognition that the U.S. military is backing away from the use of force to win these wars and dragging the public with it. Such a development promises better policy in the days ahead, a hope that stems from the unlikely source of the 300-year war of contact Americans waged against Native Americans.

Chapter Notes

Preface

1. Andrew J. Birtle, *U.S. Army Counterinsurgency and Contingency Operations Doctrine, 1860–1941* (Washington, D.C.: Center of Military History, U.S. Army, 1998).

2. Robert N. Watt, "Raiders of a Lost Art? Apache War and Society," *Small Wars and Insurgencies*, Vol. 13, Issue 3 (2004): 1–28; Wayne Lee, "Using the Natives against the Natives: Indigenes as 'Counterinsurgents' in the British Atlantic, 1500–1800," *Defense Studies*, Vol. 4, No. 3 (Autumn 2004): 88–105.

3. John M. Gates, "Indians and Insurrectos: The U.S. Army's Experience with Insurgency," *Parameters*, XIII, No. 1 (1983): 67–68.

4. Francis Parkman, *The Conspiracy of Pontiac and the Indian War after the Conquest of Canada*, 2 Vols. (Lincoln: University of Nebraska Press, 1994, 1870).

5. Francis Jennings, *The Invasion of America: Indians, Colonialism, and the Cant of Conquest* (New York: W.W. Norton, 1976), v.

6. See the charge of genocide and the refutation of discovery in Ward Churchill, *A Little Matter of Genocide: Holocaust and Denial in the Americas, 1492 to the Present* (San Francisco: Lights Books, 1997), 3–4; and the denouncement of the grave environmental degradation stemming from "contact" or "the encounter" speaking to a lost opportunity of mutual accommodation in Kirkpatrick Sale, *The Conquest of Paradise: Christopher Columbus and the Columbian Legacy* (New York: Plume, 1990), 367–368.

7. Richard White, *The Middle Ground: Indians, Empires, and Republics in the Great Lakes Region, 1650–1815* (New York: Cambridge University Press, 1991). According to Michael McConnell, Natives successfully did the same in Ohio Valley region until 1774. McConnell, *A Country Between: The Upper Ohio and Its Peoples, 1724–1774* (Lincoln: University of Nebraska Press, 1992). Mary E. Young presents a multitude of middle grounds along the "Indian frontier." See Young, "The Dark and Bloody but Endlessly Inventive Middle Ground of Indian Frontier Historiography," *Journal of the Early Republic*, Vol. 13, No. 2 (Summer 1993): 193–205.

8. Michael Scheuer, "Break Out the Shock and Awe," *Los Angeles Times,* Opinion, March 9, 2008.

9. Gil Merom, *How Democracies Lose Small Wars: State, Society, and the Failures of France in Algeria, Israel in Lebanon, and the United States in Vietnam* (New York: Cambridge University Press, 2003), 15.

10. Matthew J. Flynn, *Contesting History: The Bush Counterinsurgency Legacy in Iraq* (Santa Barbara, CA: Praeger Security International, 2010). Douglas Porch also critiques the reliance on military force by arguing that counterinsurgency operations in the modern era have generated too much destruction in the name of stability. See Porch, *Counterinsurgency: Exposing the Myths of the New Way of War* (New York: Cambridge University Press, 2013), xi–xii, 2.

11. James H. Lebovic, *The Limits of U.S. Military Capability: Lessons from Vietnam and Iraq* (Baltimore: The Johns Hopkins University Press, 2010); and David Fitzger-

ald, *Learning to Forget: U.S. Army Doctrine and Practice from Vietnam to Iraq* (Stanford, CA: Stanford University Press, 2013).

12. For Algeria, see David Galula, *Counterinsurgency Warfare: Theory and Practice* (NY: Praeger, 1964), and Roger Trinquier, *Modern Warfare: A French View of Counterinsurgency* (Westport, CT: Praeger Security International, 1964).

13. John A. Nagel, *Learning to Eat Soup with a Knife: Counterinsurgency Lessons from Malaya and Vietnam* (Westport, CT: Praeger, 2002).

14. David J. Kilcullen is best here. Many value his concerted effort to find a proscription of success in "modern" counterinsurgency operations. See Kilcullen, *Counterinsurgency* (New York: Oxford University Press, 2010).

15. A number of experts look to get past the Vietnam War and point out American successes in other COIN wars to then set the recent American effort in Iraq in better relief. See Wayne Bert, *American Military Intervention in Unconventional War: From the Philippines to Iraq* (New York: Palgrave Macmillan, 2011), Max Boot, *The Savage Wars of Peace: Small Wars and the Rise of American Power* (New York: Basic Books, 2002), and Sam Sarkesian in *America's Forgotten Wars: The Counterrevolutionary Past and Lessons for the Future* (Westport, CT: Greenwood Press, 1984).

16. For example, see Ian Steele's decision to use "Amerindians" in *Warpaths: Invasions of North America* (New York: Oxford University Press, 1994), Preface.

Introduction

1. Robert M. Utley asserts that some officers moved forward in defiance of Reno's order not to do so, suggesting Reno could have reached Custer and possibly turned the battle. See Utley, *Frontier Regulars: The United States Army and the Indian, 1866–1891* (New York: Macmillan, 1973), 267. Robert Wooster says Major Reno and Captain Benteen cautiously advanced together to find Custer but beat a hasty retreat. See Wooster, *The American Military Frontiers: The United States Army in the West, 1783–1900* (Albuquerque: University of New Mex-

ico Press, 2009), 232. The evidence reveals there was no advance. In testimony given at a court of inquiry requested by Reno to clear his name, Benteen stated under oath that he did not ask Reno if he could go find Custer and that he acted on his own initiative and ordered a limited "shift" toward the sound of some scattered gunfire. Benteen also was complimentary of Reno saying Reno was present and active along the line the entire time. See *The Official Record of a Court of Inquiry Convened at Chicago, Illinois, January 13, 1879, by the President of the United States Upon the Request Major Marcus A. Reno, 7th U.S. Cavalry, to Investigate His Conduct at the Battle of the Little Big Horn, June 25–26* (Pacific Palisades, CA: 1951), 403, 406.

2. Alan D. Gaff captures the in some ways contradictory nature of Wayne, arguing that he was "patient, thoughtful, prudent, and decisive in judgment," no matter his impulsiveness earning him the nickname "Mad Anthony." See Gaff, *Bayonets in the Wilderness: Anthony Wayne's Legion in the Old Northwest* (Norman: University of Oklahoma Press, 2004), 369.

3. There is much disagreement on Little Turtle's role in this battle, whether he did not wish to fight or lead the attack. All interpretations rely on eyewitnesses of equal credibility. John Sugden offers the most accurate view. He says Little Turtle first demurred because of his fear of the American ability to continue fighting, but when overruled by Blue Jacket, he joined the battle. See Sugden, *Blue Jacket: Warrior of the Shawnees* (Lincoln: University of Nebraska Press, 2000), 175.

4. Grant's comments during his meeting with Red Cloud cited by a correspondent with the *Washington Evening Star*, May 28, 1872, *The Papers of Ulysses S. Grant*, Volume 23, February 1–December 31, 1872, p. 146, Digital Collections, Mississippi State University. Robert M. Utley and Robert W. Larson conclude that the numbers Red Cloud witnessed in the capital shaped his move toward peace. See Utley, *The Indian Frontier of the American West 1846–1890* (Albuquerque: University of New Mexico Press, 1984), 150; and Larson, *Red Cloud: Warrior-Statesman of the Lakota Sioux* (Norman:

University of Oklahoma Press, 1997), 137, 289.

5. For Cochise's distrust, see letter, Ely S. Parker, Commissioner of Indian Affairs to Secretary of the Interior Columbus Delano, July 21, 1871, *The Papers of Ulysses S. Grant*, Volume 22, June 1, 1871–January 31, 1872, p. 66, Digital Collections, Mississippi State University.

6. For Apache embrace of the benefits of living on a reservation, see correspondent, July 3, 1872, *The Papers of Ulysses S. Grant*, Volume 23, February 1–December 31, 1872, p. 184, Digital Collections, Mississippi State University. For the delegation reporting back to Cochise, see David Roberts, *Once They Moved Like the Wind: Cochise, Geronimo, and the Apache Wars* (New York: Simon & Schuster, 1993), 91, 96.

7. "To the Most High and Vertuous Princesse Queene Anne of Great Brittanie," "Pocahontas Meeting in England with Captaine Smith," *The Complete Works of Captain John Smith*, Fourth Book, Vol. 2, Virtual Jamestown, First Hand Accounts, WWW.virtualjamestown, org/firsthand. html. Ian Steele calls attention to this exchange in *Warpaths: Invasions of North America* (New York: Oxford University Press, 1994), 40.

8. *Report of the Secretary of War, Communicating, in Answer to a Resolution of the Senate, a Report and Map of the Examination of New Mexico*, by Lieutenant J.W. Abert, of the Topographical Corps, Washington, 1848, p. 6–7. Utley stresses the impact the numbers had on Yellow Wolf in *The Indian Frontier of the American West 1846–1890*, 3.

9. "To George Washington from Blue Jacket, November 1796," *Founder's Online*, National Archives, http://founders.archives. gov/?q=blue%20jacket&s=1211311111&sa= &r=3&sr=; and "From George Washington to Indian Nations," 29 November 1796, *Founders Online*, National Archives, http:// founders.archives.gov/?q=blue%20jacket& s=1211311111&sa=&r=4&sr=.

Chapter 1

1. Ian Steele, *Warpaths: Invasions of North America* (New York: Oxford University Press,

1994), 21. Francis Jennings also identifies an initial "period of invasion." Jennings, *The Invasion of America: Indians, Colonialism, and the Cant of Conquest* (New York: W.W. Norton, 1975), v.

2. James Axtell, *The Invasion Within: The Contest of Cultures in Colonial North America* (New York: Oxford University Press, 1985), 5.

3. Perry Miller famously labeled this first Puritan goal of reforming Europe the "errand into the wilderness." See Miller, *Errand into the Wilderness* (New York: Harper & Row, 1964), 15.

4. Vernon Louis Parrington, *The Colonial Mind, 1620–1800*, Volume One in *Main Currents in American Thought* (New York: Harcourt, Brace & World, 1927), 4.

5. The "Indian way of war" designed to limit losses frames much of the discussion in Armstrong Starkey, *European and Native American Warfare, 1675–1815* (Norman: University of Oklahoma Press, 1998), viii, Chapter 2. Patrick Malone describes the warfare of southern New England Natives in this way. See Malone, *The Skulking Way of War: Technology and Tactics Among the New England Indians* (Baltimore: Johns Hopkins University Press, 1991), 9, 29. For limiting losses during combat among plains tribes, see Anthony McGinnis, *Counting Coup and Cutting Horses: Intertribal Warfare on the Northern Plains 1738–1889* (Cordillera Press, 1990), x, 8, 21; McGinnis reaffirmed this view in his more recent article, "When Courage Was not Enough: Plains Indians at War with the United States Army," *Journal of Military History*, Vol. 76, No. 2 (April 2012): 473.

6. Wayne E. Lee stresses the severity of Native warfare given surprise attack and its sustainment. See Lee, "The Military Revolution of Native North America: Firearms, Forts, and Politics," in *Empires and Indigenes: Intercultural Alliance, Imperial Expansion, and Warfare in the Early Modern World*, editor Wayne E. Lee (New York: New York University Press, 2011), 53; and Lee, "Peace Chiefs and Blood Revenge: Patterns of Restraint in Native Warfare, 1500–1800," *Journal of Military History*, Vol. 71, No. 3 (July 2007): 728. But he concludes that demographics shaped this conflict more than any

social-political changes arising from the evolving military practices of the combatants. Lee, "The Military Revolution of Native North America," 70. See Richard J. Chacon and Rubén G. Mendoza for the high frequency of Native warfare before European arrival in "Ethical Considerations and Conclusions Regarding Indigenous Warfare and Violence in North America," in *North American Indigenous Warfare and Ritual Violence*, eds. Richard J. Chacon and Rubén G. Mendoza (University of Arizona, 2007), 229. Anthropologists argue that Native warfare was too often not "efficient," that it did become so at times and when this occurred more efficiency meant more deaths in battle. Therefore, inefficiency explained the few battle deaths and not a slavish and uniform adherence to ritualized warfare purposely designed to keep losses to a minimum. See Keith F. Otterbein, "Historical Essay: A History of Research on Warfare in Anthropology," *American Anthropologist*, December 1999, 101 (4): 796. Lawrence Keeley warns that when efficiency was achieved by "damaging property and inducing terror, primitive and prehistoric warfare was just as terrible and effective as the historic and civilized version." See Keeley, *War Before Civilization* (New York: Oxford University Press, 1996), 174. Of course, Native warfare did not achieve "efficiency" very often in order to preserve numbers, and this limitation was a great point of departure from European warfare in the Americas. Neil L. Whitehead stresses the "disjuncture between the Western way of war and almost all other cultural practices of conflict and killing." See Whitehead, "A History of Research on Warfare in Anthropology—Reply to Keith Otterbein," *American Anthropologist*, December 2000, Vol. 102 (4): 835. So too does McGinnis in "When Courage Was Not Enough," 473.

7. Starkey extends the limit to battle deaths to all "seventeenth-century Indian peoples" who "could ill afford a form of warfare with a high butcher's bill," hence the "skulking way of war" where Natives functioned as a "modern commando or guerrilla fighter." Starkey, *European and Native American Warfare 1675–1815* (Nor-

man: University of Oklahoma Press, 1998), 19, 25–26. Pekka Hämäläinen describes the Comanche as expert guerrillas on horseback launching devastating attacks. See Hämäläinen, *The Comanche Empire* (New Haven: Yale University Press, 2008), 4, 32. Robert M. Utley wrote that the Apache thrived in the southwest because they mastered guerrilla warfare. See Utley, *Frontier Regulars: The United States Army and the Indian, 1866–1891* (New York: Macmillan, 1973), 172.

8. Craig S. Keener, "An Ethnohistorical Analysis of Iroquois Assault Tactics Used Against Fortified Settlements of the Northeast in the Seventeenth Century," *Ethnohistory*, Vol. 46, No 4 (Autumn 1999): 802.

9. Stan Hoig, *Tribal Wars of the Southern Plains* (Norman: University of Oklahoma Press, 1993), 20. Hoig also comments that the Natives did not always minimize the severity of conflict. See Hoig, *Tribal Wars of the Southern Plains*, 34. McGinnis argues that the horse meant that the possibility of combat increased, so to keep casualties down, stealing horses became the main act of war. See McGinnis, *Counting Coup and Cutting Horses*, 12.

10. More than a few writers label them the best of the plains' horsemen and tally the resultant benefits. See Hoig, *Tribal Wars of the Southern Plains*, 35; Odie B. Faulk, *Crimson Desert: Indians Wars of the American Southwest* (New York: Oxford University Press,1974), 23; and Hämäläinen, *The Comanche Empire*, 25, 29. Hämäläinen also makes the case of Comanche power resting on ensuring equilibrium with rival powers on the periphery of Comanche territory. See *The Comanche Empire*, 2–4.

11. Dan L. Thrapp, *The Conquest of Apacheria* (Norman: University of Oklahoma Press, 1967), vii.

12. Richard White, "The Winning of the West: The Expansion of the Western Sioux in the Eighteenth and Nineteenth Centuries," *Journal of American History*, Vol. 65, No. 2 (September 1978), 321. Pekka Hämäläinen gives a less favorable view, arguing the Sioux success came from favorable circumstances and less prowess as a horse people. See Hämäläinen, "The Rise and Fall of Plains Indian Horse Cultures,"

Journal of American History, Vol. 90, No. 3 (December 2003): 861.

13. Lee, "Peace Chiefs and Blood Revenge," 706.

14. Ronald Dale Karr, "'Why Should You Be So Furious?': The Violence of the Pequot War," *Journal of American History*, Vol. 85, No. 3 (December 1998): 889.

15. For the wording in the charter, see William Stith, *The History of the First Discovery and Settlement of Virginia, Williamsburg, VA* (New York: Joseph Sabin, 1747), 48. Explorer Christopher Newport's attempt to crown Powhatan succeeded only with coercion: "by leaning hard on his shoulders, he a little stooped, and Newport put the crown on his head." See Document 2, "Coronation of Powhatan by Captain Christopher Newport, 1608," in *Early American Indian Documents: Treaties and Laws, 1607–1789*, ed. Alden T. Vaughan, Vol. IV, *Virginia Treaties, 1607–1722* (Bethesda, MD: Congressional Information Services, 2003), 5. Challenging vassals (weroances) is in Document 3, "Instructions from the Virginia Council in London Advocating Christian Conversion of the Indians, Tributary Status for Powhatan, and Agreements with his Enemies, May 1609," in *Early American Indian Documents: Treaties and Laws, 1607–1789*, ed. Alden T. Vaughan, Vol. IV, *Virginia Treaties, 1607–1722* (Bethesda, MD: Congressional Information Services, 2003), 7.

16. R. Brian Ferguson and Neil L. Whitehead define successful warfare in a tribal zone as "the radical transformation of extant sociopolitical formations, often resulting in 'tribalization,' the genesis of new tribes." See "The Violent Edge of Empire," in *War in the Tribal Zone: Expanding States and Indigenous Warfare*, eds. Ferguson and Whitehead (Santa Fe, NM: School of American Research Press, 1992), 3.

17. Wilcomb E. Washburn, *The Governor and the Rebel: A History of Bacon's Rebellion in Virginia* (Chapel Hill: University of North Carolina Press, 1957), 46, 51.

18. Guy Chet, *Conquering the American Wilderness: The Triumph of European Warfare in the Northeast* (Amherst: University of Massachusetts Press, 2003), 19.

19. Alfred A. Cave, *The Pequot War* (Amherst: University of Massachusetts Press,

1996), 152. Ronald Dale Karr argues that the English did not see Natives as a legitimate target because the colonials refused to award Natives sovereignty, a step that ensured no "reciprocity" to then limit permissible conduct and therefore escalated the violence. Karr, "'Why Should You Be So Furious?'" 909. Adam Hirsch says the English changed how they fought in frustration since the Indians did not engage in pitched battle, so cultural mixing created wars of "devastating character" as the English pursued "total war." Hirsch, "The Collision of Military Cultures in Seventh-Century New England," *Journal of American History*, Vol. 74, No. 4 (March 1988): 1210–1211. Wayne Lee reminds us that the Natives could escalate conflict and pursue a "total war" in their own right. Lee, "Peace Chiefs and Blood Revenge," 728, 732.

20. Cave, *The Pequot War*, 122, 163. For the growing rivalry between these two colonies, see Jennings, *The Invasion of America*, 201.

21. Recent literature stresses the shared cultural relationship between Natives and settlers in the New England area on the eve of the war. Russell Bourne calls it a "biracial society" and laments that there were not enough people to make one culture out of two that ultimately were not that different from one another. See Bourne, *The Red King's Rebellion: Racial Politics in New England, 1675–1678* (New York: Oxford University Press, 1990), xii, xiii. Jill Lepore says the two sides went to war because of the loss of identity inherent in creating a mixed society. See Lepore, *The Name of War: King Philip's War and the Origins of American Identity* (New York: Alfred A. Knopf, 1998), 8, 240. James D. Drake argues the Natives lost a civil war, not just among themselves as they splintered with some supporting the English and others not, but one that ended the strong links and ties that bound colonials and Natives in the region together. See Drake, *King Philip's War: Civil War in New England, 1675–1676* (Amherst: University of Massachusetts Press, 1999), 14, 17, 198–199. Altogether, these views challenge Douglas E. Leach's history stressing a lack of coexistence between "savages" and settlers, an "us versus them" account where one side, colonialss, eliminated an inferior

opponent, the Natives. See Leach, *Flintlock and Tomahawk: New England in King Philip's War* (Woodstock, VT: The Countryman Press, 1958, 2009), 250.

22. Jennings, *The Invasion of America*, 300. Those authors who argue otherwise overstate the issue, believing the exaggerated claims of "survivors." Lapore does this in *The Name of War*, 72, 74, 176. This characterization is surprising because otherwise Lapore skillfully scrutinizes the statements of colonials.

23. For both Narragansett defiance and English coveting land at their expense, see Steele, *Warpaths*, 94, 102. Jennings, as was the case with the Pequots, repeats his view of competition among colonies as driving the English to make war on the Narragansett. See Jennings, *The Invasion of America*, 255.

24. Malone says King Philip led an "insurgency" for this reason. See Malone, *The Skulking Way of War*, 2, 119. Steele emphasizes that "Plymouth leaders had claimed to be overlords of the Natives, so the war against the Wampanoag was a rebellion rather than a war against a sovereign enemy." Steele, *Warpaths*, 107. Starkey says that when Philip took over in 1662 he signed a treaty declaring the Wampanoag's were "subjects of the English crown." Starkey, *European and Native American Warfare*, 65. The treaty reads as follows: "Phillip doth, for himselfe and his successors, desire that they may for ever remaine subject to the Kinge of England." Document 4: Conference and Treaty, Metacom (Philip) and New Plymouth, August 6, 1662, in *Early American Indian Documents: Treaties and Laws, 1607–1789*, ed. Alden T. Vaughan, Volume XIX, *New England Treaties, Southeast, 1524–1761* (Bethesda, MD: Congressional Information Services, 2003), 403.

25. Benjamin Church, *Diary of King Philip's War 1675–76* (Chester, CT: Pequot Press, 1975), 77, 79.

Chapter 2

1. Robert Wooster uses this label to define the English hopes of the Proclamation line of 1763 as a division between settlers and Natives, and then American aspirations of using the Mississippi River and later a series of forts to define a border between

Americans and Natives. Wooster, *The Military and the United States Indian Policy, 1865–1903* (Lincoln: University of Nebraska Press, 1988), 6.

2. Alan Milet and Peter Maslowski, *For the Common Defense: A Military History of the United States of America* (New York: The Free Press, 1984), 23–25; and Fred Anderson, *Crucible of War: The Seven Years' War and the Fate of Empire in British North America, 1754–1766* (New York: Vintage Books, 2000), 545.

3. Richard White says the Natives were not dependent on France in the Great Lakes region. See White, *The Middle Ground: Indians, Empires, and Republics in the Great Lakes Region, 1650–1815* (New York: Cambridge University Press, 1991), 140–141, 309. Daniel K. Richter concludes the opposite for the Iroquois living just south of the *pays d'en haut* in the Great Lakes region. See Richter, *Ordeal of the Longhouse: The Peoples of the Iroquois League in the Era of European Colonization* (Chapel Hill: University of North Carolina Press, 1992), 86–87.

4. Francis Parkman, *The Conspiracy of Pontiac and the Indian War after the Conquest of Canada*, Vol. 1 (Lincoln: University of Nebraska Press, 1994, 1870), 186; Howard Peckham, *Pontiac and the Indian Uprising* (Princeton, NJ: Princeton University Press, 1947), 105–106; and Gregory Evans Dowd, *War Under Heaven: Pontiac, the Indian Nations, and the British Empire* (Baltimore: Johns Hopkins University Press, 2002), 123. Dowd, in an earlier study, argued at variance with Parkman and himself by suggesting that the Natives propagated rumors of French return to the region as a means of influencing France to do just that. See Dowd, "The French King Wakes Up in Detroit: 'Pontiac's War' in Rumor and History," *Ethnohistory*, Vol. 37, No. 3 (Summer 1990): 255.

5. Dowd, *War Under Heaven*, 60.

6. Dowd is best here, seeking to place Pontiac in his own "middle ground," not an all-powerful chief but a key leader. See Dowd, *War Under Heaven*, 9. Dowd follows Richard White's lead in *The Middle Ground*, 288, 295, 297. David Dixon counters this view, acknowledging those scholars deemphasizing Pontiac's role but placing that

chief at the center of the rebellion because he possessed the "respect necessary to maintain a fragile coalition." Dixon, *Never Come to Peace Again: Pontiac's Uprising and the Fate of the British Empire in North America* (Norman: University of Oklahoma Press, 2005), 131–132. Dixon follows Peckman, *Pontiac and the Indian Uprising*, 321–322, and Parkman, *The Conspiracy of Pontiac*, Vol 1, 187. Peckman, however, disparages Parkman's placing of Pontiac as the focal point, in Peckman, *Pontiac and the Indian Uprising*, n, 108–111.

7. See Dowd, *War Under Heaven*, 96, 104. Dowd again follows Richard White's lead in *The Middle Ground*, 288.

8. Dowd, *War Under Heaven*, 70, 75, 82–83.

9. William R. Nester relays the familiar effort of the English trying to spread smallpox among the Natives, a design primarily between Amherst and Colonel Henry Bouqet. Nester, *"Haughty Conquerors": Amherst and the Great Indian Uprising of 1763* (Westport, CT: Praeger, 2000), 114–115. Dowd emphasizes that more than Amherst favored extermination. See Dowd, *War Under Heaven*, 189–190. One scholar traces the use of this "biological warfare" by some Natives and colonials in North America far beyond the French and Indian War. See Elizabeth A. Fenn, "Biological Warfare in Eighteenth-Century North America: Beyond Jeffery Amherst," *Journal of American History*, Vol. 86, No. 4 (March 2000): 1553, 1558, 1565.

10. Dowd, *War Under Heaven,* 162, 167.

11. Conquest and resistance is arguably Parkman's view of the struggle. See Francis Parkman, *The Conspiracy of Pontiac*, Vol. 1, viii, Preface to the First Edition, xxi.

12. Daniel J. Herman, "Romance on the Middle Ground," *Journal of the Early Republic*, Vol. 19, No. 2 (Summer 1999): 283.

13. Colin G. Calloway stresses that while the Natives were badly hurt by the American Revolution, they emerged intact. The biggest problem was the outcome of the war that left the Natives with no allies, and since many Natives had sided with England, the Americans now sought removal of Natives, not assimilation. See Calloway, *The American Revolution in Indian Country: Crisis and Diversity in Native American Communities* (Cambridge: Cambridge University Press, 1995), 273, 291, 293.

14. The literature almost uniformly praises Tecumseh for his efforts at Native diplomacy. David Edmunds complicates this view by arguing that Tenskwatawa had more success in rallying Native support given his appeal to mysticism, a far stronger pull than Tecumseh's appeal to power politics. See Edmunds, "Tecumseh, the Shawnee Prophet, and American History: A Reassessment," *The Washington Historical Quarterly*, Vol. 14, No. 3 (July 1983): 275. Alfred Cave goes further, arguing that Tenskwatawa remained a key figure even after defeat at Tippecanoe. Cave, "The Shawnee Prophet, Tecumseh, and Tippecanoe: A Case Study of Historical Myth-Making," *Journal of the Early Republic*, 22 (Winter 2002): 640.

15. Preaching a race war is in Glenn Tucker, *Tecumseh: Vision of Glory* (New York: Bobbs-Merrill, 1956), 209. Recent scholarship also offers more nuance, arguing race is a poor measure explaining the cause of the fighting. More compelling is that tribes such as the Miamis in league with the French rejected the call of unity among Natives seeing such a goal as a threat to their "local interests." The Americans believed interfering French or English as one and the same thing driving a supposed Native unity, something that did not exist. Multiethnic alliances between Natives and Europeans trumped racial divides. See Patrick Bottiger, "Prophetstown for Their Own Purposes: The French, Miamis, and Cultural Identities in the Wabash-Maumee Valley," *Journal of the Early Republic*, Vol. 33, No. 1 (Spring 2013): 30–31, 52, 59. Dowd argues that Natives did act beyond "locality" as part of a militant nativist movement expressing a larger continental commonality. Gregory Dowd, *A Spirited Resistance: The North American Indian Struggle for Unity, 1745–1815* (Baltimore: The Johns Hopkins University Press,1992), xiii, xv.

16. Sugden, *Tecumseh*, 300. A less flattering view, although not intended as such, is to see Brock's support of Tecumseh as more evidence of Brock's rashness born of that general's inflated sense of honor. See Jonathon Riley, *A Matter of Honor: The Life,*

Campaigns, and Generalship of Isaac Brock (Montreal: Robin Brass Studio, 2011), 243, 304.

17. John Sugden tries to offer a more balanced view of the relationship between Tecumseh and Procter, one not all bad but clearly ineffective. See Sugden, *Tecumseh*, 322, 342. So too does Tucker, *Tecumseh*, 285, 295.

18. Robert Remini, *Andrew Jackson and His Indian Wars* (New York: Viking, 2001), 76.

19. Gregory A. Waselkov, *A Conquering Spirit: Fort Mims and the Redstick War of 1813–1814* (Tuscaloosa: University of Alabama, 2006), 3.

20. William Belko describes Jackson's punitive strike south into Florida against the Seminoles as merely an "epilogue" to the War of 1812. Ending British interference remained his primary objective. William S. Belko, "Epilogue to the War of 1812: The Monroe Administration, American Anglophobia, and the First Seminole War," in *America's Hundred Years' War: U.S. Expansion to the Gulf Coast and the Fate of the Seminole, 1763–1858*, ed. William S. Belko (Gainesville: University Press of Florida, 2011), 53, 67, 96. Dowd says Jackson saw only English intrigues behind Native disturbances in the south. Dowd, *A Spirited Resistance*, 119. The Creeks saw more local concerns, striking Fort Mims to send a message to factions within their polity in order to shore up their front when opposing American land encroachment. Karl Davis, "'Remember Fort Mims': Reinterpreting the Origins of the Creek War," *Journal of the Early Republic*, 22 (Winter 2002): 613, 635.

21. Belko points out that both houses of Congress were as fearful of British interference in Florida as Jackson. That view did not prevent a Senate committee from rebuking Jackson. Belko, "Epilogue to the War of 1812," 92, 93.

22. Douglas Hurt, *The Indian Frontier, 1763–1846* (Albuquerque: University of New Mexico Press, 2002), 119, 126, 131; and Susan Richbourg Parker, "So in Fear of Both the Indians and the Americans," in *America's Hundred Years' War: U.S. Expansion to the Gulf Coast and the Fate of the Seminole, 1763–1858*, ed. William S. Belko (Gainesville: Uni-

versity Press of Florida, 2011), 30. David Weber stresses the lasting cultural impact of Spanish rule in North America no matter its feeble political reach. Weber, *The Spanish Frontier in North America* (New Haven, CT: Yale University Press,1992), 9–12. This lasting Spanish legacy in the region could not reverse Native eclipse stemming from limited Spanish support of Native resistance to American expansion.

23. Many Americans viewed Spain as functioning as a "trustee," nominally in control of areas that would pass to the United States given American settlement. See John M. Murrin, "The Jeffersonian Triumph and American Exceptionalism," *Journal of the Early Republic*, Vol. 20, No. 1 (Spring 2000): 10. Obviously, Spain's aiding and abetting of Natives upended this rosy American view.

Chapter 3

1. John Grenier, *The First Way of War: American War Making on the Frontier, 1607–1814* (New York: Cambridge University Press, 2005), 1, 10–11.

2. Grenier, *The First Way of War*, 1. For French encouragement of Native frontier raiding, see Fred Anderson, *Crucible of War: The Seven Years' War and the Fate of Empire in British North America, 1754–1766* (New York: Vintage Books, 2000), 151, 238.

3. Grenier, *The First War of War*, 62. Armstrong Starkey calls Rogers' rangers "the most famous Anglo-American frontier fighters of the time." See Starkey, *European and Native American Warfare, 1675–1815* (Norman: University of Oklahoma Press, 1998), 3.

4. Starkey, *European and Native American Warfare*, 4, 101. Starkey references Colin G. Calloway's use of the label of psychological warfare in *The Western Abenakis of Vermont, 1600–1800: War, Migration, and the Survival of an Indian People* (Norman: University of Oklahoma Press, 1990), 177–179.

5. James Pritchard, *In Search of Empire: The French in the Americas, 1670–1730* (New York: Cambridge University Press, 2004), xx-xxi, 421.

6. Starkey, *European and Native American Warfare*, 125. No doubt military conflict badly hurt the Iroquois, but so too did the

constant and remorseless American push for settlement. See Alan Taylor, *The Divided Ground: Indians, Settlers and the Northern Borderland of the American Revolution* (New York: Alfred A. Knopf, 2006), 6, 8.

7. Barbara Mann, *George Washington's War on Native America* (Westport, CT: Praeger, 2005), 111.

8. Jon Mack Faragher, *Daniel Boone: The Life and Legend of an American Pioneer* (New York: Henry Holt, 1992), 77, 114. Faragher is Boone's foremost biographer but he shrinks from calling Boone's actions in terms of making Native Americans more vulnerable to expansion anything more than merely leading an "intrusion." See Faragher, *Daniel Boone*, 144. A more recent and also very good biography goes further, overtly stating Boone's role in aiding settlement that went far in helping to end "Indian power." See Meredith Mason Brown, *Frontiersman: Daniel Boone and the Making of America* (Baton Rouge: Louisiana State University Press, 2008), xiv.

9. Faragher, *Daniel Boone*, 55.

10. Both quotes in Faragher, *Daniel Boone*, 230, 264.

11. James A. Shackford, *David Crockett: The Man and the Legend* (Chapel Hill: University of North Carolina Press, 1956), 25.

12. Michael Lofaro is best here. He asserts that if you strip away the legend, Crockett is but an ordinary man and not really that noteworthy. See Lofaro, *Davy Crockett: The Man, the Legend, the Legacy, 1786–1986* (Knoxville: University of Tennessee, 1985), 7–8. Lofaro emphasizes Crockett's dual persona of hero and fallible man in his edited book, *Crockett at Two Hundred: New Perspectives on the Man and the Myth*, ed. Michael Lofaro (Knoxville: University of Tennessee, 1989).

13. Shackford, *David Crockett*, 212.

14. William C. Davis, *Lone Star Rising: The Revolutionary Birth of the Texas Republic* (New York: Free Press, 2004), 229–230.

15. For Travis and Bowie, see William C. Davis, *Three Roads to the Alamo: The Saga of David Crockett, James Bowie, and William Barret Travis* (New York: HarperCollins, 1998), 206, 61. For Crockett, see Shackford, *David Crockett*, 211. Davis argues Crockett was caught in between a search for land and the need to fight for Texas independence.

Davis, *Three Roads to the Alamo*, 408–409, 411, 414.

16. Carroll Smith-Rosenberg, *Disorderly Conduct: Visions of Gender in Victorian America* (New York: Oxford University Press, 1986), 101, 106–108.

17. For American apprehension over European claims, see Alan Taylor, "The Science of Distant Empire, 1768–1811," in Douglas Seefeldt, ed., *Across the Continent* (Charlottesville, VA: University of Virginia, 2005), 16–17.

18. For "demographic imperialism" excused by American Exceptionalism, see Gordon S. Wood, *Empire of Liberty: A History of the Early Republic, 1789–1815* (New York: Oxford University Press, 2009), 357, 398. Brian Steele says Jefferson allowed for Native inclusion in the American republic should they surrender their way of life and commit "cultural suicide." See Steele, *Thomas Jefferson and American Nationhood* (Cambridge: University of Cambridge, 2012), 173, 176. Peter S. Onuf argues Jefferson looked for something better, that Natives would join in union with Americans and not "disappear from the earth." See Onuf, *Jefferson's Empire: The Language of American Nationhood* (Charlottesville, VA: University Press of Virginia, 2000), 52, 51.

19. See two essays by James Ronda in *Voyages of Discovery: Essays on the Lewis and Clark Expedition*, ed. James P. Ronda (Helena: Montana Historical Society, 1998), 304, 333. Other scholars push back and stress that the expedition delivered scientific import. See a series of essays in Robert S. Cox, ed., *The Shortest and Most Convenient Route: Lewis and Clark in Context* (Philadelphia: American Historical Society, 2004), 201–203, 231–233, 246–248.

20. "Boots on the ground" is in Frederick E. Hoxie, "Introduction: What Can We Learn from a Bicentennial?" in *Lewis and Clark and the Indian Country: The Native American Perspective*, eds. Frederick E. Hoxie and Jay T. Nelson (Chicago: University of Illinois Press, 2007), 8. Characterizing the expedition as an "advance guard" is in Peter S. Onuf and Jeffrey L. Hantman, "Introduction: Geopolitics, Science, and Culture Conflicts," in *Across the Continent: Jefferson, Lewis and Clark, and the Making of America*, eds.

Douglas Seefeldt, Jeffery L. Hantman, and Peter S. Onuf (Charlottesville, VA: University of Virginia Press, 2005), 4.

21. James P. Ronda, *Lewis and Clark Among the Indians* (Lincoln: University of Nebraska Press, 1984), 113.

22. Nicholas Biddle, Tuesday, March 18, 1806, *History of the Expedition under the Command of Lewis and Clark*, ed. Elliot Coues, Vol. II (New York: Dover Publications, 1965), 816.

23. For Sacagawea's contributions, see Stephen E. Ambrose, *Undaunted Courage* (New York: Simon & Schuster, 1997), 197–198, 225.

24. Ronda, *Lewis and Clark Among the Indians,* 213. For Bernard DeVoto, see *The Course of Empire* (Boston: Houghton Mifflin, 1952), 411.

25. Richard White, *"It's Your Misfortune and None of My Own": A New History of the American West* (Norman: University of Oklahoma Press, 1991), 46–47. The duality contributed to the lack of recognition bestowed on mountain men by those streaming west since these settlers accepted these heroic figures in the name of a nationalism demanding the marginalization of mountain men and Natives alike. See Jon T. Colman, *Here Lies Hugh Glass: A Mountain Man, a Bear, and the Rise of the American Nation* (New York: Hill and Wang, 2012), 209–210.

Chapter 4

1. Francis P. Prucha, *Great Father: The United States Government and the American Indians* (Lincoln: University of Nebraska Press, 1984), 16, 59.

2. Prucha, *Great Father*, 52–58.

3. Jeffrey Ostler covers very well expansion on behalf of liberty premised on the yeoman farmer. See *The Plains Sioux and U.S. Colonialism from Lewis and Clark to Wounded Knee* (New York: Cambridge University Press, 2004), 13, 18. With settlement, American expansion was to be different from, and better than, European claims in the west due to an American ability to "conquer without war." See Robert W. Tucker, *Empire of Liberty: The Statecraft of Thomas Jefferson* (New York: Oxford, 1990), ix, x. A

darker side is settlers wielding the term "American" in the name of liberty only for themselves. See John M. Murrin, "The Jeffersonian Triumph and American Exceptionalism," *Journal of the Early Republic*, Vol. 20, No. 1 (Spring 2000): 4.

4. Anthony F.C. Wallace, *Jefferson and the Indians: The Tragic Fate of the First Americans* (Cambridge, MA: Harvard University Press, 1999), 20; and Peter S. Onuf, *Jefferson's Empire: The Language of American Nationhood* (Charlottesville, VA: University Press of Virginia, 2000), 19, 28. Bernard W. Sheehan faults Jefferson as well as his generation for legitimizing Removal due to the "white man's proclivity for conceptualization and idealization" of the Native. See Sheehan, *Seeds of Extinction: Jeffersonian Philanthropy and the American Indian* (Chapel Hill: University of North Carolina Press, 1973), 7–8.

5. For Clark, see Murrin, "The Jeffersonian Triumph and American Exceptionalism," 3. For Harrison, see Robert M. Owens, "Jeffersonian Benevolence on the Ground: The Indian Land Cession Treaties of William Henry Harrison," *Journal of the Early Republic*, Vol. 23, No. 2 (Fall 2002): 435.

6. Brian Steele, *Thomas Jefferson and American Nationhood* (Cambridge: University of Cambridge Press, 2012), 239; Onuf, *Jefferson's Empire*, 53.

7. Robert Utley presents these choices as the product of the "Permanent Indian Frontier," the promise of a sanctuary allowing Natives to define their civilization after Removal as either gradual incorporation into the new nation or adhering to a separate sovereignty within U.S. borders. Utley, *The Indian Frontier, 1846–1890*, 33. Other scholars attribute less clarity to Jefferson, that the fate of the Natives hung on the ambiguity in the "dual policy" of both offering a separate status on reservations or allowing civilized Natives incorporation into the nation. When Americans spread west, neither would be honored as Anthony F.C. Wallace presents in *Jefferson and the Indians: The Tragic Fate of the First Americans* (Cambridge, MA: Harvard University Press, 1999), 17, 19. Kevin Bruyneel argues that the ambiguity meant tribes straddled the boundary of existing in or outside of the United States, so a third space of sovereignty, creating a harmful colonial

status that still limits the development of indigenous peoples. See Bruyneel, *The Third Space of Sovereignty: The Postcolonial Politics of U.S.-Indigenous Relations* (Minneapolis: University of Minnesota Press, 2007), xv, xvii. Brian Steele sees only one, harmful outcome; Natives would have to assimilate and "cease being Indians." See Steele, *Thomas Jefferson and American Nationhood*, 174.

8. Jacksonian democracy as more than a geographical divide between east and west underscores this point. See Jackson's rise to the presidency as a result of a shift in democracy toward a popular mandate favoring "liberated capitalism" in order to restore egalitarianism in the face of an entrenched elite, something not geographically specific to the west. Richard Hofstadter, *The American Political Tradition and the Men Who Made It* (New York: Vintage Books, 1959), 55–56. The politics of that time represented the "movement of ideas" and examining the "beliefs and motives" of a "business community" emerging in the east and south realigns assumptions of "Western influence in American government." Arthur M. Schlesinger, Jr., *The Age of Jackson* (Boston: Little, Brown and Company, 1953), x.

9. Robert V. Remini, *Andrew Jackson and His Indian Wars* (New York: Viking, 2001), 228. Remini in particular endorses this view as presented in Paul Prucha, "Andrew Jackson's Indian Policy: A Reassessment," *Journal of American History* (December 1969), LVL: 534–536. Other scholars reject this tolerant view of Removal. Michael Paul Rogin sees a Jackson pathology in the act. See Rogin, *Fathers and Children: Andrew Jackson and the Subjugation of the American Indian* (New Brunswick, NJ: Transaction Publishers, 1991), xxiii-xxiv. Ronald N. Satz faults more than Jackson, laying blame on the instruments of government in *American Indian Policy in the Jacksonian Era* (Norman: University of Oklahoma Press, 2002, 1975), 293, 294.

10. Andrew Denson, *Demanding the Cherokee Nation: Indian Autonomy and American Culture, 1830–1900* (Lincoln: University of Nebraska Press, 2004), 50, 51. This pursuit included establishing a racial hierarchy with themselves at the top. That definition allowed the Cherokee to emulate American racial ideology and appeal to a Cherokee racial standing as a badge of Cherokee sovereignty. So again they acted both within the U.S. state and independent of it. Fay A. Yarbrough, *Race and the Cherokee Nation: Sovereignty in the Nineteenth Century* (Philadelphia: University of Pennsylvania Press, 208), 5, 7.

11. Remini, *Andrew Jackson and His Indian Wars*, 257.

12. Federal inaction allowed the state courts to "conform to public opinion" and use the judicial system to legitimize Removal. Tim Alan Garrison, *The Legal Ideology of Removal: The Southern Judiciary and the Sovereignty of Native American Nations* (Athens: University of Georgia Press, 2009, 2002), 238.

13. Frank Pommersheim, *Broken Landscape: Indians, Indian Tribes, and the Constitution* (New York: Oxford University Press, 2009), 105.

14. David E. Wilkens, *American Indian Sovereignty and the U.S. Supreme Court: The Masking of Justice* (Austin: University of Texas Press, 1997), 22, 63.

15. Samuel J. Watson, *Jackson's Sword: The Army Officer Corps on the American Frontier, 1810–1821* (Lawrence: University Press of Kansas, 2012), 143.

16. Paul Prucha, *Documents of United States Indian Policy* (Lincoln: University of Nebraska Press, 1990), 50–51.

17. Americans also drew the support of a number of tribes such as the Sioux, Chippewas, Winnebagos, and Foxes. See John W. Hall, *Uncommon Defense: Indian Allies in the Black Hawk War* (Cambridge, MA: Harvard University Press, 2009), 8–10.

18. For Regulars disdaining the killing, see Kerry A. Trask, *Black Hawk: The Battle for the Heart of America* (New York: Henry Holt, 2006), 290, 293. Patrick Jung presents a more mixed picture, militia certainly leading the slaughter but also joined by some Regulars. See Jung, *The Black Hawk War of 1832* (Norman: University of Oklahoma Press, 2007), 170–174.

19. Tena L. Helton, "What the White 'Squaws' Want from Black Hawk: Gendering the Fan-Celebrity Relationship," *American Indian Quarterly*, Vol. 34, No. 4 (Fall 2010): 500, 517.

20. John Missall and Mary Lou Missall, *The Seminole Wars: America's Longest Indian Conflict* (Gainesville: University Press of Florida, 2004), 7. John H. Mahan says the term Seminoles meant "wild people" as designated by a British agent in the region. See Mahon, *History of the Second Seminole War, 1835–1842* (Gainesville, FL: University Press of Florida, 1967), 7.

21. Kevin Mulroy sees a strong break between Seminoles and Maroons. See Mulroy, *Freedom on the Border: The Seminole Maroons in Florida, the Indian Territory, Coahuila, and Texas* (Lubbock: Texas Tech University Press, 1993), 10–11. Kenneth Wiggins Porter sees the groups as closely allied. See Porter, *The Black Seminoles: History of a Freedom-Seeking People*, rev. & ed. Alcione M. Amos and Thomas P. Senter (Gainesville, FL: University Press of Florida, 1996), 5–7.

22. For Abraham's role and that of "Negro Seminoles" "allied" to the Seminoles, see Kenneth Wiggins Porter, "Negros and the Seminole War, 1835–1842," *The Journal of Southern History*, Vol. 30, No. 4 (Nov. 1964): 432–433, 438–439. Missal says Abraham did not distort his message; any confusion arose from a "gap" in language. Missall, *The Seminole Wars*, 85. Porter also stresses Jesup's declaration of a Negro War as an effort to separate Blacks from the Seminoles to speed an end to the resistance. Porter, "Negros and the Seminole War," 427, 436. Matthew Clavin emphasizes this move as an indication of the extent of American fears of fighting in Florida spurring on slave revolts beyond that territory, making that war less an "Indian" war. See Clavin, "'It is a Negro, Not an Indian War,'" in *America's Hundred Years' War: U.S. Expansion to the Gulf Coast and the Fate of the Seminole, 1763–1858*, ed. William S. Belko (Gainesville: University Press of Florida, 2011), 182, 183.

23. Missall, *The Seminole Wars*, 90.

24. Peters, *The Florida Wars*, 144.

25. Missall, *The Seminole Wars*, 146.

26. Missall, *The Seminole Wars*, 216.

Chapter 5

1. Attacking enemy settlements increasingly absorbed American efforts over this prolonged struggle and suggests a "first way of war" long after 1815, the date when John Grenier ends his study, *The First Way of War: American War Making on the Frontier, 1607–1814* (New York: Cambridge University Press, 2005).

2. For the characterization of neutrality, see William W. Newcomb, *The Indians of Texas: From Prehistoric to Modern Times* (Austin: University of Texas Press, 2002, 1961), 345. Natives in the southwest maintained vibrant communities that were independently trading and interacting with Spaniards and Mexicans. The Americans greatly altered this equilibrium. See Elizabeth A.H. John, *Storms Brewed in Other Men's Worlds: The Confrontation of Indians, Spanish, and French in the Southwest, 1540–1795* (Norman: University of Oklahoma Press, 1996, 1975), xvii–xx; and Gary Clayton Anderson, *The Indian Southwest, 1580–1830: Ethnogenesis and Reinvention* (Norman: University of Oklahoma Press, 1999), 4, 6.

3. John Edward Weems, *To Conquer a Peace: The War Between the United States and Mexico* (College Station: Texas A&M University Press, 1988, 1974), 67, 101, 111.

4. Brian DeLay, *War of a Thousand Deserts: Indian Raids and the U.S.-Mexican War* (New Haven, CT: Yale University Press, 2008), 283, 291, 294. Irving Levinson presents a much different picture, one of guerrilla activity threatening American forces and Mexican elites. See Levinson, "A New Paradigm for an Old Conflict: The Mexico-United States War," *Journal of military History*, Vol. 73, No. 2 (April 2009): 394; and again in his book, *Wars Within War: Mexican Guerrillas, Domestic Elites, and the United States of America, 1846–1848* (Fort Worth: TCU Press, 2005), xv–xvi, 112–113.

5. Gary Clayton Anderson, *The Conquest of Texas: Ethnic Cleansing in the Promised Land, 1820–1875* (Norman: University of Oklahoma Press, 2005), 179.

6. Walter Prescott Webb, *The Texas Rangers: A Century of Frontier Defense* (Austin: University of Texas Press, 1935), xv, 15. Michael Collins responds to Webb's too "sanitized history" by stressing that to Spanish-speakers, Rangers were the devil personified. One could say Natives had the same reaction. See Collins, *Texas Devils: Rangers and Regulars on the Lower Rio*

Grande, 1846–1861 (Norman: University of Oklahoma Press, 2008), 5, 257–258.

7. William H. Leckie, *The Military Conquest of the Southern Plains* (Norman: University of Oklahoma Press, 1963), 13.

8. Anderson, *The Conquest of Texas*, 9, 246.

9. Robert Utley, *Lone Star Justice: The First Century of the Texas Rangers* (New York: Oxford University Press, 2002), 91.

10. Utley, *Lone Star Justice,* 202.

11. Pekka Hamalainen, *The Comanche Empire* (New Haven, CT: Yale University Press, 2008), 2. Anderson stresses the small number of raids from 1860 to 1865 in *The Conquest of Texas*, 328. F. Todd Smith also stresses this decrease as a watershed in *From Dominance to Disappearance: The Indians of Texas and the Near Southwest, 1786–1859* (Lincoln: University of Nebraska Press, 2005), 246. Gregory Michno says the war climaxed in the 1860s so that after that decade Native raiding markedly decreased. See Michno, *The Settler's War: The Struggle for the Texas Frontier in the 1860s* (Caldwell, ID: Caxton Press, 2011), 398.

12. Anderson, *The Conquest of Texas*, 303.

13. Gray H. Whaley is best here. Given the mixed Native resistance, there were multiple, closely related wars in the region. Natives enjoyed some unity but suffered just as many limitations. Thus there was no "grand tribal alliance," but instead some "contingency planning." See Whaley, *Oregon and the Collapse of Illahee: U.S. Empire and the Transformation of an Indigenous World, 1792–1859* (Chapel Hill: University of North Carolina Press, 2010), 216. Alexandra Harmon says Natives shared a system of communication with outsiders that helped them forge an "Indian" identity. See Harmon, *Indians in the Making: Ethnic Relations and Indian Identities Around Puget Sound* (Berkeley: University of California Press, 1998), 6, 8, 248.

14. E.A. Schwartz, *The Rogue River Indian War and Its Aftermath, 1850–1980* (Norman: University of Oklahoma Press, 1997), 93.

15. Robert Wooster, *The American Military Frontiers: The United States Army in the West, 1783–1900* (Albuquerque: University of New Mexico Press, 2009), 139.

16. Whaley, *Oregon and the Collapse of Illahee*, 217. Efforts like this prompt Nathan Douthit to argue the war never did reach that of extermination thanks to a limited but present middle ground. See Douthit, *Uncertain Encounters: Indians and Whites at Peace and War in Southern Oregon, 1820s-1860s* (Corvallis: Oregon State University Press, 2002), 3–4. In fact, this middle ground reemerged after the war as the reservation system failed to keep Americans and Natives apart from one another. See Douthit, *Uncertain Encounters*, 189–190. Brad Asher says legal action allowed Natives to integrate into local society despite confinement to reservations. See Asher, *Beyond the Reservation: Indians Settlers, and the Law in Washington Territory, 1853–1889* (Norman: University of Oklahoma Press, 1999), 5, 14–15.

17. Odie B. Faulk, *Crimson Desert: Indian Wars of the American Southwest* (New York: Oxford University Press, 1974), 155; and David Roberts, *Once They Moved Like the Wind: Cochise, Geronimo, and the Apache Wars* (New York: Simon & Schuster, 1993), 31, 33.

18. For Pinos Altos, see Roberts, *Once They Moved Like the Wind*, 37; for Tucson, see Faulk, *Crimson Desert*, 166.

19. Accounts are consistent in the ambiguity of blame for the killing. Donald E. Worcester, *The Apaches: Eagles of the Southwest* (Norman: University of Oklahoma Press, 1979), 89–90; Paul I. Wellman, *Death in the Desert: The Fifty Years' War for the Great Southwest* (Norman: University of Nebraska Press, 1987), 88–89.

20. Dan L. Thrapp, *The Conquest of Apacheria* (Norman: University of Oklahoma Press, 1967), xii.

21. Wooster, *The American Military Frontiers*, 172.

22. The Camp Grant travesty is well known. See Faulk, *Crimson Desert*, 163, 166. Other scholarship stresses a broad pattern of racism producing sham trials unduly convicting Apache defendants and destroying Apache legal customs in the process. See Claire V. McKanna, *White Justice in Arizona: Apache Murder Trials in the Nineteenth Century* (Lubbock: Texas Tech University Press, 2005), 15, 165, 183.

23. Wooster, *The American Military Frontiers*, 206.

24. Thrapp, *The Conquest of Apacheria,* 24–25.

25. Wooster, *The American Military Frontiers,* 210.

26. The first quote is in Wellman, *Death in the Desert,* 135; the second is in Thomas C. Leonard, "Red, White, and the Army Blue: Empathy and Anger in the American West," *American Quarterly,* Vol. 26, No. 2 (May 1974): 181.

Chapter 6

1. Paul VanDevelder, *Savages and Scoundrels: The Untold Story of the Road to Empire Through Indian Territory* (New Haven, CT: Yale University Press, 2009), 180, 199. Rather than harmony, Richard White suggests the Sioux and their allies dominated the meeting and imposed any accord, and continued expanding their territory after 1851 until 1876. See White, "The Winning of the West: The Expansion of the Western Sioux in the Eighteenth and Nineteenth Centuries," *Journal of American History,* Vol. 65, No. 2 (September 1978), 340.

2. Robert M. Utley, *The Indian Frontier, 1846–1890,* Revised Edition (Albuquerque: University of New Mexico Press, 1984), 44–45.

3. Paul N. Beck says after Harney's attack, the Sioux resolved to resist further American advances. See Beck, *The First Sioux War: The Grattan Fight and Blue Water Creek, 1854–1856* (Lanham, MD: University Press of America, 2004), 131–132. Paul VanDevelder says Harney, with this attack, dispelled any plains Natives' beliefs in accord with Americans. See VanDevelder, *Savages and Scoundrels,* 218–219.

4. Beck, *The First Sioux War,* 134; R. Eli Paul, *Blue Water Creek and the First Sioux War, 1854–1856* (Norman: University of Oklahoma Press, 2004), 164.

5. John D. Unruh, *The Plains Across: The Overland Emigrants and the Trans-Mississippi West, 1840–1860* (Urbana: University of Illinois Press, 1979), 201. The numbers are inconsistent but stress the extreme difficulty of the Army "policing" the west due to low numbers. Andrew Birtle says a number just over 27,000 had to man 116 posts in the west alone. See Birtle, *U.S.*

Army Counterinsurgency and Contingency Operations Doctrine, 1860–1941 (Washington, D.C.: Center of Military History, 2003), 59. Utley says that number of 27,000 came in 1874 after drastic reduction in the Army, so a marginally larger force was available before this date. See Utley, *Frontier Regulars: The U.S. Army and the Indian, 1866–1891* (New York: Macmillan, 1973), 16.

6. Robert Utley reviews the fighting qualities of soldiers and Natives before and during the Civil War in *Frontiersmen in Blue: The U.S. Army and the Indian, 1848–1865* (New York: Macmillan, 1967), 6–9, and also after the war in *Frontier Regulars: The U.S. Army and the Indian, 1866–1891* (New York: Macmillan, 1973), 6–7, 25, 49–50, 73–74, 87–88. See also Ball, *Army Regulars,* 36–37.

7. David Roberts, *Once They Moved Like the Wind: Cochise, Geronimo, and the Apache Wars* (New York: Simon & Schuster, 1993), 39–40. Other accounts say the local Confederate commander acted on his own and the Rebel government relieved him in favor of a more moderate policy of selling Natives as slaves. Donald E. Worcester, *The Apaches: Eagles of the Southwest* (Norman: University of Oklahoma Press, 1979), 81–82.

8. Clifford E. Trafzer, *Kit Carson Campaign: The Last Great Navajo War* (Norman: University of Oklahoma Press, 1982), 224–25, 237–38.

9. William H. Leckie, *The Military Conquest of the Southern Plains* (Norman: University of Oklahoma Press, 1963), 21.

10. Utley, *The Indian Frontier,* 93.

11. For the charge of murder, see Wooster, *The American Military Frontiers,* 184; for prisoners of war, see Jerome A. Green, *Washita: The U.S. Army and the Southern Cheyennes, 1867–1869* (Norman: University of Oklahoma Press, 2004), 19. Declaring this event a "massacre" is still being debated among the public and scholars; that debate resolved only in the good news that the "tragedy" will never be forgotten. See Ari Kelman, *A Misplaced Massacre: Struggling Over the Memory of Sand Creek* (Cambridge, MA: Harvard University Press, 2013), 262.

12. Utley, *The Indian Frontier,* 102.

13. For Chivington's failure to continue to attack, see Anthony's letter to his brother cited in Elliott West, *The Contested Plains:*

Indians, Goldseekers, and the Rush to Colorado (Lawrence: University of Kansas Press, 1998), 306. Anthony testified that he had opposed the attack, a claim that the investigators found suspect. See Hoig, *The Sand Creek Massacre*, 167. Jerome Greene says Anthony gave the attack his "wholehearted support." See Greene, *Washita*, 19.

14. Wooster, *The American Military Frontiers*, 186.

15. Mark Clodfelter, *The Dakota War: The U.S. Army Versus the Sioux, 1862–1865* (Jefferson, NC: McFarland, 1998), 204.

16. Dee Brown, *Fort Phil Kearny: An American Saga* (New York: GP Putnam's Sons, 1962), 150. Brown faults Fetterman for rushing into battle. See Brown, *Fort Phil Kearny*, 166, 177. John H. Monnett exonerates Fetterman, faults the post commander, Colonel Henry B. Carrington, for blaming Fetterman, and concludes that Lieutenant George W. Grummond forced the rash attack by pushing the cavalry far in front of the infantry accompanying Fetterman. Fetterman had to move forward in support. Nor did Fetterman ever make the boast attributed to him. See Monnett, *Where a Hundred Soldiers Were Killed: The Struggle for the Powder River Country in 1866 and the Making of the Fetterman Myth* (Albuquerque: University of New Mexico Press, 2008), xxvi–xxvii, 153, 159. Shannon D. Smith goes further, arguing that Carrington's first and second wives demonized Fetterman to rebuke Carrington's condemnation by Grant and Sherman. See Smith, *Give Me Eighty Men: Women and the Myth of the Fetterman Fight* (Lincoln: University of Nebraska Press, 2008), 188–189.

17. Utley, *The Indian Frontier*, 106. Dee Brown also notes the killing of the dog but fails to mention the reason why. See Brown, *Bury My Heart at Wounded Knee*, 137.

18. Robert Wooster, *The Military and United States Indian Policy, 1865–1903* (New Haven, CT: Yale University Press,1988), 118.

19. Michael Tate stresses the Army's primary role as one well beyond merely the use of military force and instead as a "medium through which American culture and institutions were transferred from the Appalachian frontier to the Pacific coast." See Tate, *The Frontier Army in the Settlement of*

the West (Norman: University of Oklahoma Press, 1999), 308. An earlier study of the Army in the Pacific Northwest said the Army's "presence was felt in all stages of the pioneering process." See Francis Paul Prucha, *Broadax and Bayonet: The Role of the United States Army in the Development of the Northwest, 1815–1860* (Madison, WI: State Historical Society of Wisconsin, 1953), viii. Wooster agrees to some extent that military policy was more complex than allowed for with "labels of terror, annihilation and extermination." See Wooster, *The Military and United States Indian Policy, 1865–1903* (New Haven, CT: Yale University Press, 1988), 4. But in a later study, he advances more the military effort by saying soldiers executed federal policy violently and this was the key to gaining resources that defeated the Natives. See Wooster, *The American Military Frontiers*, 272–275.

20. Stan Hoig, *The Battle of the Washita: The Sheridan-Custer Indian Campaign of 1867–1869* (New York: Doubleday, 1976), 20.

21. John H. Monnett, *The Battle of Beecher Island and the Indian War of 1867–1869* (Niwot: University Press of Colorado, 1992), 132.

22. For the changing labels of this command from scouts, to rangers, to frontiersmen, see Monnett, *The Battle of Beecher Island and the Indian War of 1867–1869*, 113, 115, 121.

23. For the articulation of "total war," see Utley, *The Indian Frontier*, 122; again Utley, *Frontier Regulars*, 52; and Wooster, *The Military and United States Indian Policy, 1865–1903*, 141. Natives unleashed their own "total war" at times, particularly in southwestern Minnesota in 1862 when striking at civilians. See Clodfelter, *The Dakota War*, 41.

24. Wooster, *The American Military Frontiers*, 204.

Chapter 7

1. Reginald Horsman, *Race and Manifest Destiny: The Origins of American Racial Anglo-Saxonism* (Cambridge, MA: Harvard University Press, 1981), 300–301.

2. Robert M. Utley, *A Life Wild and Perilous: Mountainmen and the Paths to the Pa-*

cific (New York: Henry Holt, 1997), 205, 224, 241.

3. Utley, *A Life Wild and Perilous*, 187.

4. While nominally these Native states succumbed to American control after the Civil War, William E. Unrau shows how American migration west undermined Native control of the Indian Territory in the 1850s before that war. See Unrau, *The Rise and Fall of Indian Country, 1825–1855* (Lawrence: University of Kansas Press, 2007), 137, 147, 149.

5. Clarissa W. Confer, *The Cherokee Nation in the Civil War* (Norman: University of Oklahoma Press, 2007), 148, 156.

6. Laurence M. Hauptman, *Between Two Fires: American Indians in the Civil War* (New York: The Free Press, 1995), 42.

7. Annie Heloise Abel, *The American Indian and the End of the Confederacy, 1863–1866* (Lincoln: University of Nebraska Press, 1993), 362.

8. John D. Unruh, *The Plains Across: The Overland Emigrants and the Trans-Mississippi West, 1840–1860* (Urbana: University of Illinois Press, 1979), 94.

9. Michael L. Tate, *Indians and Emigrants: Encounters on the Overland Trails* (Norman: University of Oklahoma Press, 2006), 61.

10. Unruh, *The Plains Across*, 9. Richard White says Native attacks were rare. White, *"It's Your Misfortune and None of My Own": A New History of the American West* (Norman: University of Oklahoma Press, 1991), 199.

11. Robert M. Utley, *Frontiersmen in Blue: The United States Army and the Indians, 1848–1865* (New York: Macmillan, 1967), 4.

12. Tate, *Indians and Emigrants*, 229.

13. Stan Hoig, *The Battle of the Washita: The Sheridan-Custer Indian Campaign of 1867–1869* (Garden City, NY: Doubleday, 1976), 22.

14. J.E. Kaufmann, *Fortress America: The Forts that Defended America, 1600 to the Present* (Cambridge, MA: Da Capo, 2004), 186.

15. Unruh, *The Plains Across*, 385. Richard White says 300,000. See White, *"It's Your Misfortune and None of My Own,"* 189.

16. White, *"It's Your Misfortune and None of My Own,"* 183–184.

17. Patricia Nelson Limerick writes: "Frontier history has become much more inclusive and dynamic," a story of a region more than a place of opportunity for American advancement. See Limerick, "The Adventures of the Frontier in the Twentieth Century," in *The Frontier in American Culture: An Exhibition at the Newbury Library, August 26, 1994-January 7, 1995*, ed. James R. Grossman (Berkeley: University of California Press, 1994), 78, 77, 79–80. An inclusive west forms a region settlers conquered but the inhabitants of that region still endure many of the consequences of that conquest, meaning the frontier did not end in 1890 but continues into the 20th Century (and beyond). Again, Limerick, *The Legacy of Conquest: The Unbroken Past of the American West* (New York: Norton, 2006), 26. Nor did the frontier start with a westward push by Americans, but had been ongoing amongst Natives prior to and after their contact with Europeans. See White, *"It's Your Misfortune and None of My Own,"* 4; Collin G. Calloway, *One Vast Winter Count: The Native American West Before Lewis and Clark* (Lincoln: University of Nebraska Press, 2003), 429; and Ned Blackhawk, *Violence Over the Land: Indians and Empires in the Early American West* (Cambridge, MA: Harvard University Press, 2006), 11. In this view, the Turner thesis takes a hit as both destination and process are folded into one and those impacted include more than enterprising Americans.

18. William H. Leckie, *The Military Conquest of the Southern Plains* (Norman: University of Oklahoma Press, 1963), 124.

19. Robert M. Utley, *The Indian Frontier, 1846–1890*, Revised Edition (Albuquerque: University of New Mexico, 1984), 167.

20. For the decline of the buffalo herds before 1870, see Dan Flores, "Bison Ecology and Bison Diplomacy: The Southern Plains from 1800 to 1850," *Journal of American History*, Vol. 78, No. 2 (Sept. 1991): 467, 485. For multiple factors negatively impacting the herds, not simply the Army but the human activity of both Natives and settlers on an already fragile environment, see Andrew C. Isenberg, *The Destruction of the Bison: An Environmental History, 1750–1920* (New York: Cambridge University Press,

2000), 11. David D. Smits argues the Army did have a great impact. See Smits, "The Frontier Army and the Destruction of the Buffalo: 1865–1883," *Western Historical Quarterly*, Vol. 25, No. 3 (Autumn 1994): 338.

21. Utley, *The Indian Frontier*, 124. Wooster paints Grant as more conciliatory toward Natives in the years leading up to taking office as president. See Wooster, *The Military and United States Indian Policy, 1865–1903* (New Haven, CT: Yale University Press,1995), 45, 78. Captain Grant expressed similar understanding commenting in a letter to his wife, "the whole race would be harmless and peaceable if they were not put upon by the whites." Ball, *Army Regulars on the Western Frontier, 1848–1861* (Norman: University of Oklahoma Press, 2001), 16.

22. Utley, *The Indian Frontier*, 101.

23. Utley, *The Indian Frontier*, 117.

24. Sherman expected Army deficiencies in personnel to be made good by technology. Thomas C. Leonard, "Red, White, and the Army Blue: Empathy and Anger in the American West," *American Quarterly*, Vol. 26, No. 2 (May 1974): 187. Robert Utley says Sherman made this connection between the railroads, settlement, and the Army as early as 1866. See Utley, *Frontier Regulars*, 3.

Chapter 8

1. Inaugural Address, March 4, 1869, *The Papers of Ulysses S. Grant*, Volume 19, July 1, 1868–October 31, 1869, p. 142, Digital Collections, Mississippi State University.

2. Robert W. Galler, Jr., "Sustaining the Sioux Confederation: Tanktonai Initiatives and Influence on the Northern Plains, 1680–1880," *Western Historical Quarterly*, Issue 39 (Winter 2008): 490. Richard White characterizes Sioux unity as less politically based and more one stemming from social, demographic, and economic reasons. It was enough so that the Sioux rarely clashed among themselves. White, "The Winning of the West: The Expansion of the Western Sioux in the Eighteenth and Nineteenth Centuries," *Journal of American History*, Vol. 65, No. 2 (September 1978): 328, 321. Those extolling key individuals as central to Sioux resistance to outside aggressors in-

clude Robert W. Larson, *Red Cloud: Warrior-Statesman of the Lakota Sioux* (Norman: University of Oklahoma Press, 1997); Robert M. Utley, *Sitting Bull: The Life and Times of an American Patriot* (New York: Henry Holt, 2008); and for Crazy Horse, see Mari Sandoz, *Crazy Horse: The Strange Man of the Oglalas* (Lincoln: University of Nebraska Press, 2008), and Kingsley M. Bray, *Crazy Horse: A Lakota Life* (Norman: University of Oklahoma Press, 2006).

3. Dee Brown, *Bury My Heart at Wounded Knee: An Indian History of the American West* (New York: Henry Holt, 1970), 132.

4. The Sioux stopping an invasion is in Jeffery Oslter, *The Plains Sioux and U.S. Colonialism from Lewis and Clark to Wounded Knee* (New York: Cambridge University Press, 2004), 49–50. Robert W. Larson portrays the U.S. government's decision to make peace with Red Cloud as one reflecting that growing nation's position of strength, creating more opportunity rather than a liability (setback). See Larson, *Red Cloud*, 117–118. John H. Monnett says despite the battlefield success, the Natives "ultimately lost the peace." See Monnett, *Where a Hundred Soldiers Were Killed: The Struggle for the Powder River Country in 1866 and the Making of the Fetterman Myth* (Albuquerque: University of New Mexico Press, 2008), 239.

5. Robert M. Utley, *The Indian Frontier, 1846–1890*, rev. ed. (Albuquerque: University of New Mexico Press, 1984), 63.

6. Paul L. Hedren, *After Custer: Loss and Transformation in Sioux Country* (Norman: University of Oklahoma Press, 2012), xii-xiii. Jeffrey Ostler suggests the Sioux still have a valid claim. See Ostler, *The Lakotas and the Black Hills: The Struggle for Sacred Ground* (New York: Viking, 2010), 191.

7. It is deemed the most costly war due to the expense incurred in sending a large number of troops in pursuit of an extremely limited number of Natives. Keith A. Murray, *The Modocs and Their War* (Norman: University of Oklahoma Press, 1959), 80.

8. See first Sherman's and then Gillem's reaction in Murray, *The Modocs and Their War*, 202, 212.

9. Jeff C. Riddle, *The Indian History of the Modoc War* (Mechanicsburg, PA: Stackpole Books, 2004), 188.

10. Both quotes in Jerome A. Greene, *Nez Perce Summer 1877: The Army and the Nee-Me-Poo Crisis* (Helena: Montana Historical Society, 2000), xi.

11. The friendly relations made one of the last Plains wars one against an "Indian people who could claim the longest friendship and firmest alliance with the [United States]." Elliott West, *The Last Indian War: The Nez Perce Story* (New York: Oxford University Press, 2009), xxii.

12. West, *The Last Indian War*, 282.

13. Robert M. Utley, *Frontiersmen in Blue: The United States Army and the Indians, 1848–1865* (New York: Macmillan, 1967), 325.

14. West, *The Last Indian War*, 291.

15. With the focus on Chief Joseph, or because of this focus, Robert McCoy traces how difficult it is to offer the Nez Perce point of view of this campaign. See McCoy, *Chief Joseph, Yellow Wolf, and the Creation of the Nez Perce History in the Pacific Northwest* (New York: Routledge, 2004), xiv-xv.

16. In this sense, Joseph's final words applied to all Natives. See West, *The Last Indian War*, 290, 292.

17. Angie Debo, *Geronimo: The Man, His Times, His Place* (Norman: University of Oklahoma Press, 1976), 13.

18. More recent writing has called attention to other figures besides Geronimo. See Kathleen Chamberlain, *Victorio: Apache Warrior and Chief* (Norman: University of Oklahoma Press, 2007), and Bud Shapard, *Chief Loco: Apache Peacemaker* (Norman: University of Oklahoma Press, 2010).

19. Those extolling his memory as paramount among Apache resistance figures cast a much more favorable light. See Debo, *Geronimo*, 454, and Odie B. Faulk's description of him living on in memory as a "great American" in *The Geronimo Campaign* (New York: Oxford University Press, 1969), 220.

20. Debo, *Geronimo*, 240–241.

21. Falk, *Geronimo Campaign*, 58.

22. This is General Miles' assessment of Geronimo's surrender. Odie B. Faulk, *The Geronimo Campaign* (New York: Oxford University Press, 1969), 170.

23. Heather Cox Richardson, *Wounded Knee: Party Politics and the Road to an American Massacre* (New York: Basic Books, 2010), 18, 298–299.

Chapter 9

1. In a forum titled, "The Middle Ground Revisited," published in the *William and Mary Quarterly*, a number of scholars, Richard White among them, discuss and review White's concept and, in so doing, reinforce the ties of the middle ground to counterinsurgency, albeit unintentionally. The connection is made by describing the middle ground as an "event and cultural process," one where negotiation displaced confrontation as new cultural forms came into existence due to adaptation and compromise among those attempting to gain a desired end via conflict but failing to do so. Forum, "The Middle Ground Revisited," *The William and Mary Quarterly*, Third Series, Vol. 63, No. 1 (Jan. 2006): 3–4, 9, 13, 16.

2. Wayne Lee, "Projecting Power in the Early Modern World: The Spanish Model?," Introduction in *Empires and Indigenes: Intercultural Alliance, Imperial Expansion, and Warfare in the Early Modern World* (New York: New York University Press, 2011), 2.

3. David G. Gutiérrez, "Significant to Whom?: Mexican Americans and the History of the American West," *Western Historical Quarterly*, Vol. 24, No. 4 (Nov. 1993): 520.

4. Guy Chet disputes the impact of the "first way of war" when he rejects the characterization of these attacks as "search and destroy missions" in favor of a "ranger campaign of attrition." The distinction comes from his view that the English continued to rely on massed firepower utilized on the tactical defensive, more than adopting an Indian way of war, or skulking, i.e., hit and run, raids, ambush, retreats. See Chet, *Conquering the American Wilderness: The Triumph of European Warfare in the Northeast* (Amherst: University of Massachusetts Press, 2003), 2, 5, 40, 69. In making this case, he differs with Patrick Malone and Armstrong Starkey. Malone argues that the colonists were forced to "adopt a new doctrine for forest warfare," the "skulking war

of war," in order to triumph in these wars. See Malone, *The Skulking Way of War: Technology and Tactics Among the New England Indians* (Baltimore: Johns Hopkins University Press, 1991), 128. Starkey believes that the Natives outpaced the colonists in transitioning to "frontier warfare conditions," allowing tribes to extend this conflict for 140 years even when overmatched in terms of arms and numbers. Starkey, *European and Native American Warfare, 1675–1815* (Norman: University of Oklahoma Press, 1998), 82, 168. Wayne Lee rejects the skulking way of war paradigm as defined by Malone and Starkey for overly weighing ambush as the Native's preferred method of warfare, and for unduly stressing a fear of losses as the Native's chief concern in combat. Lee, "The Military Revolution of Native North America: Firearms, Forts, and Politics," in *Empires and Indigenes,* 52.

5. For the rush to employ a middle ground everywhere, see Susan Sleeper-Smith, "Introduction," Forum, "The Middle Ground Revisited," *The William and Mary Quarterly,* Third Series, Vol. 63, No. 1 (Jan. 2006): 4–5. White says even a misreading of the middle ground can be "fruitful" and that such a process is "common" if not "universal." White, "Creative Misunderstandings and New Misunderstandings," Forum, "The Middle Ground Revisited," *The William and Mary Quarterly,* Third Series, Vol. 63, No. 1 (Jan 2006): 9–10.

6. Robert Utley argues that Native resistance required the Army to become a "counter-guerrilla" force. See Utley, *Frontiersmen in Blue: The United States Army and the Indian, 1848–1865* (New York: Macmillan, 1967), 9.

7. Frederick Hoxie, *This Indian Country: American Indian Activities and the Place They Made* (New York: Penguin, 2012), 398–401; and Nichols G. Rosenthal, *Reimagining Indian Country: Native American Migration and Identity in 20th Century Los Angeles* (Chapel Hill: University of North Carolina Press, 2012), 8–9.

8. The famous Turner thesis decries the closing of the frontier and the resulting crisis for American democracy because U.S. citizens had no more land to settle. See Frederick Jackson Turner, "The Significance

of History," in *The Early Writings of Frederick Jackson Turner,* ed. Everett E. Edwards (Madison: University of Wisconsin Press, 1938). See Patricia Limerick for the rejection of the Turner thesis as too rigid, ignoring a multitude of peoples and events. Limerick, *The Legacy of Conquest: The Unbroken Past of the American West* (New York: W.W. Norton, 1987), 20–21. Gerald Nash calls for the same recognition of the Turner thesis as too restrictive, and he favors "pluralism" as the norm. Nash, "The Great Adventure: Western History, 1890–1990," *Western Historical Quarterly,* Vol. 22, No.1 (February 1991): 18. His book reviewing the historiography of the American west indicates the push among scholars to see a more "complex tapestry" reflecting successes and failures. Nash, *Creating the West: Historical Interpretations, 1890–1990* (Albuquerque: University of New Mexico Press, 1991), 261. William Cronon emphasizes that even with the criticism, the Turner thesis remains "the central and most persistent story of American history." Cronon, "Revisiting the Vanishing Frontier: The Legacy of Frederick Jackson Turner," *Western Historical Quarterly,* Vol. 18, No. 2 (April 1987): 176.

9. David J. Weber best captures this tension of defining borderlands as not negating frontiers. He emphasizes the need to account for inclusion, not exclusion as a frontier might suggest. Frontier history done well gets to what happens when peoples meet, a look at process that does not then neglect the story of some of those peoples. See Weber, *The Spanish Frontier in North America* (New Haven, CT: Yale University Press, 1992), 7–8. Responding to Limerick's *The Legacy of Conquest,* Weber suggests that Turner's "frontier thesis" could be combined with Limerick's call to see the West as a conquered region. In this way, the frontier does not necessarily exclude a distinctive process in favor of stressing a place or region. See "*The Legacy of Conquest,* by Patricia Nelson Limerick: A Panel of Appraisal," *The Western Historical Quarterly,* Vol. 20, No. 3 (Aug. 1989): 316. This borderlands approach allows for a series of *wests,* for a process to unfold in terms of a region finding its place due to that process unfolding in a national context. To follow this thinking one step further, the

story of the west is a process tracking western expansion out of Europe to allow that region to achieve a global hegemony. See Walter P. Webb, *The Great Frontier* (Boston: Houghton Mifflin, 1952), 31–32; William H. McNeill, *The Great Frontier: Freedom and Hierarchy in Modern Times* (Princeton, NJ: Princeton University Press, 1983), 8, 58–61. Limerick got to this point in terms of having western American historians reflect on global history. Patricia Nelson Limerick, "Going West and Ending Up Global," *The Western Historical Quarterly*, No. 32 (Spring 2001): 22. The same can be said of COIN theory. That effort amounts to applying a distinct process in a declared region, but one that can be—and perhaps should be—repeated any number of times as the counterinsurgents look to find accommodation among clashing peoples. That process of interaction does not end, even if the expectation is that the contested regions will become conquered regions and cease to exist as dangerous areas in need of control. So a COIN success ends that war but by that very success perpetuates the need for a process of counterinsurgency.

10. See Sarah Sewall's introduction to *The U.S. Army, Marine Corps Counterinsurgency Field Manual, FM 3–24*, where she states this manual "adopts a population-centric approach" to counterinsurgency based on "insights" from "French counterinsurgency guru David Galula." This reliance is affirmed in John A. Nagl's foreword to the manual. See *FM 3–24* (Chicago: Uni-

versity of Chicago Press, 2007, 2006), xxiv-xxv, xix. It is not an absolute that Galula's main work, *Counterinsurgency Warfare: Theory and Practice* (New York: Praeger, 1964; reprint, New York: Praeger, 2006), features population-centric COIN.

11. The heroic struggle of Native chiefs is conveyed in Alvin M. Josephy, *The Patriot Chiefs: A Chronicle of American Indian Resistance* (New York: Penguin, 1993). Gordon M. Sayre follows the emergence of these figures as a unifying symbol only after their defeat in *Indian Chief as Tragic Hero: Native Resistance and the Literatures of America from Moctezuma to Tecumseh* (Chapel Hill: University of North Carolina Press, 2005).

12. One book sets key American and Native leaders next to one another as both sides engage in war in the west. See Richard Etulain and Glenda Riley, eds., *Chiefs and Generals: Nine Men Who Shaped the American West* (Golden, CO: Fulcrum Press, 2004).

13. See Mao's expression of the guerrilla living among the people as fish in water, and a host of western efforts to deny this very thing. This effort assumed local proportions with wholesale relocation of inhabitants to safe zones, such as the "strategic hamlets" program in Malaysia and Vietnam. See John A. Nagel, *Learning to Eat Soup with a Knife: Counterinsurgency Lessons from Malaya and Vietnam* (Westport, CT: Praeger, 2002), 130. For Mao, see *Mao Tse-Tung on Guerrilla Warfare*, trans. Samuel B. Griffith (New York: Praeger, 1961), 93.

Bibliography

Abel, Annie Heloise. *The American Indian and the End of the Confederacy, 1863–1866.* Lincoln: University of Nebraska Press, 1993.

Ambrose, Stephen E. *Undaunted Courage: Meriwether Lewis, Thomas Jefferson, and the Opening of the West.* New York: Simon & Schuster, 1997.

Anderson, Fred. *Crucible of War: The Seven Years' War and the Fate of Empire in British North America, 1754–1766.* New York: Alfred A. Knopf, 2000.

Anderson, Gary Clayton. *The Conquest of Texas: Ethnic Cleansing in the Promised Land, 1820–1875.* Norman: University of Oklahoma Press, 2005.

_____. *The Indian Southwest, 1580–1830: Ethnogenesis and Reinvention.* Norman: University of Oklahoma Press, 1999.

Asher, Brad. *Beyond the Reservation: Indians, Settlers, and the Law in Washington Territory, 1853–1889.* Norman: University of Oklahoma Press, 1999.

Axtell, James. *The Invasion Within: The Contest of Cultures in Colonial North America.* New York: Oxford University Press, 1985.

_____. *Natives and Newcomers: The Cultural Origins of North America.* New York: Oxford University Press, 2001.

Ball, Durwood. *Army Regulars on the Western Frontier, 1848–1861.* Norman: University of Oklahoma Press, 2001.

Barr, Daniel P., ed. *The Boundaries Between Us: Natives and Newcomers Along the Frontiers of the Old Northwest Territory, 1750–1850.* Kent, OH: Kent State University Press, 2006.

Beal, Merrill D. *"I will Fight no more Forever": Chief Joseph and the Nez Perce War.* Seattle: University of Washington Press, 1963.

Beck, Paul N. *The First Sioux War: The Grattan Fight and Blue Water Creek, 1854–1856.* Lanham, MD: University Press of America, 2004.

Beckham, Stephen Dow. *Requiem for a People: The Rogue Indians and the Frontiersmen.* Corvallis: Oregon State University Press, 1996, 1971.

Belko, William S. *America's Hundred Years' War: U.S. Expansion to the Gulf Coast and the Fate of the Seminole, 1763–1858.* Gainesville: University Press of Florida, 2011.

Bert, Wayne. *American Military Intervention in Unconventional War: From the Philippines to Iraq.* New York: Palgrave Macmillan, 2011.

Birtle, Andrew J. *U.S. Army Counterinsurgency and Contingency Operations Doctrine, 1860–1941.* Washington, D.C.: Center of Military History, U.S. Army, 1998.

Blackhawk, Ned. *Violence Over the Land: Indians and Empires in the Early American West.* Cambridge, MA: Harvard University Press, 2006.

Blaufarb, Douglas S. *The Counterinsurgency Era: U.S. Doctrine and Performance, 1950 to the Present.* New York: Free Press, 1977.

Boot, Max. *The Savage Wars of Peace: Small Wars and the Rise of American Power.* New York: Basic Books, 2002.

Bottiger, Patrick. "Prophetstown for Their Own Purposes: The French, Miamis, and Cultural Identities in the Wabash-Maumee Valley." *Journal of the Early Republic,* Vol. 33, No. 1 (Spring 2013): 29–60.

Bourne, Russell. *The Red King's Rebellion:*

Racial Politics in New England, 1675–1678. New York: Oxford University Press, 1990.

Bray, Kingsley M. *Crazy Horse: A Lakota Life.* Norman: University of Oklahoma Press, 2006.

Brown, Dee Alexander. *Bury My Heart at Wounded Knee: An Indian History of the American West.* New York: Bantam Books, 1972, 1970.

_____. *Fort Phil Kearny: An American Saga.* New York: Putnam, 1962.

Brown, Meredith Mason. *Frontiersman: Daniel Boone and the Making of America.* Baton Rouge: Louisiana State University Press, 2008.

Bruyneel, Kevin. *The Third Space of Sovereignty: The Postcolonial Politics of U.S.-Indigenous Relations.* Minneapolis: University of Minnesota Press, 2007.

Calloway, Colin G. *The American Revolution in Indian Country: Crisis and Diversity in Native American Communities.* Cambridge: Cambridge University Press, 1995.

_____. *One Vast Winter Count: The Native American West Before Lewis and Clark.* Lincoln: University of Nebraska Press, 2003.

_____. *The Western Abenakis of Vermont, 1600–1800: War, Migration, and the Survival of an Indian People.* Norman: University of Oklahoma Press, 1990.

Carter, Harvey Lewis. *The Life and Times of Little Turtle: First Sagamore of the Wabash.* Urbana: University of Illinois Press, 1987.

Cave, Alfred A. *The Pequot War.* Amherst: University of Massachusetts Press, 1996.

_____. "The Shawnee Prophet, Tecumseh, and Tippecanoe: A Case Study of Historical Myth-Making." *Journal of the Early Republic,* Vol. 22, No. 4 (Winter 2002): 637–673.

Chacon, Richard J., and Rubén G. Mendoza, eds. *North American Indigenous Warfare and Ritual Violence.* Tucson: University of Arizona Press, 2007.

Chaffin, Tom. *Pathfinder: John Charles Frémont and the Course of American Empire.* New York: Hill and Wang, 2002.

Chamberlain, Kathleen. *Victorio: Apache Warrior and Chief.* Norman: University of Oklahoma Press, 2007.

Chet, Guy. *Conquering the American Wilderness: The Triumph of European Warfare in the Colonial Northeast.* Amherst: University of Massachusetts Press, 2003.

Church, Benjamin. *Diary of King Philip's War 1675–76.* Chester, CT: Pequot Press, 1975.

Clodfelter, Mark. *The Dakota War: The United States Army Versus the Sioux, 1862–1865.* Jefferson, NC: McFarland, 1998.

Coleman, Jon T. *Here Lies Hugh Glass: A Mountain Man, a Bear, and the Rise of the American Nation.* New York: Hill & Wang, 2012.

Collins, Michael L. *Texas Devils: Rangers and Regulars on the Lower Rio Grande, 1846–1861.* Norman: University of Oklahoma Press, 2008.

Colwell-Chanthaphonh, Chip. *Massacre at Camp Grant: Forgetting and Remembering Apache History.* Tucson: University of Arizona Press, 2007.

Confer, Clarissa W. *The Cherokee Nation in the Civil War.* Norman: University of Oklahoma Press, 2007.

Connell, Evan S. *Son of the Morning Star.* New York: Harper & Row, 1985.

Coues, Elliot, ed. *History of the Expedition under the Command of Lewis and Clark.* New York: Dover Publications, 1965.

Cox, Robert S., ed. *The Shortest and Most Convenient Route: Lewis and Clark in Context.* Philadelphia, PA: American Philosophical Society, 2004.

Cronon, William. "Revisiting the Vanishing Frontier: The Legacy of Frederick Jackson Turner." *Western Historical Quarterly,* Vol. 18, No. 2 (April 1987): 157–176.

Davis, Karl. "'Remember Fort Mims': Reinterpreting the Origins of the Creek War." *Journal of the Early Republic,* Vol. 22, No. 4 (Winter 2002): 611–636.

Davis, William C. *Lone Star Rising: The Revolutionary Birth of the Texas Republic.* New York: Free Press, 2004.

_____. *Three Roads to the Alamo: The Saga of David Crockett, James Bowie, and William Barret Travis.* New York: HarperCollins, 1998.

Debo, Angie. *Geronimo: The Man, His Times, His Place.* Norman: University of Oklahoma Press, 1976.

DeLay, Brian. *War of a Thousand Deserts: Indian Raids and the U.S.-Mexican War.* New Haven, CT: Yale University Press, 2008.

Denson, Andrew. *Demanding the Cherokee*

Nation: Indian Autonomy and American Culture, 1830–1900. Lincoln: University of Nebraska Press, 2004.

Derr, Mark. *The Frontiersman: The Real Life and Many Legends of Davy Crockett.* New York: W. Morrow, 1993.

De Voto, Bernard A. *The Course of Empire.* Boston: Houghton Mifflin, 1952.

Dillon, Richard. *Burnt-out Fires.* Engle Woods Cliff, NJ: Prentice-Hall, 1973.

Dixon, David. *Hero of Beecher Island: The Life and Military Career of George A. Forsyth.* Lincoln: University of Nebraska Press, 1994.

_____. *Never Come to Peace Again: Pontiac's Uprising and the Fate of the British Empire in North America.* Norman: University of Oklahoma Press, 2005.

Documents of United States Indian Policy. Ed. Francis Paul Prucha. Lincoln: University of Nebraska Press, 1990.

Donovan, James. *A Terrible Glory: Custer and the Little Bighorn—The Last Great Battle of the American West.* New York: Little, Brown, 2008.

Douthit, Nathan. *Uncertain Encounters: Indians and Whites at Peace and War in Southern Oregon, 1820s-1860s.* Corvallis: Oregon State University Press, 2002.

Dowd, Gregory Evans. "The French King Wakes Up in Detroit: 'Pontiac's War' in Rumor and History." *Ethnohistory,* Vol. 37, No. 3 (Summer 1990): 254–278.

_____. *A Spirited Resistance: The North American Indian Struggle for Unity, 1745–1815.* Baltimore, MD: Johns Hopkins University Press, 1992.

_____. *War Under Heaven: Pontiac, the Indian Nations, and the British Empire.* Baltimore, MD: Johns Hopkins University Press, 2002.

Drake, James D. *King Philip's War: Civil War in New England, 1675-1676.* Amherst: University of Massachusetts Press, 1999.

Dunlay, Tom W. *Kit Carson and the Indians.* Lincoln: University of Nebraska Press, 2000.

Early American Indian Documents: Treaties and Laws, 1607-1789. Ed. Alden T. Vaughan. Bethesda, MD: Congressional Information Services, 2003.

Edmunds, David. "Tecumseh, the Shawnee Prophet, and American History: A Reassessment." *Western Historical Quarterly,* Vol. 14, No. 3 (July 1983): 261–276.

Etulain, Richard W., and Glenda Riley, eds. *Chiefs and Generals: Nine Men Who Shaped the American West.* Golden, CO: Fulcrum Publisher, 2004.

Falk, Odie B. *Crimson Desert: Indian Wars of the American Southwest.* New York: Oxford University Press, 1974.

_____. *The Geronimo Campaign.* New York: Oxford University Press, 1969.

Faragher, John Mack. *Daniel Boone: The Life and Legend of an American Pioneer.* New York: Henry Holt, 1992.

Fenn, Elizabeth A. "Biological Warfare in Eighteenth-Century North America: Beyond Jeffery Amherst." *Journal of American History,* Vol. 86, No. 4 (March 2000): 1552–1580.

Ferguson, R. Brian, and Neil L. Whitehead, eds. *War in the Tribal Zone: Expanding States and Indigenous Warfare.* Santa Fe, NM: School of American Research Press, 1992.

Fitzgerald, David. *Learning to Forget: U.S. Army Doctrine and Practice from Vietnam to Iraq.* Stanford, CA: Stanford University Press, 2013.

Flores, Dan. "Bison Ecology and Bison Diplomacy: The Southern Plains from 1800 to 1850." *Journal of American History,* Vol. 78, No. 2 (Sept. 1991): 465–485.

Flynn, Matthew J. *Contesting History: The Bush Counterinsurgency Legacy in Iraq.* Santa Barbara, CA: Praeger Security International, 2010.

Gaff, Alan D. *Bayonets in the Wilderness: Anthony Wayne's Legion in the Old Northwest.* Norman: University of Oklahoma Press, 2004.

Galler, Robert W., Jr. "Sustaining the Sioux Confederation: Yanktonai Initiatives and Influence on the Northern Plains, 1680–1880." *Western Historical Quarterly,* Vol. 39, No. 4 (Winter 2008): 467–490.

Galula, David. *Counterinsurgency Warfare: Theory and Practice.* New York: Praeger, 1964; Reprint, New York: Praeger, 2006.

Garrison, Tim Alan. *The Legal Ideology of Removal: The Southern Judiciary and the Sovereignty of Native American Nations.* Athens, GA: University of Georgia Press, 2002.

Gates, John M. "Indians and Insurrectos: The U.S. Army's Experience with Insurgency." *Parameters,* XIII, No. 1 (1983): 59–68.

Gatewood, Charles B. *Lt. Charles Gatewood and His Apache Wars Memoir.* Ed. Louis Kraft. Lincoln: University of Nebraska Press, 2005.

Greene, Jerome A. *Nez Perce Summer 1877: The U.S. Army and the Nee-Me-Poo Crisis.* Helena, Mont: Montana Historical Society Press, 2000.

_____. *Washita: The U.S. Army and the Southern Cheyenne, 1867–69.* Norman: University of Oklahoma Press, 2004.

Grenier, John. *The First Way of War: American War Making on the Frontier, 1607–1814.* New York: Cambridge University Press, 2005.

Gutiérrez, David G. "Significant to Whom?: Mexican Americans and the History of the American West." *Western Historical Quarterly,* Vol. 24, No. 4 (Nov. 1993): 519–539.

Haley, James L. *The Buffalo War: The History of the Red River Indian Uprising of 1874.* Norman: University of Oklahoma Press, 1985, 1976.

Hall, John W. *Uncommon Defense: Indian Allies in the Black Hawk War.* Cambridge, MA: Harvard University Press, 2009.

Hämäläinen, Pekka. *The Comanche Empire.* New Haven: Yale University Press, 2008.

_____. "The Rise and Fall of Plains Indian Horse Cultures." *Journal of American History,* Vol. 90, No. 3 (Dec. 2003): 833–862.

Handbook of North American Indians: History of Indian-White Relations. Ed. Wilcomb E. Washburn. Washington, D.C.: Smithsonian Institution, 1988.

Harmon, Alexandra. *Indians in the Making: Ethnic Relations and Indian Identities Around Puget Sound.* Berkeley: University of California Press, 2000.

Hauptman, Laurence M. *Between Two Fires: American Indians in the Civil War.* New York: Free Press, 1995.

Hedren, Paul L. *After Custer: Loss and Transformation in Sioux Country.* Norman: University of Oklahoma Press, 2011.

Helton, Tena L. "What the White 'Squaws' Want from Black Hawk: Gendering the Fan-Celebrity Relationship." *American Indian Quarterly,* Vol. 34, No. 4 (Fall 2010): 498–520.

Herman, Daniel J. "Romance on the Middle Ground." *Journal of the Early Republic,* Vol. 19, No. 2 (Summer 1999): 279–291.

Hirsch, Adam J. "The Collision of Military Cultures in Seventh-Century New England." *Journal of American History,* Vol. 74, No. 4 (March 1988): 1187–1212.

Hofstadter, Richard. *The American Political Tradition and the Men Who Made It.* New York: Vintage Books, 1959.

Hoig, Stan. *The Battle of the Washita: The Sheridan-Custer Indian Campaign of 1867–69.* Garden City, NY: Doubleday, 1976.

_____. *The Sand Creek Massacre.* Norman: University of Oklahoma Press, 1961.

_____. *Tribal Wars of the Southern Plains.* Norman: University of Oklahoma Press, 1993.

Horsman, Reginald. *Race and Manifest Destiny: The Origins of American Racial Anglo-Saxonism.* Cambridge, MA: Harvard University Press, 1981.

Hoxie, Frederick E., Jay T. Nelson, eds. *Lewis and Clark and the Indian Country: The Native American Perspective.* Urbana: University of Illinois Press, 2007.

_____. *This Indian Country: American Indian Activists and the Place They Made.* New York: Penguin, 2012.

Hurt, Douglas. *The Indian Frontier, 1763–1846.* Albuquerque: University of New Mexico Press, 2002.

Isenberg, Andrew C. *The Destruction of the Bison: An Environmental History, 1750–1920.* New York: Cambridge University Press, 2000.

Jennings, Francis. *The Invasion of America: Indians, Colonialism, and the Cant of Conquest.* New York: W.W. Norton, 1975.

John, Elizabeth A.H. *Storms Brewed in Other Men's Worlds: The Confrontation of Indians, Spanish, and French in the Southwest, 1540–1795.* 2nd ed. Norman: University of Oklahoma Press, 1996, 1975.

Josephy, Alvin M. *The Patriot Chiefs: A Chronicle of American Indian Resistance.* New York: Penguin, 1993.

Jung, Patrick J. *The Black Hawk War of 1832.* Norman: University of Oklahoma Press, 2007.

Kaufmann, J.E., and H.W. Kaufmann. *Fortress America: The Forts that Defended America, 1600 to the Present*. Cambridge, MA: Da Capo, 2004.

Karr, Ronald Dale. "'Why Should You Be So Furious?': The Violence of the Pequot War." *Journal of American History*, Vol. 85, No. 3 (December 1998): 876–909.

Keeley, Lawrence H. *War Before Civilization*. New York: Oxford University Press, 1996.

Kelman, Ari. *A Misplaced Massacre: Struggling Over the Memory of Sand Creek*. Cambridge, MA: Harvard University Press, 2013.

Kenner, Craig S. "An Ethnohistorical Analysis of Iroquois Assault Tactics Used Against Fortified Settlements of the Northeast in the Seventeenth Century." *Ethnohistory*, Vol. 46, No. 4 (Autumn 1999): 777–807.

Kilcullen, David J. *Counterinsurgency*. New York: Oxford University Press, 2010.

Larson, Robert W. *Gall: Lakota War Chief*. Norman: University of Oklahoma Press, 2007.

_____. *Red Cloud: Warrior-Statesman of the Lakota Sioux*. Norman: University of Oklahoma Press, 1997.

Laxer, James. *Tecumseh and Brock: The War of 1812*. Toronto: House of Anansi, 2012.

Leach, Douglas E. *Flintlock and Tomahawk: New England in King Philip's War*. New York: Norton, 1966, 1958.

Lebovic, James H. *The Limits of U.S. Military Capability: Lessons from Vietnam and Iraq*. Baltimore, MD: Johns Hopkins University Press, 2010.

Leckie, William H. *The Military Conquest of the Southern Plains*. Norman: University of Oklahoma Press, 1963.

Lee, Wayne E. "Early American Ways of War: A New Reconnaissance, 1600–1815." *The Historical Journal*, Vol. 44, No. 1 (March 2001): 269–289.

_____. "Fortify, Fight, or Flee: Tuscarora and Cherokee Defensive Warfare and Military Culture Adaptation." *Journal of Military History*, Vol. 68, No. 3 (July 2004): 713–770.

_____. "The Military Revolution of Native North America: Firearms, Forts, and Polities." In *Empires and Indigenes: Intercultural Alliance, Imperial Expansion, and Warfare in the Early Modern World*, Ed. Wayne E. Lee. New York: New York University Press, 2011.

_____. "Peace Chiefs and Blood Revenge: Patterns of Restraint in Native Warfare, 1500–1800." *Journal of Military History*, Vol. 71, No. 3 (July 2007): 701–741.

_____. "Using the Natives against the Natives: Indigenes as 'Counterinsurgents' in the British Atlantic, 1500–1800." *Defense Studies*, Vol. 4, No. 3 (Autumn 2004): 88–105.

"*The Legacy of Conquest*, by Patricia Nelson Limerick: A Panel of Appraisal." *Western Historical Quarterly*, Vol. 20, No. 3 (Aug. 1989): 303–322.

Leonard, Thomas C. "Red, White, and the Army Blue: Empathy and Anger in the American West." *American Quarterly*, Vol. 26, No. 2 (May 1974): 176–190.

Lepore, Jill. *The Name of War: King Philip's War and the Origins of American Identity*. New York: Alfred A. Knopf, 1998.

Levinson, Irving W. "A New Paradigm for an Old Conflict: The Mexico-United States War." *Journal of military History*, Vol. 73, No. 2 (April 2009): 393–416.

_____. *Wars Within War: Mexican Guerrillas, Domestic Elites, and the United States of America, 1846–1848*. Fort Worth, TX: TCU Press, 2005.

Limerick, Patricia N. "The Adventures of the Frontier in the Twentieth Century." In *The Frontier in American Culture: An Exhibition at the Newberry Library, August 26, 1994-January 7, 1995*. Ed. James R. Grossman. Berkeley: University of California Press, 1994.

_____. "Going West and Ending Up Global," *Western Historical Quarterly*, No. 32, No. 1 (Spring 2001): 4–23.

_____. *The Legacy of Conquest: The Unbroken Past of the American West*. New York: Norton, 2006.

Lofaro, Michael A. *Crockett at Two Hundred: New Perspectives on the Man and the Myth*. Knoxville: University of Tennessee Press, 1989.

_____. *Davy Crockett: The Man, the Legend, the Legacy, 1786–1986*. Knoxville: University of Tennessee Press, 1985.

Mahon, John K. *History of the Second Seminole War, 1835–1842*. Gainesville: University Presses of Florida, 1985, 1967.

Malone, Patrick M. *The Skulking Way of War: Technology and Tactics Among the New England Indians*. Baltimore, MD: Johns Hopkins University Press, 1993.

Mandell, Daniel R. *King Philip's War: Colonial Expansion, Native Resistance, and the End of Indian Sovereignty*. Baltimore, MD: Johns Hopkins University Press, 2010.

Mann, Barbara Alice. *George Washington's War on Native America*. Westport, CT: Praeger, 2005.

Mao Tse-Tung. *Mao Tse-Tung on Guerrilla Warfare*. Trans. Samuel B. Griffith. New York: Praeger, 1961.

McChristian, Douglas C. *Fort Laramie: Military Bastion of the High Plains*. Norman, OK: Arthur H. Clark, 2009.

McConnell, Michael N. *A Country Between: The Upper Ohio Valley and Its Peoples, 1724–1774*. Lincoln: University of Nebraska Press, 1992.

McCoy, Robert R. *Chief Joseph, Yellow Wolf, and the Creation of the Nez Perce History in the Pacific Northwest*. New York: Routledge, 2004.

McGinnis, Anthony. *Counting Coup and Cutting Horses: Intertribal Warfare on the Northern Plains 1738–1889*. Evergreen, CO: Cordillera Press, 1990.

_____. "When Courage Was Not Enough: Plains Indians at War with the United States Army." *Journal of Military History*, Vol. 76, No. 2 (April 2012): 455–473.

McKanna, Clare V. *White Justice in Arizona: Apache Murder Trials in the Nineteenth Century*. Lubbock, TX: Texas Tech University Press, 2005.

McLoughlin, William G. *After the Trail of Tears: The Cherokees, Struggle for Sovereignty, 1839–1880*. Chapel Hill: University of North Carolina Press, 1993.

McNeill, William H. *The Great Frontier: Freedom and Hierarchy in Modern Times*. Princeton, NJ: Princeton University Press, 1983.

Merom, Gil. *How Democracies Lose Small Wars: State, Society, and the Failures of France in Algeria, Israel in Lebanon, and the United States in Vietnam*. New York: Cambridge University Press, 2003.

Michno, Gregory. *The Settler's War: The Struggle for the Texas Frontier in the 1860s*. Caldwell, ID: Caxton Press, 2011.

"The Middle Ground Revisited." *The William and Mary Quarterly*, Third Series, Vol. 63, No. 1 (Jan. 2006): 3–96.

Miller, Perry. *Errand into the Wilderness*. New York: Harper & Row, 1964, 1956.

Millett, Alan R., and Peter Maslowski. *For the Common Defense: A Military History of the United States of America*. New York: The Free Press, 1984.

Missall, John, and Mary Lou Missall. *The Seminole Wars: America's Longest Indian Conflict*. Gainesville: University Press of Florida, 2004.

Monnett, John H. *The Battle of Beecher Island and the Indian War of 1867–1869*. Niwot: University Press of Colorado, 1992.

_____. *Where a Hundred Soldiers Were Killed: The Struggle for the Powder River Country in 1866 and the Making of the Fetterman Myth*. Albuquerque: University of New Mexico Press, 2008.

Moore, Stephen L. *Savage Frontier: Rangers, Rifleman, and the Indian Wars in Texas*. Vol. 1. Plano, TX: Republic of Texas Press, 2002.

Moyar, Mark. *Phoenix and the Birds of Prey: The CIA's Secret Campaign to Destroy the Viet Cong*. Annapolis, MD: Naval Institute Press, 1997.

Mulroy, Kevin. *Freedom on the Border: The Seminole Maroons in Florida, the Indian Territory, Coahuila, and Texas*. Lubbock, TX: Texas Tech University Press, 1993.

Murray, Keith A. *The Modocs and Their War*. Norman: University of Oklahoma Press, 1959.

Murrin, John M. "The Jeffersonian Triumph and American Exceptionalism." *Journal of the Early Republic* Vol. 20, No. 1 (Spring 2000): 1–25.

Nagel, John A. *Learning to Eat Soup with a Knife: Counterinsurgency Lessons from Malaya and Vietnam*. Chicago, IL: University of Chicago Press, 2005.

Nash, Gerald D. *Creating the West: Historical Interpretations, 1890–1990*. Albuquerque: University of New Mexico Press, 1991.

_____. "The Great Adventure: Western History, 1890–1990." *Western Historical Quarterly*, Vol. 22, No. 1 (February 1991): 4–18.

Nester, William R. *"Haughty Conquerors":
Amherst and the Great Indian Uprising of
1763.* Westport, CT: Praeger, 2000.

Nevins, Allan. *Frémont: Pathmarker of the
West.* New York: Ungar, 1962, 1955.

Newcomb, William Wilmon. *The Indians of
Texas: From Prehistoric to Modern Times.*
Austin: University of Texas Press, 2002,
1961.

O'Donnell, Terence. *An Arrow in the Earth:
General Joel Palmer and the Indians of
Oregon.* Portland, OR: Oregon Historical
Society, 1991.

Onuf, Peter S. *Jefferson's Empire: The Language of American Nationhood.* Charlottesville: University Press of Virginia,
2000.

Ostler, Jeffrey. *The Lakotas and the Black
Hills: The Struggle for Sacred Ground.*
New York: Viking, 2010.

_____. *The Plains Sioux and U.S. Colonialism
from Lewis and Clark to Wounded Knee.*
New York: Cambridge University Press,
2004.

Otterbein, Keith F. "Historical Essay: A History of Research on Warfare in Anthropology." *American Anthropologist,* Vol.
101, No. 4 (Dec 1999): 794–805.

Owens, Robert M. "Jeffersonian Benevolence on the Ground: The Indian Land
Cession Treaties of William Henry Harrison." *Journal of the Early Republic,* Vol.
23, No. 2 (Fall 2002): 405–435.

The Papers of Andrew Jackson. The University of Tennessee Knoxville. Digital.

The Papers of George Washington. The
University Press of Virginia, Digital.

The Papers of Thomas Jefferson. Princeton
University. Digital.

The Papers of Ulysses S. Grant. Mississippi
State University. Digital.

Parkman, Francis. *The Conspiracy of Pontiac
and the Indian War after the Conquest of
Canada.* 2 Vols. Lincoln: University of
Nebraska Press, 1994, 1870.

Parrington, Vernon Louis. *The Colonial
Mind, 1620–1800.* Volume One, *Main
Currents in American Thought.* New
York: Harcourt, Brace & World, 1927.

Paul, R. Eli. *Blue Water Creek and the First
Sioux War, 1854–1856.* Norman: University of Oklahoma Press, 2004.

Peckham, Howard Henry. *Pontiac and the
Indian Uprising.* Princeton, NJ: Princeton
University Press, 1947.

Perdue, Theda, and Michael D. Green. *The
Cherokee Nation and the Trail of Tears.*
New York: Viking, 2007.

Peters, Virginia Bergman. *The Florida Wars.*
Gainesville, FL: Anchon Books, 1979.

Pommersheim, Frank. *Broken Landscape:
Indians, Indian Tribes, and the Constitution.* New York: Oxford University Press,
2009.

Porch, Douglas. *Counterinsurgency: Exposing the Myths of the New Way of War.*
New York: Cambridge University Press,
2013.

Porter, Kenneth Wiggins. *The Black Seminoles: History of a Freedom-Seeking People.*
Revised and Edited by Alcione M. Amos
and Thomas P. Senter. Gainesville, FL:
University Press of Florida, 1996.

_____. "Negros and the Seminole War,
1835–1842." The *Journal of Southern History,* Vol. 30, No. 4 (Nov. 1964): 427–450.

Pritchard, James S. *In Search of Empire: The
French in the Americas, 1670–1730.* New
York: Cambridge University Press, 2004.

Prucha, Francis Paul. "Andrew Jackson's Indian Policy: A Reassessment." *The Journal
of American History,* Vol. 56, No. 3 (December 1969), 527–539.

_____. *Broadax and Bayonet: The Role of the
United States Army in the Development of
the Northwest, 1815–1860.* Madison, WI:
State Historical Society of Wisconsin,
1953.

_____. *The Great Father: The U.S. Govern-
ment and the American Indians.* 2 Vols.
Lincoln: University of Nebraska Press,
1984.

Remini, Robert V. *Andrew Jackson & His Indian Wars.* New York: Viking, 2001.

Rice, James D. *Tales from a Revolution:
Bacon's Rebellion and the Transformation
of Early America.* New York: Oxford University Press, 2012.

Richardson, Heather Cox. *Wounded Knee:
Party Politics and the Road to an American
Massacre.* New York: Basic Books, 2010.

Richter, Daniel K. *Ordeal of the Longhouse:
The Peoples of the Iroquois League in the
Era of European Colonization.* Chapel
Hill: University of North Carolina Press,
1992.

Riddle, Jeff C. *The Indian History of the Modoc War.* Mechanicsburg, PA: Stackpole Books, 2004.

Riley, Jonathon. *A Matter of Honor: The Life, Campaigns, and Generalship of Isaac Brock.* Montreal: Robin Brass Studio, 2011.

Roberts, David. *A Newer World: Kit Carson, John C. Frémont, and the Claiming of the American West.* New York: Simon & Schuster, 2000.

_____. *Once They Moved Like the Wind: Cochise, Geronimo, and the Apache Wars.* New York: Simon & Schuster, 1993.

Rogin, Michael Paul. *Fathers and Children: Andrew Jackson and the Subjugation of the American Indian.* New Brunswick: Transaction Publishers, 1991.

Rolle, Andrew F. *John Charles Frémont: Character as Destiny.* Norman: University of Oklahoma Press, 1991.

Ronda, James P. *Lewis and Clark Among the Indians.* Lincoln: University of Nebraska Press, 1984.

_____. *Voyages of Discovery: Essays on the Lewis and Clark Expedition.* Helena: Montana Historical Society Press, 1998.

Rosenthal, Nicolas G. *Reimagining Indian Country: Native American Migration and Identity in Twentieth Century Los Angeles.* Chapel Hill: University of North Carolina Press, 2012.

Sandoz, Mari. *Crazy Horse: The Strange Man of the Oglalas.* Lincoln: University of Nebraska Press, 2008, c. 1942.

Sarkesian, Sam C. *America's Forgotten Wars: the Counterrevolutionary Past and Lessons for the Future.* Westport, CT: Greenwood Press, 1984.

_____. *Unconventional Conflicts in a New Security Era: Lessons from Malaya and Vietnam.* Westport, CT: Greenwood Press, 1993.

Satz, Ronald N. *American Indian Policy in the Jacksonian Era.* Norman: University of Oklahoma Press, 2002.

Sayre, Gordon M. *Indian Chief as Tragic Hero: Native Resistance and the Literatures of America from Moctezuma to Tecumseh.* Chapel Hill: University of North Carolina Press, 2005.

Schlesinger, Arthur M. *The Age of Jackson.* Boston: Little, Brown, 1953.

Schwartz, E.A. *The Rouge River Indian War* and *Its Aftermath, 1850–1980.* Norman: University of Oklahoma Press, 1997.

Seefeldt, Douglas, Jeffrey L. Hantman, Peter S. Onuf, eds. *Across the Continent: Jefferson, Lewis and Clark, and the Making of America.* Charlottesville: University Press of Virginia, 2005.

Shackford, James A. *David Crockett: The Man and the Legend.* Chapel Hill: University of North Carolina Press, 1956.

Shafer, Michael D. *Deadly Paradigms: The Failure of U.S. Counterinsurgency Policy.* Princeton, NJ: Princeton University Press, 1988.

Shapard, Bud. *Chief Loco: Apache Peacemaker.* Norman: University of Oklahoma Press, 2010.

Sheehan, Bernard W. *Seeds of Extinction: Jeffersonian Philanthropy and the American Indian.* Chapel Hill: University of North Carolina Press, 1973.

Sides, Hampton. *Blood and Thunder: An Epic of the American West.* New York: Doubleday, 2006.

Sklenar, Larry. *To Hell with Honor: Custer and the Little Bighorn.* Norman: University of Oklahoma Press, 2000.

Smith, Shannon D. *Give Me Eighty Men: Women and the Myth of the Fetterman Fight.* Lincoln: University of Nebraska Press, 2008.

Smith, F. Todd. *From Dominance to Disappearance: The Indians of Texas and the Near Southwest, 1786–1859.* Lincoln: University of Nebraska Press, 2005.

Smith-Rosenberg, Carroll. *Disorderly Conduct: Visions of Gender in Victorian America.* New York: Oxford University Press, 1985.

Smits, David D. "The Frontier Army and the Destruction of the Buffalo: 1865–1883." *Western Historical Quarterly,* Vol. 25, No. 3 (Autumn 1994): 312–338.

Starkey, Armstrong. *European and Native American Warfare, 1675–1815.* Norman: University of Oklahoma Press, 1998.

Steele, Brian D. *Thomas Jefferson and American Nationhood.* New York: Cambridge Unity Press, 2012.

Steele, Ian K. *Warpaths: Invasions of North America.* New York: Oxford University Press, 1994.

Stith, William. *The History of the First Dis-*

covery and Settlement of Virginia, Williams-burg, VA. New York: Joseph Sabin, 1747.

Sugden, John. *Blue Jacket: Warrior of the Shawnees.* Lincoln: University of Nebraska Press, 2000.

_____. *Tecumseh: A Life.* New York: Henry Holt, 1998.

Summers, Harry G. *On Strategy: A Critical Analysis of the Vietnam War.* Navato, CA: Presidio Press, 1982.

Svaldi, David. *Sand Creek and the Rhetoric of Extermination: A Case Study in Indian-White Relations.* Lanham, MD: University Press of America, 1989.

Sweeney, Edwin R. *From Cochise to Geronimo: The Chiricahua Apaches, 1874–1886.* Norman: University of Oklahoma Press, 2010.

Sword, Wiley. *President Washington's Indian War: The Struggle for the Old Northwest, 1790–1795.* Norman: University of Oklahoma Press, 1985.

Tate, Michal L. *Indians and Emigrants: Encounters on the Overland Trails.* Norman: University of Oklahoma Press, 2006.

Taylor, Alan. *The Divided Ground: Indians, Settlers and the Northern Borderland of the American Revolution.* New York: Alfred A. Knopf, 2006.

Thrapp, Dan L. *The Conquest of Apacheria.* Norman: University of Oklahoma Press, 1967.

Trafzer, Clifford E. *The Kit Carson Campaign: The Last Great Navajo War.* Norman: University of Oklahoma Press, 1982.

Trask, Kerry A. *Black Hawk: The Battle for the Heart of America.* New York: Henry Holt, 2006.

Trinquier, Roger. *Modern Warfare: A French View of Counterinsurgency.* New York: Praeger, 1964; reprint, Westport, CT: Praeger Security International, 2006.

Tucker, Glenn. *Tecumseh: Vision of Glory.* Indianapolis, IN: Bobbs-Merrill, 1956.

Tucker, Robert W. *Empire of Liberty: The Statecraft of Thomas Jefferson.* New York: Oxford University Press, 1990.

Turner, Frederick Jackson. "The Significance of History." In *The Early Writings of Frederick Jackson Turner.* Ed. Everett E. Edwards. Madison: University of Wisconsin Press, 1938.

The U.S. Army, Marine Corps Counterinsur-gency Field Manual, FM 3–24. Chicago, IL: University of Chicago Press, 2007, 2006.

Unrau, William E. *The Rise and Fall of Indian Country, 1825–1855.* Lawrence: University Press of Kansas, 2007.

Unruh, John D. *The Plains Across: The Overland Emigrants and the trans-Mississippi West, 1840–1860.* Urbana: University of Illinois Press, 1979.

Utley, Robert M. *A Life Wild and Perilous.* New York: Henry Holt, 1997.

_____. *Custer: Cavalier in Buckskin:George Armstrong Custer and the Western Military Frontier.* Norman: University of Oklahoma Press, 2001.

_____. *Frontier Regulars: The U.S. Army and the Indian, 1866–1891.* New York: Macmillan, 1973.

_____. *Frontiersmen in Blue: The U.S. Army and the Indian, 1848–1865.* New York: Macmillan, 1967.

_____. *Geronimo.* New Haven, CT: Yale University Press, 2012.

_____. *Indian Frontier of the American West 1846–1890.* Albuquerque: University of New Mexico Press, 1984.

_____. *Indian Wars.* Boston: Houghton Mifflin, 2002.

_____. *The Lance and the Shield: the Life and Times of Sitting Bull.* New York: Henry Holt, 1993.

_____. *Lone Star Justice: The First Century of the Texas Rangers.* New York: Oxford University Press, 2002.

_____. *Sitting Bull: The Life and Times of an American Patriot.* New York: Henry Holt, 2008.

VanDevelder, Paul. *Savages and Scoundrels: The Untold Story of America's Road to Empire Through Indian Territory.* New Haven, CT: Yale University Press, 2009.

Wallace, Anthony F. C. *Jefferson and the Indians: The Tragic Fate of the First Americans.* Cambridge, MA: Belknap Press of Harvard University, 1999.

Waselkov, Gregory A. *A Conquering Spirit: Fort Mims and the Redstick War of 1813–1814.* Tuscaloosa: University of Alabama Press, 2006.

Washburn, Wilcomb E. *The Governor and the Rebel: A History of Bacon's Rebellion in Virginia.* Chapel Hill: University of North Carolina Press, 1957.

Watson, Samuel J. *Peacekeepers and Conquerors: The Army Officer Corps on the American Frontier, 1821–1846.* Lawrence: University Press of Kansas, 2013.

Watt, Robert N. "Raiders of a Lost Art? Apache War and Society." *Small Wars and Insurgencies* Vol. 13, Issue 3 (2002): 1–28.

Webb, Walter Prescott. *The Great Frontier.* Boston: Houghton Mifflin, 1952.

_____. *The Texas Rangers: A Century of Frontier Defense.* New York: Houghton Mifflin, 1935.

Weber, David J. *The Mexican Frontier, 1821–1846: The American Southwest Under Mexico.* Albuquerque: University of New Mexico Press, 1982.

_____. *The Spanish Frontier in North America.* New Haven, CT: Yale University Press, 1992.

Weems, John Edward. *To Conquer a Peace: The War Between the United States and Mexico.* College Station: Texas A&M University Press, 1988, 1974.

Weinberg, Albert K. *Manifest Destiny: A Study of Nationalist Expansion in American History.* Chicago: Quadrangle Books, 1963, 1935.

Wellman, Paul I. *Death in the Desert: The Fifty Years' War for the Great Southwest.* Norman: University of Nebraska Press, 1987.

Werner, Fred H. *The Beecher Island Battle.* Greeley, CO: Werner Publications, 1989.

West, Elliot. *The Contested Plains: Indians, Goldseekers, and the Rush to Colorado.* Lawrence: University Press of Kansas, 1998.

_____. *The Last Indian War: The Nez Perce Story.* New York: Oxford University Press, 2009.

Whaley, Gary H. *Oregon and the Collapse of Illahee: U.S. Empire and the Transformation of an Indigenous World, 1792–1859.* Chapel Hill: University of North Carolina Press, 2010.

White, Richard. *"It's Your Misfortune and None of My Own": A History of the American West.* Norman: University of Oklahoma Press, 1991.

_____. *The Middle Ground: Indians, Empires, and Republics in the Great Lakes Region, 1650–1815.* New York: Cambridge University Press, 1991.

_____. "The Winning of the West: The Expansion of the Western Sioux in the Eighteenth and Nineteenth Centuries." *Journal of American History*, Vol. 65, No. 2 (September 1978): 319–343.

Whitehead, Neil L. "A History of Research on Warfare in Anthropology—Reply to Keith Otterbein." *American Anthropologist*, Vol. 102, No. 4 (December 2000): 834–837.

Wilkins, David E. *American Indian Sovereignty and the U.S. Supreme Court: The Masking of Justice.* Austin: University of Texas Press, 1997.

Wood, Gordon S. *Empire of Liberty: A History of the Early Republic, 1789–1815.* New York: Oxford University Press, 2009.

Wooster, Robert. *The American Military Frontiers: The United States Army in the West, 1783–1900.* Albuquerque: University of New Mexico Press, 2009.

_____. *The Military and United States Indian Policy, 1865–1903.* New Haven, CT: Yale University Press, 1988.

Worcester, Donald E. *The Apaches: Eagles of the Southwest.* Norman: University of Oklahoma Press, 1979.

Yarlbrough, Fay A. *Race and the Cherokee Nation: Sovereignty in the Nineteenth Century.* Philadelphia: University of Pennsylvania Press, 2008.

Young, Mary E. "The Dark and Bloody but Endlessly Inventive Middle Ground of Indian Frontier Historiography." *Journal of the Early Republic*, Vol. 13, No. 2 (Summer, 1993): 193–205.

Index